E SHELF   C0-ASX-338

lume XVII

No.
4. Representative American Speeches: 1943-1944. A. C. Baird. $1.25.

No.
5. Lowering the Voting Age. J. E. Johnsen. $1.25.

Volume XVI

No.
1. Representative American Speeches: 1941-1942. A. C. Baird. $1.25.
2. Plans for a Postwar World. J. E. Johnsen. $1.25.
3. Independence for India. J. E. Johnsen. $1.25.

No.
6. Representative American Speeches: 1942-1943. A. C. Baird. $1.25.
7. Reconstituting the League of Nations. J. E. Johnsen. $1.25.

Volume XV

No.
1. Representative American Speeches: 1940-1941. A. C. Baird. $1.25.
2. Universal Military Service. R. E. Summers and H. B. Summers. $1.25.
3. Federal Regulation of Labor Unions. J. V. Garland. $1.25.

No.
6. Wages and Prices. R. E. Summers. $1.25.
7. The Closed Shop. J. E. Johnsen. $1.25.
9. Permanent Price Control Policy. J. E. Johnsen. $1.25.
10. A Federal Sales Tax. E. R. Nichols. $1.25.

Volume XIV

No.
1. Representative American Speeches: 1939-1940. A. C. Baird. $1.50.
2. Interstate Trade Barriers. J. E. Johnsen. $1.25.
6. Compulsory Military Training. J. E. Johnsen. $1.25.

No.
8. International Federation of Democracies. J. E. Johnsen. $1.25.
9. Debate Index. Supplement. J. E. Johnsen. 75c.

Volume XIII

No.
4. Europe: Versailles to Warsaw. R. S. Kain. $1.25.
5. Public Housing in America. M. B. Schnapper. $1.25.
6. United States Foreign Policy (Supplement) J. E. Johnsen. 75c.

No.
9. The National Labor Relations Act. Should It Be Amended? J. E. Johnsen. $1.25.
10. Trade Unions and the Anti-Trust Laws. J. E. Johnsen. $1.25.

THE REFERENCE SHELF

Vol. 22   No. 2

SHOULD WE HAVE MORE TVA'S?

Compiled by
WALTER M. DANIELS

THE H. W. WILSON COMPANY
NEW YORK   1950

PREFACE

The Tennessee Valley Authority has "the broadest duty of planning for the proper use, conservation and development of the natural resources of the Tennessee River drainage basin and its adjoining territory for the general social and economic welfare of the nation." These words of President Roosevelt in urging its creation were substantially written into the TVA Act, which became law in 1933.

In carrying out its functions of flood control and development of navigation, TVA has made the Tennessee the first completely engineered river in history. TVA has also become one of the largest producers and distributors of hydroelectricity.

The Tennessee Valley Authority is a business corporation, its initial capital provided by Congress. It turns back its net earnings annually to the federal treasury and receives annual Congressional appropriations.

TVA policy is determined by a three-man board of directors, resident in the Valley and responsible directly to the President and Congress. A general manager with engineering training is in charge of execution of policies and programs. The principal check on this autonomy is that Congress may refuse an appropriation for any TVA project it does not approve.

Around the nine inland lakes which provide a stillwater channel, TVA has created wildlife reservations and recreational areas. Fertilizers produced at the Muscle Shoals plants are distributed throughout the nation and provide the basis for farm demonstrations teaching soil preservation and reclamation, crop rotation, contour plowing, etc. Such demonstrations have been given in forty-four states, principally by county agents and agricultural college experts paid by TVA.

New industries seeking to take advantage of the Valley's power facilities have received advice and technical assistance from TVA in the matters of sites, availability of materials, and manufacturing methods.

In its construction stages, TVA built towns for its workers, with homes, schools, churches, stores, and movie theaters. It provided library service and medical care and conducted public health programs, such as the elimination of malarial mosquitoes. Many of these activities were continued by local authorities when the construction workers moved on.

The Tennessee Valley Authority Act is the model for all but one of the bills introduced in Congress to extend the "regional authority" idea to other river basins. The debate, both in Congress and outside, centers about the question whether the TVA set up is "democratic" or "socialistic."

It is democratic in principle, its proponents argue, because it carries government to the people, vesting both administrative and policy-shaping functions in a three-man resident board. It has proved democratic in action, they say, because it has delegated tasks whenever possible to state, county and local agencies, because it has employed mainly Valley residents, and because it has concentrated on assisting industry, agriculture, and commerce in the Valley.

Its opponents call the idea socialistic because it concentrates too much power in the hands of a few individuals responsible only to the President and the Congress in Washington. They also point out that it would, if carried to its logical conclusion, greatly expand federal controls in all parts of the country.

Few would dispute that only the Federal Government is equipped to handle the task of developing and controlling the water and land resources of an entire river basin. The argument arises over whether the problem can best be dealt with as a unified whole by a single authority, or as a series of related tasks undertaken separately by federal agencies with long experience in their respective fields.

Other arguments about the desirability of river basin authorities stem from these two basic issues.

For their kindness in permitting reproduction of the copyrighted material in this volume, the compiler is indebted to the editors of the following periodicals:

American Political Science Review, Business Week, Country Gentleman, Harper's Magazine, Nation, Nation's Business, New Republic, Newsweek, New York Times, Omaha World-Herald, Oregon Journal, Reader's Digest, Saturday Evening Post, Senior Scholastic, Survey, United States News & World Report, and *Vital Speeches of the Day.*

Also to the following individuals and organizations:

Max Coffey, R. H. S. Crossman, Tom Humphrey, David E. Lilienthal, Wesley Price, the Foundation for Economic Education, Harper and Brothers, and Alfred A. Knopf, Inc.

Sincere thanks for providing copies of speeches and other information are extended to Senator Harry P. Cain, C. Girard Davidson, Lachlan Macleay, Senator Wayne Morse, Senator James E. Murray, W. G. Sloan, Brig. Gen. S. D. Sturgis, Jr., W. L. Sturdevant, the Mississippi Valley Association, the Pacific Northwest Development Association, and the TVA Department of Information.

WALTER M. DANIELS

April 24, 1950

CONTENTS

THE TENNESSEE VALLEY AUTHORITY

EDITOR'S INTRODUCTION

The Tennessee Valley Authority was created to harness a rampaging river and to raise the economic level of one of the most backward regions of the United States. With the Tennessee now the first "completely engineered" river in history, engineers and economists are now assessing TVA's progress toward these objectives in seventeen years of operation.

The criticisms most frequently made are (1) that TVA has subordinated its main operating functions, flood control and navigation, to the generation and sale of electricity; (2) that it has engaged in subsidiary activities, such as the manufacture and distribution of fertilizer, to an extent never visualized by its creators; (3) that it has charged off too much of its investment to flood control and navigation in order to hold down its electric rates, and (4) that it does not provide the advertised "yardstick" for electric rates because TVA is excused from payment of interest on its investment and of local taxes, both considerable items in the calculation of private utility electric rates.

Answers to all these charges have been offered in surveys made by the General Accounting Office and the Federal Power Commission and at hearings before congressional committees. The answers, however, have not satisfied TVA's critics, who keep alive vigorous controversies, especially over the "yardstick" rate issue. The same arguments are heard in the debate over every legislative proposal to extend the TVA principle.

A HARD LOOK AT TVA [1]

I am going to ask and attempt to answer in concrete terms a central question: Is TVA really democratic?

[1] From an article by C. Hartley Grattan, former contributing editor, *Harper's Magazine*. *Harper's Magazine*. 191:206-15. September 1945. Reprinted by permission.

I think it is. It is democratic chiefly because its administrators rely so heavily on persuasion, accompanied by cooperation with state and local authorities through negotiation and shared responsibility. But nevertheless I find it hard to convince myself that the way TVA is at present operated is the only way it could be operated under the existing law, even though that law does pretty clearly specify persuasion. I can imagine another set of directors resting on their oars and relying upon the passive coercion of federal pressure to get the required results. I can even imagine the covert use of active coercion as an instrument of policy. In short, after careful reading of the law and of a reasonable amount of the literature about TVA administration, I feel sure that the active pursuit of the correct course is a matter of the personalities of the directors, and especially of the [former] chairman, David E. Lilienthal. . . .

Mr. Lilienthal appears to have sought in an extraordinarily conscientious fashion—even, to some degree, at the expense of efficiency—the intimate cooperation of state and local authorities in carrying out TVA's duties. Thus, in realizing the farm program, the work is largely done through, and with the help of, the land-grant colleges of the Valley and the established county agents of the extension service. TVA has sought, on the one hand, to avoid absorbing what are properly local functions and, on the other, has sought to act positively to strengthen and extend local functions. It seeks to realize its purposes through local institutions, wherever feasible. This, I think, is democratic.

Moreover, it is democratic in that it does not *command* cooperation; it achieves it by negotiation and, often, by written agreement defining the responsibilities assumed by the parties; and, further, it does not seek to coerce the ultimate beneficiaries, the citizens. If TVA in its activities needs an improved county library system, it helps the local system, if one exists, or it assists in establishing a new one. But it will not maintain the new library facilities permanently. When TVA's special need—created, say by the building of a dam in some remote place—has passed, the further maintenance of the improved library system must be undertaken by the authorities normally concerned. As a rule this happens, because the people in general have welcomed the enlarged opportunities for getting books to read. But no one has ever said, "Comes TVA, books you shall read."

Nor does TVA require people to abandon old shacks for modern houses, TVA style; or even to cease following farm practices that erode the land. TVA seeks to gain cooperation all along the line by persuasion, not coercion, and to teach by example, not by compulsion. . . .

Although it is all to the good that TVA is run on democratic lines, it might be run democratically to a footless end. What is the central purpose of TVA? I assume that there will be little quarrel with the statement that its fundamental objective is the raising of living standards—particularly within the area of its operations, but with a generally favorable effect on the nation as a whole.

Everything TVA does has an effect on living standards, even though it may be hard to measure each item in dollars and cents. How would you reckon the per capita value of the sharply diminished risk of floods? Or the worth to the average man of improved navigation facilities on the Tennessee? How would you state the worth of a good library system in terms of personal income? Or better facilities for recreation? Can you calculate in money terms the significance of a sharp decline in the incidence of malaria, due to TVA's malaria-control program, in a region where it was once rife? Measuring living standards is always difficult, since there are so many intangibles involved. How much more difficult it is to measure the impact on them of so complex an institution as TVA.

Some things we know. TVA operates in an area where living standards, as indicated by dollar incomes, have long been below the national average, in some districts sharply below. The Valley includes portions of seven states (Tennessee, Alabama, North Carolina, Virginia, Georgia, Kentucky, Mississippi) in which a larger proportion of the citizens are engaged in farming for small returns than is true of the nation as a whole, while a smaller proportion are engaged in manufacturing. We know also that such an occupational distribution is not favorable to a high average level of income.

Coming into this general situation in 1933, TVA's first impact was like that of any public works program. The building of the dams gave people jobs under good conditions—exceptionally good for construction camps—at wages at least equal to those of the general vicinity. But it is obvious that something more permanent than this is needed to justify TVA, though it has continued to play a part right down to the present moment. Construction is now drawing to an end. It is at this point that the production and sale of electricity and the agricultural program begin to assume major importance.

The agricultural program has as its principal purpose the pointing of a way to improved incomes on the farms by (a) better methods of cultivation, (b) improvement of the quality of the soil, (c) development of new crops, (d) processing of crops in the immediate vicinity before final marketing. The electricity program contributes its share to improving farm methods by making possible the use of electric hay driers, refrigeration, electric milkers, and so on. Of course none of the newly introduced factors operates evenly throughout the entire Valley. The TVA approach through persuasion precludes that. But it is already possible to state that a lot of progress has been made on the farms. They cannot be turned into gold mines, but they *can* produce substantially improved incomes.

As to the general effect of TVA electricity, it can perhaps be phrased this way: cheap current caused an immediate rise in consumption per customer to 50 per cent above the national average in an area where income is below the national average; and the number of residential consumers more than doubled between 1933 and 1943. Cheap current also sharply enlarged the sale of appliances of all kinds. (TVA does not retail electricity, as it happens, but it controls the resale price through its contracts with retail distributors.) The enlarged use of electricity in homes and on farms is a definite step forward, and its effect on living standards is extremely important.

But the real road to rising standards in the area as a whole is through the development of new factory industries. In so far as TVA electricity plays a strategic role in bringing industries to the area, it is definitely setting the stage for a general advance.

TVA tries to encourage the establishment of small industries, locally owned and managed. Mr. Lilienthal has stated, "TVA took a firm stand against any policy of inducing existing industries located in other regions to move to the Tennessee Valley." Any factories established in the Valley must, therefore, be net additions to the total national plant. If, for example, TVA sees the need for a new farm implement, or an adaptation of an old one to local conditions, its technicians do the job at the technical level and then the Authority encourages the production of the machine by a local manufacturer. Or TVA technicians may tackle the problem of freezing strawberries, carrying the job up to the pilot-plant stage, but the local people are then expected to carry on the job from there.

In short, TVA may, at any given moment, be experimenting in a number of industrial lines, but it is not engaged in manufacturing on a permanent basis, except at the fertilizer works at Muscle Shoals, save in wartime when it does electro-metallurgical work as a service to national defense. But beyond its direct technological contributions, it definitely encourages industries of all kinds from cheese factories to flour mills. And it is also not averse to old industries being expanded or to large new industries being established to utilize local resources, including power. In the electro-metallurgical and chemical fields, where electricity is a primary cost, there are Alcoa, Monsanto, Victor Chemical, the Electro-Metallurgical Company, and Reynolds Metals. In 1944, indeed, electricity for non-ferrous metals constituted the largest single item of power requirements in the TVA area, with chemicals third, and municipalities and cooperatives sandwiched in between. The Valley, like the Pacific Northwest, with which it will be in fairly direct competition, looks hopefully to the light metals age. All this means that TVA can finally achieve its basic purpose only in so far as private enterprise picks up the ball and carries it across the goal line.

A close examination of TVA today reveals that while certain things, like improved farm management and cheap electric current, can cause a marked change for the better in a retarded area like the Valley, in the final analysis the way forward is along . . . strictly traditional lines . . . : progression from primary industries (agriculture, mining, and forestry) to the secondary or manufacturing industries, thus leading to the elaboration of the tertiary or service industries. The basic problem of any area seeking to improve its income position is to get these three categories of employment into proper balance.

As long as the Valley has an abnormal concentration in primary industry, it will lag behind. As it moves a proportion of its farmers into manufactures, it will improve. As manufacturing gets on a sound basis, the services will be developed more fully. When the three categories approach the balance which is characteristic of the nation as a whole, the Valley will approach the national income average.

The really hard pull in the Valley has just begun. The construction period it about over, so the public works effects will now rapidly fade away, and the rather rapid rate of improvement in incomes and living standards which they induced in a substandard region will inevitably be retarded from now on. What may be called the internal structural changes, which caused sharp improvement, have shown themselves valuable but insufficient, even should they eventually be uniformly adopted in the Valley. Now begins the long pull along a traditional road, the usual progress from a heavy concentration of manpower in primary industries to a rising proportion in factories and services. The war has helped this movement, but with what final effects it is impossible just now to calculate.

Here, beyond a question, is a crisis in TVA history, obscured by the war, but certain to be fully revealed in the postwar period. Only if industrialization moves forward rapidly can the Valley maintain its past rate of progress. Even the important job of further spreading the good effects of improved farm management and cheap electricity is really incidental to the main task now clearly defined.

It is my guess that the Valley will not industrialize at a spectacular rate and that, therefore, incomes and living standards will tend to level off at a point which is still definitely below the national average. . . .

The propaganda battle over TVA is, like the undertaking itself, definitely on the colossal side. There is an uneasy feeling in TVA circles that its friends have overpublicized it, claiming too much for it, oversimplifying the problems the Authority is up against, and giving the public the impression that not only is TVA already a subdivision of Utopia, but that it can be duplicated anywhere just by chanting the three magic letters T—V—A.

I have tried to show otherwise, emphasizing that the testing time is yet to come; that no royal road to higher living standards has been found; and that what TVA has done thus far is to clear away the underbrush and lay out the right-of-way for progress along the traditional highway. If the American economy moves forward in the next few decades, TVA also will go forward. If it hesitates or marks time, so also will TVA—though perhaps to a slightly lesser degree. Any flaming optimism, or thoughtless overvaluation of prospects, can be a distinct disservice to the men who have a hard job of work to do in the Valley.

The case which has been made out *against* TVA is not easy to state in summary since it deals both with general principles and particular issues of fact. The basic objection is to TVA's very existence—on the theory that the government should never have undertaken such an enterprise. From this standpoint the crux of the issue is the generation and sale of electricity, since flood control, navigation, agricultural extension work, and so on can hardly be ruled out of the government's province. The production and distribution of electricity is asserted to be unfair competition. (Lately 167 private utilities have banded together to support the proposition that the government may produce electricity at the dams, but should sell it all to private companies for distribution. This is a metaphysical distinction, more an evidence of a planned retreat to a new position *vis à vis* TVA and other government electricity schemes than anything else.)

When it comes to particular indictments of TVA it is my candid opinion that private enterprise critics have done a shabby job. . . .

Many of the allegations against TVA are too trivial to be refuted here. But two that may appear to carry weight are, first, that it does not pay a proper share of taxes, and, second, that it operates at a loss and therefore sells power subsidized by the taxpayer. Neither of these allegations holds water.

As a federal instrumentality TVA does not have to pay taxes to states and municipalities. This position is based on Justice Marshall's decision in *McCulloch* v. *Maryland* in 1819. But TVA is nevertheless instructed in Section 13 of the act setting it up to pay specified "percentages of the gross proceeds derived from the sale of power" to "those states and local governments in which the power operations of the corporation are carried on and in which the corporation has acquired properties previously subject to state and local taxation." As far as I can make out they are equitable payments. Today they exceed in amount taxes paid by the private utilities formerly operating in the TVA's area. Private utility spokesmen, trying to calculate the tax load they carry to compare it with TVA's liability, have included their excess profits taxes. This is nonsense.

On the profit and loss issue, the usual dodges are to ignore the question of allocation of capital costs among the several functions of TVA—flood control, navigation, fertilizer, and so on—and try to establish that *electricity should carry them all*; and likewise to charge against the income from electricity the current costs of flood control, navigation, fertilizer, and so on. Now the question of the allocation of capital costs was publicly thrashed out in detail some years ago and the present TVA practice was established by Congress, which rejected—as not consistent and not objective—the theory that all capital costs should be allocated to power. The effort to make electricity carry all capital costs is, at bottom, simply an effort to lessen TVA's ability to make profits as a preliminary to denouncing it as a failure; or, alternatively, to destroying its effectiveness as a yardstick for beating down private utility charges for power.

Why should the government manufacture but not distribute? Like Mr. McNaughton in *It Pays to Be Ignorant*, "I don't get it." As matters stand today, figures put forward by the private utilities themselves show that the government generates only 20 per cent of all the nation's electric power, and distributes only 14 per cent of it. Of course, within such areas as the Valley and the Pacific Northwest, it does tend to pre-empt large areas where private companies would be the principal suppliers if left to their own devices. The question seems to me to be:

Should the government ever, under any circumstances, engage in the production and distribution of electricity? I think there are many circumstances under which it should; and this answer has also been given by liberal and conservative Congresses alike at various times since 1906. You can't take the issue out of its context and arrive at a rational judgment on it, unless you are a fanatically doctrinaire advocate of private enterprise.

The private utilities still have ample scope for their operations in this country, and the day when they can legitimately complain of being cramped is fairly remote, though particular utilities in the areas served by government plants may have to sell out. This I cannot regard as disaster to private enterprise as a whole. An operation like TVA is of such magnitude that, on the one hand, no private group is apt to undertake it and, on the other, even if it should propose to, it should not be allowed to do so. As the *New York Times* remarked editorially, "The task was too huge for private capital to undertake; or if private capital had undertaken it the resulting monopoly would have been dangerous to the public welfare." If a few private utilities cease business (after full compensation) as a result of such a public undertaking, this must be balanced against the larger good.

One of the amusing consequences of the gaudy publicity received by the Authority is that the letters TVA have been translated from a specific into a generic term. We hear of TVA's planned in all corners of the globe. . . . The mechanical translation of TVA (specific) into TVA's everywhere will bring headaches and grief. Every project should be assessed in detail, not only in relation to the natural and human resources of the specific area but also in relation to the general social, economic, and political context in which it will have to operate. . . .

But whatever the problems raised by exporting the TVA idea, let us see our own TVA plain: It is a state capitalist enterprise operating to provide a new floor—including the power resource of electricity—on which private enterprise is to continue to operate, the whole designed by a combination of state and private effort to give a sharp fillip to the standard of living. Other nations, other purposes, no doubt. But we should not fool ourselves into believing that we have gone farther in the Tennessee Valley than we actually have. We have, of course, gone a long way beyond what is customary in this country, but only by bending old policies to new ends, as I have shown. Above all, let us keep firmly in mind that only if private capitalist enterprise does its stuff in the Valley can we hope to see TVA gain its objective in full measure. Here, therefore, is a sharp challenge to action that our capitalists must surely face and meet. If they meet it successfully, the results will be profitable to themselves, the Valley, and the whole nation.

TVA, A PAYING INVESTMENT [2]

The funds used by the TVA have all been advanced from funds appropriated by Congress with two major exceptions: 65 millions of TVA bonds and about 50 millions supplied by electric ratepayers and reinvested in dams and equipment [$186 million as of June 30, 1949—this and all other figures in brackets from the TVA annual report for the fiscal year ended June 30, 1949—Ed.]. To avoid unduly complicating the statement however, I shall treat the funds expended as if they *all* had been advanced directly from the federal treasury; the exceptions do not affect the principles. The American people who advanced these funds are entitled to a return from them.

In judging whether they have received such a return and whether the product of TVA's investment of the people's money has been worth the outlay, it must be remembered that much of the return, to the Tennessee Valley and the nation, is in benefits which cannot be exactly measured. It is only the investment in power facilities that yields the federal taxpayers a return in dollars in addition to other benefits. . . .

It is not possible to record the same precise dollar measure of navigation benefits as it is with power. But simply because they do not appear on TVA's books as income does not mean, of course, that there are no benefits.

[2] From *TVA—Democracy on the March*, by David E. Lilienthal, former chairman, Tennessee Valley Authority. Harper & Brothers, New York. Copyright, 1943, by David Lilienthal. p38-45, 66-191. Reprinted by permission.

Likewise, the benefits of flood control produced by these dams extend all the way down the Mississippi River to the mouth of the Red. But since TVA is not paid for those benefits in dollars, the taxpayers' return cannot be measured in that way. And so it is with TVA's expenditures to produce phosphate plant food, and to demonstrate its use to control soil erosion not only in the Tennessee Valley but in Minnesota, Wisconsin, New York, Iowa, and seventeen other states outside this region. So with forestry, industrial research, mapping.

The *cost* of such deveopment work appears on *TVA's books as net expense; but the benefits appear on the balance sheet of the region and of the nation.* And, as with public improvement expenditures generally the country over, it was anticipated that such expenditures would be repaid to the taxpayers not directly in dollars, but indirectly in benefits.

Turning now to TVA's expenditures, and first the cost of developing the river: TVA's financial balance sheet shows that to provide a 650-mile navigable channel, flood protection, and power supply, the TVA has an investment in completed plant as of June 30, 1943, totaling about $475 million [net plant investment, $810,961,030; net power investment, $431,432,417 —as of June 30, 1949]. . . .

What dividends for the people does this investment yield? Do the expenditures yield a product that justifies this cost?

As to power the answer is a relatively easy one; power is sold and the revenues provide a dollar measurement, and one that is reassuring. In the fiscal year ended June 30, 1943, the sale of power yielded revenues to TVA in excess of $31.5 million [$57,618,811]. Operating expenses to produce that power, including about $2 million of tax payments [$2,050,437] and $6 million [$8,663,513] (or almost 20 per cent of each dollar of revenue) in depreciation charges, left a surplus of revenue over cost of more than $13 million [$21.5 million]. . . .

The size of this net income indicates pretty clearly that the power asset of the Tennessee River certainly is worth its cost.

These calculations take into account only dollar returns to TVA, and none of the indirect benefits. But such benefits are many. Among them are the $10 million [$33 million] annual savings to consumers as a result of greatly reduced rates, the effect of providing the region's business enterprises with large amounts of low-cost power, the benefits that have resulted to business in other regions of the country, as well as the fact that 80 per cent of the equipment and materials purchased by TVA were produced in factories located in regions outside the Tennessee Valley. Nor do they seek to measure the value to the country of the fact that it was largely because of power from this river that in 1943 America was able to build huge fleets of bombers to send over Europe and the South Pacific. . . .

Revenues from power and surpluses show a favorable relation to the capital invested to produce that income. On the basis of actual experience to date, power surplus could repay the American people their total power investment in TVA without interest within the next thirty years. Since much of the investment is in land or in property of almost indefinite life—a concrete dam is almost as indestructible as the rock on which it rests—this is a brief period indeed for the repayment of this investment. [Title II of the Government Corporations Appropriation Act, 1948, provides for repayment of $348,239,240 of power investment from net power revenues over a period of forty years.] . . .

The direct stimulus that . . . channel and flood protection have provided to the growth of private business has already been shown to be great. While it cannot be proved statistically, there is every reason to believe that the value of the benefits justifies the investment allocable to navigation and flood control, which will be about $250 million [$305,601,925] and an annual operation cost, including depreciation, of about $3 million. . . .

During the ten-year period [ended June 30, 1943] the net expense of TVA's land restoration and other development work has been $39,800,000; in addition $8,383,000 has been spent on fertilizer plants and equipment, including the phosphate plant at Muscle Shoals and the phosphate ore reserves, which are, of course, capital investments. The total TVA capital expenditures for every purpose whatever to June 30, 1944 . . . [was] in the neighborhood of $750 million [$810,961,030 for plant investment as of June 30, 1949].

Are the expenditures for this development worth their cost to the country? There is, of course, no way of settling the question by statistical proof. You must look at the valley, appraise what the expenditure of these funds has done in increasing the productivity of the region and of the nation. You must look at the effect of the growing strength and new vitality of the valley on the total strength of the whole country in war and peace. One has to consider what it is worth to the country to provide opportunity to thousands of men and women in this valley— farmers, businessmen engaged in new enterprises, workers in new factories.

This is not a question that accountants or financial experts can answer for us. Whether the over-all results in this region are worth what they have cost is something the citizen must answer for himself as a matter not of arithmetic, but of the highest public policy. . . .

The TVA Act was nothing inadvertent or impromptu. It was rather the deliberate and well-considered creation of a new national policy. For the first time in the history of the nation, the resources of a river were not only to be "envisioned in their entirety"; they were to be developed *in that unity with which nature herself regards her resources*—the waters, the land and the forests together. . . .

The Tennessee Valley's resources were not to be dissected into separate bits that would fit into the jurisdictional pigeonholes into which the instrumentalities of government had by custom become divided. It was not conceded that at the hour of Creation the Lord had divided and classified natural resources to conform to the organization chart of the federal government. . . .

Because they sinned against the unity of nature, because they developed some one resource without regard to its relation to every other resource in the life of man, ancient civilizations have fallen into decay and lie buried in oblivion. . . .

There is no security or safety for us anywhere if nature's resources are exhausted. The day of machines and increasing populations multiplies our jeopardy. For this we must remember: Unless nature's laws of restoration are observed, modern technology can compress a once gradual process of resource exhaustion into a quick cycle of a generation or two. . . .

The unification of the various technical skills was a central part of our task in TVA, as indeed it is a central problem in modern life. The skills are not self coordinating. In the selection of TVA's technical staff, the importance of the expert's need for a broad view was seen. . . .

Here the men who design and build the dams, who operate the power systems, who build the terminals and roads, are working together, literally and with a conscious purpose. Their physical proximity helps. The public health physician and the many kinds of specialists are in daily touch with one another as a matter of course. They work under a single management. That helps to unify their efforts and their thinking. . . .

Decentralizing the administration of government functions that are clearly national has been carried so far in this valley that it is literally true (I can think of no exceptions) that, whenever there is a state or local institution which can perform part of the task that has been assigned by law to the TVA, we have sought to have that nonfederal agency do it. . . .

There is nothing in this region's experience to support the genuine fears or the partisan outcry of ten years ago that setting up a federal regional agency would mean the undermining and ultimate destruction of state government and local communities. The contrary has been the case. It is indisputable from the record that state government is stronger in the Tennessee Valley today than it was ten years ago, and has more functions to perform. It is notably true that the local community government and functions are more vigorous. I know of no other place in the United States of which this can be said with equal basis in performance. . . .

In TVA's charter Congress stated clearly what was to be done in the Tennessee Valley: idle resources were to be set to work—rivers, land, minerals, forests. The job to be done was defined, clearly, simply, and yet in broad inclusive terms. . . .

Not only *what* was to be done, but the fundamental policies we were to follow were likewise set out. . . .

The job having been defined and the broad policies laid down, Congress in the TVA Act did what is new in our history; it fixed upon one agency the responsibility for results in resource development in a region. . . .

The corporation is a vehicle well adapted to such fixing of responsibility. The fact that TVA was set up as a corporation, however, is not alone any guarantee that it would not be subjected to the same rituals of divided responsibility, clearances, and detailed management by Congress as any bureau; in fact, some of our public corporations are thus encumbered. But, while no guarantee, there was a psychological advantage in using the corporate device, since by established practice and custom the corporation has come to embody in people's minds this idea of managerial responsibility. . . .

Can science and politics live together without one dominating the other? Can experts and managers be kept accountable to the public despite the great power over the lives of all of us that technical knowledge puts into their hands?

TVA has, of course, inevitably faced these fundamental questions many times in the past ten years. The answers thus far have been in the affirmative. It is quite generally conceded that a high standard of technical and managerial competence has been maintained, and that the TVA has been guided by public policies laid down by Congress. It has remained responsive to the wishes of the people it serves, who warmly support TVA's resistance to political interference. . . .

In my opinion the idea of planning is still struggling for popular support in America largely for this reason: that the most spectacular plans have been drawn by men who did not have the responsibility for carrying them out. They did not have the salutary discipline which the experts of this valley had who have had to ask themselves: "Is this a plan that I can take responsibility for seeing carried out? Will the people understand it, will the people help make it effective? Will they make the plan their own?"

THE PEOPLE IN SAID BASIN [3]

TVA had been instructed by Congress to promote the "economic and social well-being of the people living in said river basin." Who were those people?

[3] From *The Valley and Its People*, by Robert L. Duffus, editorial writer, *New York Times*. p 125-49. Reprinted by permission of Alfred A. Knopf, Inc., Copyright, 1944, by Alfred A. Knopf, Inc., New York.

They certainly weren't all alike, any more than the spots of earth on which they lived were all alike. Some of them were Negroes: close to one in twenty in the whole state of Tennessee; about one in twelve in the whole state of Kentucky; about one in two in the whole state of Mississippi. There were towns where there were a great many Negroes, and towns where there weren't any. Most of them were down in the old cotton country to the south and over toward the Mississippi.

No statute could alter the psychology underlying the interracial situation. Local folkways in the Valley, as elsewhere in the South, said the races should be segregated, and TVA in its camps followed the folkways. It did pay equal wages for equal work, and when it did things for farmers the Negroes had a chance just the same as the whites.

Its work in the Valley was bound, nevertheless, to have an effect on the status of the Negro. Racial antagonisms flourish where there is a shortage of something men want: jobs, houses, opportunities. Fear has more to do with them than pride. Poverty creates tensions. When incomes and living standards go up, these tensions relax. Racial troubles in Northern war-boom cities do not prove the contrary, for in those cities, though incomes have gone up, the things that men wish to buy with their incomes —good homes, convenient access to their jobs, facilities for recreation—have remained scarce.

But the Negro, as a part of "the people living in said river basin," does benefit by everything that TVA does that adds to the Valley's prosperity. Hate and fear don't flourish when most families are fairly comfortable. The opportunities electricity and its applications produce make the Valley economically more spacious, and in that spaciousness there is room for increased good will. In the long run TVA is making it easier for Negroes and white people to live side by side without trouble. In the long run: one won't read of a sudden transformation in tomorrow morning's newspapers. . . .

The Valley is the people living on isolated farms, in little market towns, in textile towns, and in the cities. It is the people who plant crops in the dark of the moon, for luck, and people who terrace their lands and use improved phosphate fertilizers.

It is the people who believe that John Thomas Scopes was justly convicted and fined, in Dayton, Tennessee, in 1925, for teaching the forbidden doctrine that "man has descended from a lower order of animals"; and it is also the people who regard Charles Darwin, not as a dangerous innovator, but as a classicist who has been left far behind by the march of modern genetics. It is people who consider anyone from beyond the state boundaries, or sometimes even the county boundaries, as a "foreigner," and it is people who know New York City fairly well and keep up with the latest ideas in magazines and books.

The total effect is conservative. Words like "socialism," "communism," and even "trade-unionism" have always alarmed many Valley people. This was and is about the last place in America in which one would expect a revolution to begin. If TVA had been described as a revolution, or even as a wholly new idea, the Valley would not have welcomed it. And in general the people are willing to accept certain demonstrable facts and principles, whereas they might shy away from the hifalutin words that describe them. . . .

The pioneer stock hasn't gone to seed. It still has character and virility. What it needed was something outside itself of which it had been robbed by unhappy circumstances. It needed hope for the future. Hope is the pioneer's mainspring. He can't keep it wound up when every year the same amount of work brings in worse returns. But if he can inch ahead year by year, get a little more corn out of the old field, increase his milk yields, get more work done because he has electricity and machinery to help him, pay off his mortgage, paint his house, put in new plumbing and other gadgets, give his children better schooling— then he will be as good as he ever was, and as good as his ancestors were, which is pretty good. . . .

Looking back over the first decade one can see that the Valley was ready for something to awaken it to more vigorous life. It was not ready, however, to be taken over by even a benevolent outside agency. It had no desire to be a colony, however well administered. It wished to be independent or nothing—wished it as a section, as states, as counties and townships, and as families and individuals.

The TVA might have been a wretched failure if it had actually been what some careless observers supposed it to be, or what some enthusiasts wanted it to be. If it had gone into the Valley with the avowed purpose of "uplifting" the inhabitants, it would have pauperized a small minority and estranged the great majority. The sober truth is that there were some signs of a rather tactless attempt at uplift in the first year or so. They soon ceased. TVA had made its way in the Valley because it took the people into partnership. . . .

TVA was born in a time of depression, when widespread hardship could be avoided only by the use of the federal power to do many things *for* the citizens of the states. Private enterprise was paralyzed and state power was not sufficient. But TVA was so situated and its authority was so used that it ceased very early to do things for the people and passed into the phase of enabling people to do things for themselves.

No other policy could have worked well in the Valley—and this is possibly a way of saying that no other policy will permanently work well in any part of America. The Valley people were, and are, proud. They had rather be poor than dependent. The essence of TVA, from their point of view, was that it opened up to them the road to independence.

The first benefits from TVA came in the form of wages. More than forty thousand were on the payroll at the construction peak. But these wages were not regarded as doles, and were not doles. They were a fair exchange for skill and muscle. If a man got a cashable fraction of a congressional appropriation he could feel that he had earned his pay. This was no leaf-raking job.

TVA came to stand for more than a single kind of power. It was the power of man over his environment—of all men, of little men as well as big men, of unlettered men as well as the graduates of universities. It was cooperative power. The Valley people saw how out of the fathomless confusion of a beginning construction project the most exquisite sort of order could come. They saw how men working together, the planning engineers and the building engineers, skilled mechanics and laborers, could do a magnificent thing.

It was easy to believe that similar methods would work in other fields. And this, in fact, is how TVA's wider task was carried out. In the sweep of things beyond the routine of construction the key was cooperation. There was little that TVA did alone.

It worked with other governmental agencies—scores of them. It worked with voluntary agencies—dozens of them. It put energy into those local agencies that are by far the most potent influences for American democracy, and it drew energy out of them. When a rural cooperative was formed it put new responsibilities on individuals. They had to grow, and did grow, to new dimensions. Villages and cities buying or building distribution systems for TVA power had new problems thrust upon them. Demonstration farmers found themselves equal to a more exacting game with the soil and weather. Community-owned refrigerators or harvesting machinery demanded organizing skills that had long lain dormant. TVA brought libraries to its camps, and when the camps were gone some counties continued the libraries on their own money and their own initiative. Scientific control of disease in the camps stimulated a demand for a better public health service.

All over the Valley little men have been growing into bigger men because they have had bigger things to do. TVA has helped as much by standing aside as by butting in. The TVA cars, going up and down on their lawful errands, are not formidable symbols of Mr. Whiskers. They are likely to contain folks who may be familiarly addressed as Joe or Frank, and who can talk cotton, tobacco, corn, fruit, eggs, milk, livestock, fertilizers, electrical gadgets, schools, malaria, prices, the business situation, and military strategy with anyone who is interested. The composite TVA man either was born in the Valley or has settled down to grow up with it. He is one of the people among whom he circulates, and he does not put on airs. When he is hot he is not afraid to take off his coat and show his suspenders.

A normally skeptical outsider, acquainted with the ways of propagandists and properly suspicious of "spontaneous" popular movements which suddenly spring up equipped with chairmen, mailing lists, and money to hire halls, might wonder at the way the Valley rallied behind TVA when TVA was in trouble with Congress. But one such outsider, at least, after ten years of observation, hasn't been able to detect the hand of TVA behind the scenes pulling the strings.

In the early spring of 1933, when Senator McKellar was trying to introduce a monkey wrench or two into the TVA machinery, this outsider attended a protest gathering in a small Alabama city. It was not a mass meeting but rather an informal committee session. There was a preliminary dinner at the leading hotel, and a good deal of talk about plowing, weather, local business conditions, and local politics. After dinner a legal representative of TVA, present by invitation, made a speech, in which he carefully explained what would happen if the McKellar proposals were adopted. Questions were asked—by a farmer, an editor, a banker, a merchant, a doctor, and so on. There was some difference of opinion about how to proceed. Some wanted to persuade Mr. McKellar and some wanted to scare him. There were no varying opinions as to the objective, which was to do all that could be done to keep TVA a constructive agency and save it from being turned into a vehicle for political patronage.

This was obviously a group of people whose emotions were deeply rooted in old ways, and whose thoughts were their own, not TVA's. They were individualists. Some had been on principle opposed to public ownership and originally hadn't cared for the TVA experiment. They were now united to the extent that they thought they had discovered in TVA an agency and influence which was favorable to men's happiness and well-being in the Valley. They were friendly to it as they might be to the river itself or to the Great Smoky Mountains.

They weren't consciously rejecting anything they had learned at home, at school or in church. They weren't seeking a new way of life, but the old way made richer and safer. They wanted better homes, better schools, better churches.

Each of them represented some kind of private enterprise that could be more successfully operated when electricity was cheap and plentiful than when it was scarce and expensive. Each of them owned something he was trying to hang on to and add to. But each of them was glad, without any prompting, to own a share in dams, generators, switchboards, and wires that could never be anybody's private property. Private business in the Valley seemed to them better off because there was this much public business.

At this particular meeting organized labor wasn't represented. Indeed, organized labor might have had its quarrels with some of those present. But any labor leader in the Tennessee Valley would have endorsed the resolutions adopted. Here was one principle that cut across traditional, sectional and economic lines.

The Valley people, in short, have accepted TVA. They have a pride in it. They do not yet know quite what they will do with it, any more than the pioneers knew what they would do with the new lands when they started coming down the Valleys of the Holston, the Clinch, and the French Broad. But they can see the dawn breaking above the Smokies and streaming westward to the Mississippi. The adventure lies ahead. Like their ancestors, resolute and unafraid, they press forward.

TVA, MIRACLE OR MONSTER? [4]

TVA, in its original intent and purpose, is an instrument for controlling one of the orneriest, most exasperating, most unpredictable, most devastating rivers in all America.

It has done just that. Done it with neatness and dispatch.

The Tennessee's development into a great hydroelectric power stream is supposedly incidental. Actually, it is a tail-wags-dog phenomenon, planned all the way. . . .

You get out the Tennessee River survey maps prepared by Maj. Lewis H. Watkins, Hugh B. Hooper and the corps of engineers at Chattanooga back in 1928—five years before TVA

[4] From twelve articles by Tom Humphrey, associate editor, *Oregon Journal*. *Oregon Journal.* March-April 1949. Published as a pamphlet and distributed by the Pacific Northwest Development Association. 205 Multnomah Hotel. Portland, Oregon. Reprinted by permission.

was anything but a frustrated dream. You compare it with the latest map you picked up at TVA. And they are so much alike that at first glance you think they are the same.

You ask about that and find that TVA simply picked up the army engineers' program for the comprehensive development of the river, refined it a bit, put a TVA label on it, and had at it—after the great depression gave the plan urgency and Messrs. Roosevelt, Norris and McKellar and the Congress gave it the nod. . . .

And you wonder about the five ALCOA plants that have finally been integrated into the TVA system after five years of resistance. ALCOA really did the hydroelectric pioneering on the Little Tennessee, you know, starting way back in 1916 and perhaps it had some pride of authorship, besides a need for great blocks of TVA power.

You ask, finally, if TVA really does what it is billed to do, that is, really controls floods in Tennessee Valley and really serves as a boon to navigation. You are assured by everyone in TVA that it does. . . .

TVA had to have land—more than a million acres of it—for dams and reservoirs, for transmission lines and towns. So if it couldn't negotiate deals with owners, it exercised its powers of eminent domain. It sued.

It even evolved an ingenious technique for blanket takeovers. Individual suits were too time-consuming. TVA, therefore, worked out its "non-trading" scheme, ostensibly to protect the government against land speculators.

The scheme was simple and effective. Appraisers set the price. TVA made the offer. There could be no "trading." The owner had to take it or leave it. Most of them took it, but many went to court to defend themselves against condemnation.

Remember, the war hadn't come with its insatiable demand for the light metal and chemical industries and for explosives. So TVA had to have customers, preferred customers. The TVA Act had directed that preference be given municipalities, rural electric cooperatives and other public agencies. And there simply weren't any worth mentioning in the Tennessee Valley area. Ergo, TVA had to promote them. And it did so.

It used as weapons (a) its broad bond issuing powers, (b) the relatively high rates of the private companies of the region (the southern power companies weren't as far-sighted about rates as those of the Pacific Northwest), (c) the PWA grants Mr. Ickes held out to any public power group that was interested, and (d) TVA's own wholesale and retail rate structures. "Yardstick" rates, they called them. And they were so low, by the current standards, that they made people's eyes stick out. . . .

Finally nineteen companies joined together in the famous Ashwander case which attacked the constitutionality of the TVA Act and all that it implied. Their case made supreme court history, the dissenting opinion was caustic, but they lost it just the same.

The Congress, after a bitter fight, amended the TVA Act to permit the authority not only to acquire the transmission lines and water-power properties of Wendell Willkie's Commonwealth & Southern group, but also to acquire its steam plants. TVA could do anything from then on.

And Mr. Roosevelt obligingly called Mr. Willkie to the White House and laughingly told him that he'd better sell Tennessee Electric Power Company while he still had something to sell.

That did it. Willkie sold for $78.6 million—about 80 per cent of the real value of the properties. The other power companies gave up, either selling or making deals to cede parts of their territories to TVA distributors. They were paid $116 million, lost 288 thousand customers in the deal. The TVA team had won. It had an unbeatable hand. . . .

It's ironic, in a way, that the power program which was mentioned only in whispers in the early TVA days and always last even today, is by far the most successful operation in the TVA book. . . .

TVA's twenty-seven hydro and six steam plants produced 14.25 billion kilowatt-hours of energy last fiscal year. TVA sold it for almost $49 million to distributors who sold it in turn to almost one million customers for more than $60 million.

That's a lot of power from a lot of plants for a lot of customers.

It's a lot of power, even by Northwest standards.

TVA has taken this power and created a power empire, the greatest power monopoly in the United States, bar none. For, you see, TVA is the sole supplier of power for 80 thousand square miles of territory containing 5 million people. This is power, king size.

TVA is answerable to no one (except nominally to the President) for its costs, its rates or its methods of operation. It can plow its earnings back into system improvements or fertilizer or recreation or fish or seedling trees or traveling libraries or towns or what have you—without going back to Congress for permission.

It has had to go to the Congress for permission to build the new $54 million New Johnsonville steam plant, an unprecedented proposal that makes many congressmen, many United States Chamber of Commerce members very unhappy, but that's another story and another issue.

TVA controls the rates and the operations of its 140 public power outlets, controls them absolutely. States and municipalities have nothing to say about it. Neither has the Federal Power Commission or any other governmental regulatory body. TVA and its affiliated distributors can do anything and everything with power—anything but eat it. . . .

No one is stupid enough to assume that a great multiple purpose project like TVA—with its vast construction program and its regionalization of 80 thousand square miles of America —can be consummated without dislocations of various sorts.

You can't spend almost a billion dollars anywhere or in any manner or for any purpose whatsoever without touching a lot of lives, without pushing people around.

You assume all this when you enter the Tennessee Valley. . . .

You ask at TVA and at the University of Tennessee and else-where how many people TVA had to move to get that more than a million acres for dams, locks and reservoirs, for fertilizer plants and construction towns. How many pieces of property?

They sidestep a bit (just as they look blank when you ask about self-liquidating projects such as those of the Pacific North-west). But finally they reduce it to families—about 14 thousand of them, they say, counting some 225 displacements at South Holston and Watauga dams, still under construction. More than 30 thousand different tracts of land, averaging about forty acres. About a half million acres of it agricultural land (the extension service estimated) that produced $27 million worth of crops an-nually—at prewar prices.

Do a little mental arithmetic and you see that at least 75 thousand persons were actually forced to leave their homes, farms and businesses to make way for the taming of a river. And this does not include the thousands of persons who lived on higher ground and worked on lowland farms or in lowland canneries, flour mills and other small establishments. . . .

Of course, TVA handled the displaced persons thing with kid gloves. It persuaded the extension service and the county agents—they knew these about-to-be-displaced people, these vic-tims of progress, personally—to do the job and they did it skill-fully. TVA didn't haggle over prices, either, though it had to take some cases to court. . . .

The TVA board has absolute control over the hiring and firing of its employees—13,581 when I was in Tennessee Valley in March, more than 42 thousand at the peak of construction. And when I say absolute, I mean absolute. The TVA Act sees to that.

Once the TVA board is appointed (for nine-year terms at $10 thousand a year) by the President and confirmed by the Senate, they're the works.

The law specifically exempts all TVA employees from the Civil Service Act. . . .

True, the board is directed to pay the "prevailing rates of wages for work of a similar nature" and to take into consideration such wage rates as have been secured through collective bargaining in the area. But the board is not directed to make contracts with established labor unions, nor has it done so. And if workers are not satisfied with the wage rates established by the board, their only appeal is to the Secretary of Labor whose decision is final.

So in TVA you have no civil service, no formal agreements with organized labor. Each year TVA holds a "conference" with the fifteen or so representatives of organized labor in the region. At this conference, wage scales and working conditions are determined. TVA then hires its men on an individual basis, without consulting union leaders or employing union hiring halls. . . .

It has set up its own retirement plan (it applies to workers on an annual basis only.) You see, TVA employees are specifically excluded from the benefits of the Social Security Act. That means, of course, that workers on an hourly basis can work for TVA for ten or twelve years, as some of them have, and they have no old-age retirement insurance whatever, and they're not covered by TVA's own retirement program. . . . You talk to some TVA employees who got enough and took a walk. . . .

Appointments and advancements to or in the good jobs are on a personal, political and ideological basis, they charge.

"TVA merit system? What's that?

"If TVA could get rid of twenty or thirty of the lodge brothers," they add, "it would be all right. Ninety-five per cent of its employees are OK."

There it is. All sides of the case for you to judge.

You look back at the copy of the TVA act Senator McKellar sent you. You find at least a partial answer to a question that grows in your mind: How is this thing? It's in paragraph (h) of Section II. It sets forth the only qualification for appointment to the TVA board that you can find. It says simply:

"All members of the board shall be persons who profess a belief in the feasibility and wisdom of this act."

They and their employees like them. . . .

You make a deal with yourself when you enter the Tennessee Valley.

Try to do a reporting job. Look at both sides of that shining TVA shield. Divide your time equally between the pro and con —if that be possible. Subject yourself to the standard TVA treatment, then break away and talk to the opposition, if there is any. Soak up as much of that fascinating Tennessee Valley history as possible. Work days, fly nights, move around.

So you do just that.

First, you make an interesting discovery:

The pro side of the TVA story is a lead pipe cinch. It's all around you—the dams, the electroprocess industry, the navigation and flood control angles. Just like the Pacific Northwest. Easy for a Pacific Northwest reporter to grasp. . . .

Then tiny cracks appear in the shining shield. Some of the irreconcilables begin to talk. Editors, former TVA employees, labor leaders, chamber of commerce managers, city councilmen who can't understand why their power boards are flush and their city government floundering in high taxes and debt. Some of them can't be quoted, they say, but they refer you to others who can.

Business members of chamber boards who vote for pro-TVA resolutions, including the New Johnsonville steam plant, but privately hate TVA's gaudy guts. Former employees who took all the TVA guff they could stomach, then took a walk. Some of them talk freely. Labor leaders and employees who pay lip service to TVA's force account policy and its merit system, admit privately their unhappiness over having wage rates and working conditions handed down from on high—no contract, no social security, no civil service, no appeal. . . .

Some educators who subscribe to the tenets of the TVA program admit to their close friends that its socialistic implications "scare the hell out of them."

Editors like Guy L. Smith of the *Knoxville Journal* and Brainard Cooper of the *Chattanooga News-Free Press* who sometimes blast away at some phases of TVA, admit that every time they do so the heat's on. They tell you quite frankly, however, that they are concerned about the autonomy of the region. They indicate their abhorrence of the sapping of the moral fiber of the Tennessee country, by arousing its selfish sectionalism, by appealing to its desire for subsidized power, subsidized fertilizer, subsidized recreation.

Others break down and confess that you couldn't run for dog catcher and win—not on an anti-TVA platform, not in Tennessee, anyway. . . .

Finally, you come to the conclusion that no one in Tennessee (and to a lesser degree, in bordering states) can say a word against TVA or any of its works and get away with it—no one, that is, but Senator McKellar.

You see, Senator McKellar has been in the Senate so long, he has done so much for TVA (Norris Dam should have been named for him, not the late Nebraskan) that he can take Lilienthal apart and get away with it. But no one else can—not in Tennessee. . . .

Anyway, you begin to get the picture.

You simply don't oppose TVA any more. Not in Tennessee Valley. Not if you want to stay in business and in one piece.

You try to analyze this. You talk it over with people. You take a look around, a good look, and you find part of the answer —TVA in everything.

First, TVA has undisputed control of the water resources of the Tennessee watershed and in large measure its land resources.

TVA is in absolute control of the manufacture and distribution of power for 5 million people.

TVA has the bordering power companies buffaloed, companies like the Southern Company system (Georgia Power, Mississippi Power, Gulf Power, Alabama Power), companies like Birmingham Electric.

Oh, they'll talk about their operating relations with TVA. Very good. They'll talk about their own power plants, services and community relations. Very sound. Georgia Power Company is particularly proud of its annual home-town contest, and with reason; it's a honey.

They'll even talk about their rates—TVA rates plus taxes, in general terms. But they won't talk about challenging TVA—not after what TVA did to Willkie's power empire. They know that if they want a fight, Mr. Clapp and his boys will be glad to oblige—the minute TVA has the power capacity to do so and despite gentlemen's agreements dividing service areas.

TVA is in the fertilizer business in a big way—$16 million a year. It's one of the biggest manufacturers and distributors of phosphate fertilizers in the world. It isn't worried about costs. And it controls its distribution to test-demonstration farms, which it supplies with free fertilizer, and selects the co-operatives which get it at cost and pass it on under TVA rules.

TVA is in all the land-grant colleges, their extension services and the offices of their county agents. It sets up attractive research projects in the universities, paying all the bills. It allows the extension service and their county agents to handle the free fertilizer, test-demonstration deal. It pays the salaries of assistant county agents where needed to carry on the TVA land-use program.

And TVA is in the planning commissions of the various states. It set up most of them, manned them, still helps some. And some of them are excellent, don't misunderstand me, particularly the Tennessee state planning commission, which is certainly doing a job (wish we had as good in the Pacific Northwest).

TVA provides free seedling trees for state forestry departments, as well as thousands of privately owned farms, helps set up fire districts, makes good deals with federal, state and local agencies on fish and wildlife projects, parks and recreation sites along its chain of man-made lakes. All under contract, all according to the TVA pattern.

You recall that list of thirty businesses TVA was supposed to be in a few years ago. You find, on checking, that TVA has unloaded some of them. It's disposed of Norris and Fontana villages, for instance. It doesn't run drugstores or service stations any more. But it's still engaged in a lot of enterprises, besides power and fertilizer, flood control and navigation.

TVA has a big malaria control program, a successful one, despite the fact that much of the malaria problem was of its own devising—those man-made lakes and mosquitoes, you see.

It's in the banking business. It may issue bonds up to $100

million for its own use or to finance its public power distributors. It competes with the private contractors by doing all its own construction work. It quarries limestone and marble. It does engineering work both inside and outside the valley. It is in the recreation business, either on its own or through contracts with private operators. It builds and operates river terminals, docks and piers. It promotes food processing and marketing associations and cooperatives to handle TVA fertilizer. It engages in widespread research and development projects, such things as deep freeze, wood products, agricultural machines.

TVA has contracts with other federal agencies, with states, cities, counties, cooperatives, utility boards, industries, schools, libraries and universities—hundreds of them. And its work is well publicized, in reports, booklets, special brochures, movies, news and radio releases. They go everywhere.

As we say, TVA is in everything—all within the broad terms of the TVA act, all on a cooperative, grass-roots basis, all very smoothly handled.

TVA doesn't engage in personal politics.

TVA doesn't interfere with state and local governments of the Tennessee Valley.

TVA doesn't have to. For TVA *is* the government in Tennessee Valley.

There is nothing, no one above it.

WHAT'S WRONG WITH TVA? [5]

Since the TVA "idea" has been defined as the *decentralized administration of centralized authority* [*Democracy on the March*, by David E. Lilienthal, page 143], let's take a look at how that purpose was to be accomplished. First of all TVA is a federal agency, with all the powers of the federal government behind it. TVA supersedes state and local governments just as much as the federal government supersedes them. TVA has been given the power to *force* state and local officials to conform to its decrees and decisions.

[5] From *The TVA Idea*, by Dean Russell, staff writer, Foundation for Economic Education. Foundation for Economic Education. Irvington-on-Hudson, N.Y. 1949. p44-93. Reprinted by permission.

The defenders of TVA, while admitting that such power exists, maintain that it has seldom been used. In fact, a vital part of the TVA "idea" is to secure the voluntary cooperation of local officials and of all the residents within the region. What if they don't volunteer? Mr. Lilienthal gives us the answer on page 119: "Of course there are clashes which as of any given moment cannot be harmonized. The private interests must then be subordinated." . . .

The advocates of TVA maintain that Congress does have some control over it because the Senate must approve the President's selection of TVA board members, and the House of Representatives must make yearly appropriations of additional money to make up the TVA annual deficits.

That is all true, but with the possible exception of the Atomic Energy Commission, TVA is still probably less responsive to Congress and the people than any other administrative branch of the government. . . .

He [Mr. Lilienthal] says that the advantage lies in federal ownership and its power to get things done. But the danger is that the holders of that coercive power—officials of the federal government—will misuse it. His solution is to retain the federal power, but to place that power in *appointed* officials who are not directly responsible to the representatives *elected* by the people. . . .

If it is agreed that *authority* is a dangerous thing, why not restrict the *authority* itself instead of placing it in other hands? If the *authority* is not to be restricted, then our elected representatives in Congress are just as capable of handling it as are the appointed officials on the TVA Board. . . .

Today, whether we are aware of it or not, our country is largely dominated by government administrative agencies. TVA is one example in the field of electricity production. There are also administrative agencies for housing, banking, labor, insurance, farming, communications, shipping, railroads, and a host of others covering almost any phase of our economy that you care to mention. . . .

The advocates of administrative agencies and authorities claim that "simplicity of procedure and nontechnical methods" result from this new type of administrative "justice." Admittedly this "justice" is simple and nontechnical. The authority issues an order, and you must obey—or raise the money for a long court battle. . . . For purposes of "simple nontechnical procedure," *the official has been given what amounts to the right to make up laws as he goes along*. That is the equivalent of saying that what government does *is* law. . . .

One of the main arguments advanced for river development by government is that private enterprise cannot or will not do the job. Demonstrably, this is not true. For example, the Southern California Edison Company's Big Creek development shows what private power companies have done—and are doing—on many rivers in various parts of the United States.

In the High Sierras, Southern California Edison Company has constructed a $100 million project. Beginning thirty-six years ago, this company (and its predecessor companies) built access railways and highways, a thirteen-mile tunnel, hydroelectric power houses and dams. In addition to furnishing a steadier water flow for power production, these dams also provide valuable flood control for the lower San Joaquin River. They flood no good or tillable land. They store water to be released for power production during the dry season. This water is then automatically available for irrigation in the valley below. Not only do the taxpayers make no contribution to this project but also they receive contributions from all these improvements through taxes paid on them by Southern California Edison. Contrasted to the tax-supported TVA project, this job is taxed while the people get the resulting incidental flood control and irrigation benefits without charge. . . .

Actually there are three power lobbies. There are, of course, the public power lobby and the private power lobby. But the third lobby is not so well known because it is informal and unorganized. Possibly it should be called an "attitude" instead of a lobby. It is composed of certain private interests—including private power companies—and government officials who want the government to produce electricity to be distributed by private companies. . . .

Thus we have one of the main reasons why government ownership of the means of production is increasing in America.

Many of the leaders of private industry themselves are either in favor of it or have given up all hope of stopping it. Many of them are now saying: "But we've got to be practical about this matter. The interests of our stockholders and employees demand that we compromise on certain issues in order to keep any business at all." . . .

Admittedly many private producers of electricity have been maneuvered—or have maneuvered themselves—into a position where they now feel that they must either sell out to government, bow to government control, or face bankruptcy. . . . But if freedom of enterprise is to survive in America, this much is certain: As harsh as it may sound—and as tempting and expedient as compromise or surrender may seem—private utilities everywhere must continue to resist both the threats and promises of the advocates of government power production. This must be done *if freedom is to survive in America.* . . .

The advocates of government ownership and operation of the means of production generally place the power industry at the top of their list. They offer various reasons for this. First it is claimed that the power industry is "clothed with the public interest." True. But so is the baking industry and the shoe industry. In fact, it would be difficult to find any industry that is not "clothed with the public interest."

The second—and most effective—weapon being used to socialize the electrical industry is the idea that the production of electrical energy is a "natural monopoly." . . .

It is true that usually only one power company serves a given area or community. But this is not always the case. And even when there is only one power company, the extent of actual and potential competition is far greater than appears on the surface. First of all, according to Federal Power Commission data, in 1944 there were over a hundred cities with populations of more than twenty-five hundred where two or more power producers were in a position to compete directly. . . .

Then there are certain forms of direct competition that *all* power companies must meet. For instance, manufacturing plants, apartment houses, stores, hotels, farms and many other types of business can *and frequently do* install and operate their own electric generating equipment. . . .

In addition, all power companies—including TVA—must meet direct competition from substitute forms of heat and energy. For instance, electricity, gas, oil, coal, wood, bottled gas, and waste steam are competing ways of cooking, heating water, and heating houses and plants. Electricity, gas and oil are alternate methods for refrigeration and air conditioning. Steam, gas and Diesel engines under many circumstances are alternates for electric power.

And, finally, there remains the most effective competition of all. *The electric companies must compete with everyone else for the consumer's dollar.* . . .

That is one of the main reasons why the average revenue per kilowatt hour of residential electricity has dropped from eleven cents in 1906 to about three cents in 1947 [*Statistical Bulletin,* November 15, 1948, Edison Electric Institute, page 28]. Since 1939, according to the United States Bureau of Labor Statistics, electricity and commercial gas are the only consumer items which have gone down in price. . . .

TVA represents a step backward instead of forward. It means reduced competition as one giant arm of the state replaces many private companies. It means that an agency of government, with an exclusive and perpetual franchise, replaces voluntary associations with nonexclusive and limited franchises. It means that instead of private companies conforming to competitive markets and economic trends, there is an agency that sets its own course, fixes its own rates, and makes up its losses by compulsory levies on the taxpayers. . . .

If most editors and publishers of newspapers and magazines continue to support TVA—and to advocate more TVA's—it will doubtless mean that in due time this nation will be covered with valley authorities. There will be no more private ownership and operation of the means of producing electricity. In that respect, at least, the United States will not differ greatly from socialistic England and communistic Russia. . . .

Woodrow Wilson, when he was a candidate for President, correctly weighed the fundamentals of this issue in these two quotations from his speeches as reported by *The New York Times* of September 9 and 10, 1912: "The history of liberty is the history of limitations of governmental powers, not the increase of it." And: "Has justice ever grown in the soil of absolute power? Has not justice always come from the . . . heart and spirit of men who resist power? Liberty has never come from the government, but always from the subjects of it."

Is there not a thought here worthy of deep consideration by those American editors, publishers, teachers and others who favor TVA and more TVA's?

REBUTTAL OF "THE TVA IDEA" [6]

The Foundation [for Economic Education] . . . has announced it needs $1.5 million a year to promote "an understanding of individual liberty, the voluntary society, and the free market economy" and to scotch "collectivism," which it scents in many places, including TVA. One of its recent staff-written books—*Liberty*, by F. A. Harper—said taxing people and spending the money for things people don't want was slavery, even in a democracy, but didn't explain how it discovered people didn't want the things their elected representatives voted for.

With this background, it is not difficult to understand why Russell's book is characterized by a propaganda approach rather than an objective one. . . . On page 54, Russell says:

For instance, TVA has the legal right to approve or disapprove all drainage projects and plans within its area. . . . Theoretically at least, all property owners must have TVA's permission before building a pond, cutting a ditch, terracing a field, or doing any project that affects "drainage." No unit of local government within the TVA area can build a road, change the course of a stream, or even build a culvert if TVA decides against the project under its "drainage and flood control powers."

TVA has no such powers. The only provision in the TVA Act which even faintly resembles this description is section 26a, which provides that no dams or other obstructions which might

[6] Department of Information, Tennessee Valley Authority, Knoxville, Tenn. October 27, 1949. 38p. Mimeographed.

affect navigation, flood control, or public lands or reservations
can be built or operated "across, along, or in said river or any
of its tributaries" until plans have been approved by the TVA
Board. Except for the power of condemnation of land rights
needed for its projects, a power which is also exercised by private utilities, TVA has no other powers of compulsion.

One of Russell's major theses is that the TVA power operations are subsidized. He declares on page 17 that

Much of the cost of its electricity production is charged off to supposed
gains from its flood control program.

The allocation of investment to navigation, he adds on page 23,

. . . correspondingly reduces the costs charged to power production,
permits lower electricity rates to TVA customers, and puts a larger share
of the load on the taxpayers.

The Federal Power Commission, in a report made at the
request of a subcommittee of the Senate Committee on Public
Works and published before Russell's book appeared, found that
the estimated flood control and navigation benefits would justify
investments for those purposes nearly $140 million greater than
the actual investments under the TVA allocation of investment
in its multiple-purpose system. . . .

On page 23, Russell says:

Fortunately, for purposes of rough comparison, the Army Engineers
made an estimate of the cost of a separate navigation project for the
Tennessee River in 1930. This report to Congress concerned a contemplated project to do for navigation on the Tennessee just what TVA later
did. The estimate for the total project was $75 million. Yet, in a period
of much lower construction costs, TVA allocated $149 million for the
project. . . .

This report, House Document 328, 71st Congress, did not
"concern" a single-purpose navigation project; practically the
whole of its more than seven hundred pages were "concerned"
with a multiple-purpose development for flood control, navigation, and power encompassing some 150 dams in the Tennessee
Valley . . . .

Finally, he discussed traffic in terms of tons rather than ton-miles. This is equivalent to comparing the value of moving a ton of sand and gravel a dozen miles with the value of moving a ton of wheat or gasoline the full 630-mile length of the channel. . . .

On page 37, Russell says that

TVA has taken over many tax-paying industries, and it has taken many thousands of acres of productive farm land off the tax rolls. . . .

TVA has "taken over" no industries. It has purchased a part of the facilities of one industry, the transmission and generating facilities of electric power producers in the region. Local groups bought the distribution facilities. . . .

TVA is entirely a wholesaler of power, and comparisons of the taxes paid by private utilities which combine both production and retail operations should be made with combined payments of TVA and the local distributors. . . .

The fact is that TVA's payments in lieu of taxes in the fiscal year 1948, amounting to $2,008,000, exceeded the state and local ad valorem taxes on the utility properties it has acquired and on *all* reservoir lands by more than $500,000. The payments by TVA plus the payments by municipal and cooperative distributors of TVA power amounted to $4,538,000 and exceeded former state and local ad valorem taxes by $1,404,000.

On page 33, Russell says:

The fact that the TVA electricity rates do not include interest and other inescapable costs of doing business does not mean that these costs are thereby avoided. . . .

Regulatory commissions have long held that interest, for rate-making purposes, cannot be included as an operating cost. As the Oklahoma Supreme Court held twenty-six years ago:

To allow appellant (a gas utility) a return on the money invested, and also the interest paid on the bonds with which this money was procured, would be to impose upon the public a burden it should not carry. . . .

Russell attempts to minimize the national defense contributions of TVA. For example, although it is widely known that one of the major reasons for the location of the Oak Ridge atomic energy plant in the Tennessee Valley was the ability of TVA to supply large amounts of power on a fast schedule, Russell refers at page 30 to "whatever electricity TVA may have sold" to Oak Ridge as though it were a small contribution. . . .

The Congressional Record of June 15, 1948, page 8537, reveals that as of that date the Atomic Energy Commission had a contract for 225 thousand kilowatts of power from TVA and its average demand on the TVA system was 211 thousand kilowatts. It further revealed that future developments or an emergency might result in a need for 50 thousand kilowatts additional and "possibly several times that figure." Two hundred and twenty-five thousand kilowatts is a great deal of power— more than that purchased by any other customer of TVA, including the cities of Memphis and Chattanooga.

He likewise minimizes the contribution of TVA power to aluminum production, although the fact is that the ability of TVA to build dams in record time and thus supply power quickly enabled the rapid expansion of aluminum production at Alcoa, Tennessee. In fact, early in the war, the Office of Production Management, after canvassing the possibilities, determined that the Tennessee Valley was the only place in the country where a needed block of power, upwards of one hundred thousand kilowatts, could be made available within a year's time. . . .

Russell . . . at page 16 sets the loss of agricultural production on all TVA-purchased lands at $27 million, and attempts to compare this solely against flood control benefits, disregarding the many other benefits of multiple-purpose river control. . . .

The value of agricultural production on the lands now under water—approximately 300 thousand acres of crop and pasture land—was nowhere near $27 million, but rather, on the basis of careful calculations based on prices at the time most of it was acquired, no more than $8 million. Even this is a gross exaggeration of "loss." Much more than land enters into the making of a crop or of agricultural production—management, labor, seed, fertilizer, farm machinery, livestock—and none of these are "lost" by reason of construction of the reservoirs. The actual "loss," therefore, amounts to no more than the rental value of the land, for which the owners were compensated in the purchase prices. At 6 per cent return on the value of the land, this amounted, at a generous estimate, to $1 million. . . .

Russell's chapter 12, in which he seeks to make out that electric service is not a natural monopoly but is subject to competition just like the corner grocery or the main street department store, is lavishly sprinkled with italics. . . .

For in this, as in several other respects, Russell goes far beyond even the private utilities themselves, which recognize that they are one of the businesses which have long been recognized as "affected with a public interest" and are thus subject to regulation. . . .

In 1898, the United States Supreme Court held in the case of *Smyth* v. *Ames*, with respect to the status of a utility (in this case a railroad):

Such a corporation was created for public purposes. It performs a function of the state. Its authority to exercise the right of eminent domain and to charge tolls was given primarily for the benefit of the public. . . .

Russell also goes beyond the private utilities in contending that the government should not develop the public streams, for even the power companies have come to recognize that only the government can fully develop the potentialities of the nation's water resources.

On page 30, Russell says:

Private companies have doubled and trebled their production in many other sections of the country before—and after—TVA came into existence. Can it be logically assumed that they would not also have continued to meet the full demand for electricity in Tennessee if the government had not forced them out of business?

In the Tennessee Valley, power production has been not doubled or trebled, but multiplied ten times. Quite aside from the fact that private interests would not have developed the River on a multiple-purpose basis, for navigation and flood control and other subsidiary but substantial benefits, there is ample evidence they would not have developed the power potentialities either.

HIDDEN RED INK IN TVA'S BOOKS [7]

In 1916 war raged in Europe. To insure a supply of nitrates, Congress voted funds for two nitrate plants at Muscle Shoals and a dam to produce hydroelectric power to run the plants. The dam, finished in 1925, became a government headache. Finally in 1933 Senator George Norris put through a bill creating the Tennessee Valley Authority to operate the plants for fertilizer and the dam for navigation, flood control and power.

But TVA is no longer just a plant and a dam. There are 28 dams on 650 miles of rivers running through 7 states. TVA owns ten steam plants, has built villages, parks, stores; makes fertilizer; carries on forestry, agricultural and recreational operations. Moreover, it is now proposed to establish as many as nine more TVA's all over the country for the Missouri, Columbia, Arkansas and other valleys.

I strongly advocated TVA. But in the interest of TVA and the country I think TVA's financial picture should be set straight. Its managers have made extravagant claims. Dr. Arthur E. Morgan, its first chairman, told Congress in 1934:

After a preliminary period . . . this program will be amortized in 25 years.

David Lilienthal, its next chairman, said in 1944:

Even if the total investment in power, navigation and flood control— the entire $700 million—were charged against power, revenues would pay the entire cost in less than sixty years.

It cost $762 million to build TVA. The government borrowed and put up the money and pays interest on it. In addition the plant must be operated. The operation costs over fourteen years up to June 1946, including the interest paid by the government, were $339 million. The revenues were $209 million. Thus there was actually a deficit of $130 million.

[7] From an article by John T. Flynn, journalist, frequent contributor to *The Reader's Digest,* author of *The Road Ahead. Reader's Digest.* 308:129-35. December 1947. Reprinted by permission.

But TVA has a different figure. It arrives at it by leaving out of its accounts the $129 million paid by the government as interest on the loans.

TVA carries out many activities. Power production is only one of them. The figures given above are for the entire program, including power. Now let us look at the power enterprise alone. TVA insists it is selling power cheaper than private companies and doing so at a profit. Let us see.

The total investment in TVA power—using TVA's own accounting assumptions—is $462 millions. All of this was borrowed by the government. A TVA propaganda book claims that "the total net profit from power since the beginning in 1933 to June 30, 1944" was $38 million. But alas, this left out the fact that $53 million was paid by the government as interest on the money borrowed to build the power plants. Hence a power deficit of $15 million.

TVA, of course, will never accept these figures. If one questions its accounts, it replies: "Go to our reports. It is all there, verified by a firm of independent accountants." But it is not all there. Nowhere can you find any record of the interest charges paid by the government. The firm of accountants it cites took particular pains to point this out, saying: "The net results stated for this program do not include any charge for interest." And the General Accounting Office of the United States, in an official report, expressly calls attention to this same failure and wants it corrected.

The government has financed hundreds of housing projects. There is a loss of over $4 million a year on these. But the projects faithfully record their interest costs. If, following TVA, they ignored this item, they could boast a profit of $14 million a year.

On the government-financed Bonneville Dam project the Treasury charges 2.5 per cent interest. Why not on TVA's power debt? As a matter of fact, TVA's debt for its power investment alone is split into two classes. There is a small one of $58 million and a large one of $404 million. The government holds both. TVA does pay one per cent on the small one but nothing on the big one. Why is the interest on the small debt—however inadequate—a proper cost item while the interest on the big one is suppressed in its accounts?

If TVA were a private corporation the law would require it to state its debt and interest payments with exactitude. TVA ignores this. Each year it reports its revenues and expenses (without interest). It calls the difference "net income." This is inexcusable in any case. It is doubly so in TVA, which started out as a "scientific yardstick" to measure public utility rates. But a yardstick must control all thirty-six inches. The interest costs actually amount to more than a third of TVA's annual power costs. What sort of yardstick is it which leaves out a whole foot?

No one need take my word for this. The United States General Accounting Office says:

> Unless all costs for TVA's power operations are included in its income statement . . . it cannot be conclusively shown that the power operations are self-supporting.

It then insists that the interest on the government loans must be included and that the proper rate is 2.5 per cent.

The TVA, of course, greatly improved its showing during the war. The whole Valley was turned into a war arsenal. TVA revenues doubled, as did those of many corporations. However, TVA reports its war record for power with the same two-foot yardstick. It reports "net income" for the six years from 1941 to 1946 as $72 million. But what it omits is a bill for $57 million of government interest on the power debt.

However, these years do show a net power income, even when interest is included. At least, they seem to do so. But the General Accounting Office is unwilling to say so. It points in its TVA report to various costs left out, one alone amounting to as much as $500 thousand a year, and concludes that

> Power rates appear to produce gross revenues in excess of the costs of power production, [but] there can be no consistent showing of whether TVA is self-supporting and liquidating unless every element of cost is recorded on its books and shown in its final statement.

The TVA Act says its power project must be self-liquidating. The GAO says it will never be until its electric rates produce enough to liquidate its debt. The Appropriations Committee of the House says it should liquidate its debt in forty years. This alone would mean an annual minimum payment to the government of $11 million. Who should pay the cost of the power plant which produces power if not the people who enjoy the use of that power as is done by the customers of every private utility in the land?

The General Accounting Office has said the books do not tell the whole story: It is not all there. All of which recalls the complaint of Dr. Arthur Morgan, the first TVA chairman, who declared that there ought to be an impartial investigation of the "obscure financial record of the power program."

We may now ask: Is TVA selling power at less than it costs? What should power costs include? Obviously the following: (1) All operation costs. The GAO says all are not included. (2) State taxes. It pays some but less than a private company of the same size. (3) Federal taxes. It pays none. Other utilities pay large sums. TVA boasts that other utilities pay only a part of their profits in taxes, while TVA pays all its profits. But it has no profits. (4) Interest on the government power debt to build TVA. (5) Liquidation of the debt incurred to build TVA.

Actually, the estimates of the cost of TVA power given above are probably much too low. They are based on certain assumptions made by TVA directors. Upon these assumptions I have put the debt for power at $462 million. I believe, however, that a more rational allocation of power costs would put that debt at not less than $600 million.

Many of the great dams in the Tennessee River and tributaries are called "multi-purpose" dams. It is claimed they were built not only to produce hydroelectric power but to control navigation and floods. The directors of TVA have declared how much of the structure is for power and how much for navigation and flood control. But no one has ever officially checked this allocation. The private accounting firm which audited TVA's books specifically disclaimed any responsibility for the allocation used. And the General Accounting Office has made the same disclaimer.

Competent engineers have disputed TVA's claims and have insisted that the dams are almost wholly for power production and that the element of flood protection or navigation control in them is small. They are supported in this by the leading authority on flood control in Congress, Will M. Whittington, a Democrat, former Chairman of the House Committee on Flood Control, a supporter of TVA and a Representative of Mississippi, which enjoys a large measure of benefits from TVA. In a speech in the House he declared that "TVA is primarily for the development of power."

There can never be any authoritative accounting of the cost of TVA power until the total amount of the investment in power has been settled. It is this that the General Accounting Office referred to when it recently reported that "the power debt should be finally determined."

I have examined patiently most of the evidence on both sides of this subject and have gone to the TVA country to check on the respective claims. I believe there is no escaping the conclusion that the allocation of power investment and costs made by TVA is arbitrary and that if it is ever audited by a competent board of impartial engineers and accountants it will be found that the power investment and debt is not $462 million but $600 million at the lowest.

The reason for TVA's official claim of lower power investment is plain. The more costs TVA can unload on navigation and flood control, the less the costs of power will seem. By the accounting trick here described TVA has cut more than $150 million from the debt due for power. They can also reduce the seeming cost of operating the dams, because they now charge off most of the cost of operating the "common purposes" of the dams to navigation and flood control.

Do I want TVA destroyed? Certainly not. But we must submit TVA to the yardstick which it now tries to forget. Just as we had to have commissions to stop private utilities from soaking the customers, we should have some authority to prevent publicly owned power projects from soaking the taxpayers.

What should be done seems to me inescapable: (1) The outstanding government debt on the power enterprise should be determined definitely and the TVA should pay interest on it. (2) The TVA should pay off this debt in forty years. (3) These items and all other costs should be included in the rates charged for power. (4) The TVA directors should not be the sole judges of the amount of the investment in power. (5) All the non-power activities of TVA—agriculture, fertilizer production, forestry and other projects—should be transferred to appropriate departments of the government. They should be divorced from the TVA power project to which they have no rational relationship. (6) The costs of these activities should be paid out of authorized Congressional appropriations like any other costs of government.

There is an aspect of TVA which disturbs me more than its fiscal vagaries. It has operated as a federal corporation under a charter which has enabled it to do an incredible number of things and to escape government scrutiny. The federal charter is a comparatively new device to enable the Federal Government to expand its powers immensely. Mr. Lilienthal, in his book, *TVA—Democracy on the March*, calls attention to the vast growth of federal power. It has become so great that, he says, it cannot be wisely administered from Washington. But the power must not go back to the governors, mayors, legislatures and councils elected by the people. It must go to great regional areas administered by directors appointed by the President, to a corporation cunningly devised to accumulate power and to elude congressional authority. We will see the country split into a few great regional provinces run by corporate provincial governors. This is what Mr. Lilienthal calls "democracy on the march." I think it is democracy in retreat, a return to the European system of centrally controlled provincial governors. With TVA as a beginning the advocates of regionalism are planning under the guise of flood, navigation and forestry control and other excuses to blanket America with this new type of government which represents a complete revolution in our political system.

The TVA should be specifically instructed by Congress that it is not a provincial government agency of a regional province but a government-owned power enterprise. If the people of the United States want to adopt the regional form of government they should do so—but only after full discussion and a formal decision. I do not think it should be presented to them suddenly as an accomplished fact.

CHANGES IN TVA ACCOUNTING [8]

You ask about the recommendations made in the 1945 GAO audit report on TVA [see page xxx]. We assume that you are aware that few of the recommendations related to accounting proper, but rather were recommendations that Congress change policies which it had incorporated in the original TVA Act. Congressional action for such changes would of course be required.

A number of recommendations made in the 1945 audit report have been dropped or greatly modified in subsequent audit reports. . . . Some changes have been made as follows:

[It was] recommended that the TVA determine and show separately on its books the portion of its capital derived from appropriations and invested in the power system. This determination has been made and is reflected on the books and in the TVA annual report (1949), page A 5.

[It was] recommended that a definite plan be adopted for repayment of appropriated funds invested in power and for payment of interest. In the Government Corporations Appropriations Act, 1948, Congress enacted a plan for repayment of the Treasury investment in the TVA power system over a period of forty years. The Congress has not adopted the recommendation that payment of interest on such funds be required in addition.

[It was] recommended that TVA be permitted to combine all of its funds in one depository account. Legislation granting this permission has been enacted in the Independent Offices Appropriations Act, 1950, but the combination has not been made by TVA pending completion of a study being made of the effects of such action by the Department of the Treasury, the Bureau of the Budget, and the General Accounting Office.

[8] From a letter to the editor of this compilation by W. L. Sturdevant, Director of Information, Tennessee Valley Authority. Knoxville, Tenn. February 10, 1950. Quoted by permission.

[It was] recommended that the act of November 21, 1941, containing the requirement that TVA render accounts to the General Accounting Office under the Budget and Accounting Act, 1921, be repealed. The act in question has not been repealed, but the purposes of the recommendation have been met by regulations issued by the General Accounting Office under the provisions of the Government Corporation Control Act. In effect, the change means that GAO makes a commercial-type audit of individual transactions in Washington.

LABOR-MANAGEMENT RELATIONS IN TVA [9]

Management and labor have learned to work together, to their mutual satisfaction and in the interest of the public, on projects of the Tennessee Valley Authority, which was established in 1933. For collective bargaining purposes, most of the employees are represented by the Tennessee Valley Trades and Labor Council, composed of fourteen AFL unions. TVA also deals separately with several other unions, representing white-collar workers for the most part.

Some of the reasons for the good labor-management relations are set forth in a recent report of a congressional committee (Congressional Joint Committee on Labor-Management Relations. Report No.372):

Management has proved by its deeds that it is constantly striving to deal fairly and squarely with labor; labor has confidence in the motives of TVA; both labor and management know the value and meaning of cooperation; the Tennessee Valley Trades and Labor Council is composed of responsible unions; the officers of the council are real labor leaders, men of exceptional ability and character; TVA keeps the council fully informed of all events that are of interest to the council; TVA officers, on the whole, have been competent, intelligent, and realistic individuals.

As it began building up the working force from the Tennessee watershed area, the TVA adopted an employee-relationship policy of nondiscrimination between union and non-union

[9] *Monthly Labor Review.* 69:41-2. July, 1949.

employees, freedom of workers to organize or to join unions of their choice, and majority rule in selection of union representatives. Work continued under this policy, without a written union-management agreement, from 1935 to 1940, when the first written agreement was signed by the TVA and the Tennessee Valley Trades and Labor Council. The closed or union shop at TVA operations, according to the congressional committee's report, has never become an issue, chiefly because

The council has complete faith in the labor policy of the Authority. . . . [TVA officials] all have proven by their actions and deeds that they are constantly striving to deal honestly and aboveboard with all the unions with whom TVA has relations, and with the Tennessee Valley Trades and Labor Council as an over-all trades and labor body.

On the unions' side, the leaders have been men who have worked with tools. They have risen through the ranks, and have developed into efficient and practical leaders.

Joint labor-management committees have been used to give the workers an effective voice in working out problems of job classification, operating efficiency, education and training, health and safety, strengthening of morale, etc. Employees' suggestions are solicited and evaluated under a system of nonmonetary rewards. An apprenticeship program and a retirement system have been developed and carried on with the assistance of joint committees. Wage rates are set on the basis of rates prevailing in the vicinity. When wages are negotiated, the TVA and the council make separate surveys and then compare results to determine the prevailing rates. Disputes over this question may be referred to the United States Secretary of Labor for final determination. Only four such disputes have been so referred, according to the Senate committee's report.

With respect to the settlement of grievances, adjustment is first sought through supervisory channels, with privilege of appeal to the director of personnel, whose decision is final in cases involving salaried employees. For trades and labor employees, this procedure has been supplemented by the general agreement between the TVA and the Tennessee Valley Trades and Labor Council. The agreement provides that where a dispute is not settled by the means described above it is to be considered by representatives of the council, the international representative of the union involved or his agent, and, for the TVA, the director of personnel or his representative, in joint session. If not settled at this point, it goes to a joint board of adjustment. If no satisfactory decision is reached within sixty days after completion of hearings, this board, with the concurrence of either party, submits the dispute to an impartial referee for final determination.

TVA has had few strikes or work stoppages of any consequence. In the first sixteen years of its existence only one strike has had the backing of the international union officers; this was a jurisdictional strike which lasted, at different points of construction, from three days to a week. Jurisdictional disputes are kept to a minimum by advance discussions of work assignments and by settling claims of the unions involved before projects actually get under way.

THE FIRST FIFTEEN YEARS [10]

The Tennessee Valley Authority's greatest accomplishment may not be its magnificent dams, but its demonstration that democracy can be efficient. TVA today provides the standing answer to the contention that whenever the people try to do something for themselves, the undertaking bogs down in legislative delays, bureaucratic rivalries, extravagance and graft.

Under the chairmanship of David Lilienthal, TVA has shown that the corporation device can be as useful in the public service as for private gain. While properly subject to ultimate congressional control, TVA is largely divorced from Washington. Its work is done in the region which it serves. And it is done with all the engineering and accounting facilities which modern management commands. Along the Tennessee there are none of those interdepartment battlefields that scar the valleys of the Columbia and Missouri. . . .

[10] From an article by Ernest Kirschten, staff writer, the *St. Louis Post-Dispatch*. *The Nation*. 166:656-9. June 12, 1948. Reprinted by permission.

The latest opposition argument runs along the line that it is all right for TVA to develop natural resources—meaning water power—but it should not be allowed to generate enough thermal power to enable it to market hydroelectric current in an orderly manner. [The issue involves a bill to permit TVA to build a steam generating plant at New Johnsonville, Tennessee.] . . .

The critics still say that TVA is being run mostly "for other purposes." Actually it has been remarkably faithful to its mandate. A score of dams have been built between Gilbertsville in Kentucky and Fontana in North Carolina. They have turned a once shoal-dotted and troublesome stream into a succession of beautiful inland lakes which in 1947 carried an estimated 341 million ton-miles of freight, exclusive of sand and gravel. This was more than ten times the traffic in 1933.

As for flood control, TVA reduced by ten feet the crest of last February's flood and saved Chattanooga alone about $6 million in flood losses. It is estimated that $27 million in flood losses has been saved since Norris Dam went into operation in 1936. Nor can it be overlooked that control of the Tennessee has lowered flood crests on the Ohio and the Mississippi.

TVA has always been well aware that flood control begins on the land. Again faithful to the act, it has planted thousands of trees and fostered contour plowing. To reclaim marginal land it has made progress in breaking the one-crop habit. It has demonstrated that grass—in the form of meat and dairy products—is more profitable than cotton. It has shown that fertilizers, especially phosphates, can make well-nigh barren land fertile. Thus, while tobacco acreage is down 8 per cent, the yield is up 48 per cent. Corn acreage is down 19.7 per cent, but the yield is up almost 20 per cent. Between 1939 and 1944 farm prices rose 105 per cent, but the value of Tennessee Valley farm products went up 147 per cent—from $110,803,000 to $274,466,000.

The once backward valley has been transformed into an industrial region of increasing importance. Between 1933 and 1945 employment opportunities in factories went up 161 per cent, or 30 per cent more than in the rest of the country. Since

1933 more than eighteen hundred new plants have been opened in the area. And as Mr. Clapp [Gordon R. Clapp, TVA chairman] said in a recent speech, "so far as is known, only four of these new plants were moved in from other regions."

Per capita income in the valley is rising more rapidly than in the United States as a whole. In 1933 it was only 40 per cent of the national average. By 1946 it had risen to 58 per cent. The dollar figure for 1945 was a round $2.1 billions—or $680 million more than it would have been had it increased only at the national rate. Income-tax figures show how this has benefited the nation. In 1933 collections in the valley represented 3.4 per cent of the total. By 1946 the figure was up to 6 per cent. Also, of that extra $680 million, no less than $450 million was used to buy products of other sections of the United States.

The big chapter in TVA's story, of course, is power. Increased incomes in industry and agriculture alike are based on it. It also has enabled TVA to make its prescribed contribution to the national defense. TVA electricity made the aluminum that filled the air with American planes. TVA electricity runs Oak Ridge.

TVA produced 14,797,000,000 kilowatt hours in 1947 [15,734,764,000 in the 1949 fiscal year], compared with 12,314,000,000 in the previous year. (Incidentally 92 per cent of the 1947 output came from hydroelectric plants.) But the demand still is rising. Between June 20 of last year and the end of February, 1948, the number of consumers increased from 743,000 to 810,000 [984,600 for the 1949 fiscal year]. And the use per consumer is mounting. The average for 1947 was 2,197 kilowatt-hours; by the end of last February it was up to 2,446 [2,762 by June 30, 1949].

Surely this is proof of the theory that low costs will promote widespread use of power. And TVA power is cheap. The average price at the end of February was 1.59 cents per kilowatt hour, compared with a national average of 3.08 cents. [TVA's average price for the 1949 fiscal year was 1.54 cents and the country's average was 2.98 cents.] For 100 kilowatt hours the residential rate in the TVA area is $2.50. In New York it is $4.86; in Chicago, $3.35; in St. Louis, $2.85; in San

Francisco, $2.82. In McMinnville, Oregon, served by Bonneville, it is $2.50 as in the TVA area.

And now the storm breaks! Sure, TVA rates are low, but they are subsidized, runs the charge. Well, at least Congress is satisfied that TVA is not allocating to navigation and other activities expenses properly chargeable to the power account. Of TVA's bookkeeping the General Accounting Office has said that it probably is "the finest accounting system in the entire government and probably one of the best accounting systems in the world." So no facts are concealed. But known facts can be variously interpreted.

TVA does not pay interest on the sums appropriated by the federal government for construction of its facilities. It regards this money as an investment rather than as a loan. And TVA does not pay federal taxes. Certainly, these factors should be considered in comparisons with private power rates. Privately owned utilities cannot raise money in quite the same way. On this point Mr. Clapp says:

The charge of subsidy can best be answered by examining what the books show for the fiscal year ending June 30, 1947. In that year TVA showed a net operating revenue of $21.8 million [$20,944,915 for 1948-49 fiscal year], representing a 5.5 per cent return on all the money—$400 million—invested in the power system. This is the sum remaining after state and local ad valorem tax payments, straight-line depreciation and all operating expenses incurred in generating and transmitting power. The $21.8 million therefore, corresponds to the sum which a private corporation, utility or otherwise, has to divide among those who have invested money in the business and to pay federal income taxes. It is the significant figure in determining the financial soundness of the enterprise.

All of this $21.8 million or 5.5 per cent return, is the property of the federal government. It can be divided up according to any theory you care to use. For example, if interest were charged at 2 per cent, the average cost of money to the government during the period, on the entire TVA average net power investment of $400 million, there would still remain $13.8 million. If income taxes were calculated at the rate charged large corporations, 38 per cent on net income after interest, or roughly and generously $5.3 million, there still remains a surplus of $8.5 million. . . .

And the last word: in the 1948 appropriation bill Congress provided a formula whereby the government's investment in

TVA power facilities—set at $348,249,000 rather than the round figure of $400,000,000 used by Mr. Clapp—is to be paid back into the Treasury in forty annual instalments. After that, TVA power earning will be virtually a windfall for the American taxpayer. In less obvious and less easily calculated ways TVA's other activities also in the long run are bound to pay for themselves.

This, it seems, ought to be the answer not only to the critics of TVA but to those who regard this world-famous enterprise merely as a rich nation's gift to a backward section or, as a friend puts it, restitution by the North for the carpetbagging of Reconstruction days.

BIG PUSH AGAINST THE VALLEY [11]

The South is in many ways the social laboratory of America. A constant search goes on here for ways of improving relations with minority groups, extending political democracy, and bringing the fruits of industrialization within the reach of the people of the region. . . .

This last effort is perhaps the most spectacular and encouraging. And almost none of its inspiration can be traced to communism; the South knows little about communism as a theory and has too few resident Communists to be affected by their words or actions. This is doubly important just now when the TVA is being assailed as never before by the private power interests and their political henchmen. While the real purpose of the TVA's enemies—to regain control of the power business— has not changed, new slogans have been coined to take advantage of the present drive against world communism and its corollary, public ownership in the country. The reactions of the people in the Tennessee Valley to these slogans are singularly illuminating. Is the TVA employee resentful or fearful because his boss is the government? Is the employee of the Alabama Power Company, which serves adjacent areas, glad that the company for which he

[11] From "Dixie in Black and White," by A. G. Mezerik, editor and business consultant. *The Nation.* 164:655-8. May 31, 1947. Reprinted by permission.

works is privately owned? It turns out that neither is concerned about this aspect of his work. Both think well of their employers; both discuss their jobs in terms of hours, wages, and security.

When they compare the two utilities they speak of conditions of work, or the opportunities for advancement, or the pension system. "Regimentation," "collectivism," "capitalism"—these ideas do not creep into their talk.

The consumers of power, the people who use it in their homes or factories or on their farms, are just as little concerned with the bogy of communism. They are interested in the cost of power, and they favor the TVA because it sells power more cheaply than private companies. In the hills that march up almost to the borders of the city of Chattanooga, mountaineers have lived for generations, remote and isolated in their unpainted cabins. Now the city of Chattanooga is bringing TVA power to these people. And though the Tennessee mountaineers have long been celebrated in song and story as fanatical individualists, not one has refused the chance to get light or heat because it is supplied by a publicly owned generating plant. Nor have any of the other three and a quarter million people in the seven states of the valley refused for that reason. Even the gigantic monopolies, by using so much of TVA's power, testify to the irrelevancy of arguing about the sin or virtue of public ownership.

Dupont, Alcoa, Monsanto, and Eastman are organizations which Representative Rankin himself could hardly accuse of collectivist leanings; yet they are among the ten great corporations which, with the United States installation at Oak Ridge, use 48 per cent of all the power developed by the TVA. America's great monopolies have built huge plants in the Valley. TVA power is cheap and abundant. The presidents of these companies, however, damn public ownership every time they speak at their 1947 versions of Liberty League dinners. . . . Recently Gwilym A. Price, president of Westinghouse, one of the world's greatest producers of equipment for utility companies, went all out against collectivism. He was afraid people might fall for it in the belief that government ownership would lower prices. A survey made by the Psychological Corporation, he said, has discovered that almost one third of the people of the United States believed government ownership might bring lower prices. "This means," he added, "that one third of our population has swallowed the Communist party line and doesn't know it." Perhaps they have, but have Du Pont, Union Carbon and Carbide, and Alcoa also fallen for it? They seem to be convinced that the government sells its product more cheaply than do private plants or they would not have located in the Valley. The private-utility bloc must think the same thing or they would not be trying to get Congress to make them the sole recipients and sales agents of all government-owned power.

Their actions, of course, have nothing to do with communism. They do, however, raise another kind of doubt. The TVA was developed with public money, yours, mine, and that of 135 million other taxpayers. Monopolies use almost 48 per cent of TVA's electric power in their industrial operations; an additional 20 per cent is surplus and exported to the power lines of privately owned utility companies. On every cent's worth of that 68 per cent of TVA's power output these huge companies, in and outside the Valley, are getting a subsidy from the rest of us, for our taxes made possible the savings in power costs which they now enjoy. The success of private enterprise may be more dependent on public ownership than anyone has guessed—an idea not likely to attract the study or the sympathy of the NAM [National Association of Manufacturers].

Public subsidy works queer changes. In neighboring North Carolina a textile bourbon who has opposed not only the TVA at every stage, from planning through completion, but also the REA [Rural Electrification Administration] and everything connected with either, has had a conversion. When I talked to him the other day, he described with great enthusiasm a new electrically powered knitting machine designed for home use on farms. (The textile industry would like to revive the old work-at-home contracting business, which might develop into a strike-breaking and union-busting business, especially if the farmer's wife could be listed as a textile employee with a vote in the National Labor Board elections.) I asked my bourbon acquaintance whether he had changed his mind and come to the conclusion that public power was really a fine thing. The answer was pithy: "It doesn't make any difference what I think about it; TVA is here to stay, and the textile industry is going to get what benefits it can from it."

The left hand of industry—it must be the left—takes the subsidy of cheap power rates and tries to find new ways to increase its share of the subsidy. But evidently the left hand says nothing at all to the right hand, which is busy trying to cripple the source of the subsidy. . . .

Rates may be lowered to consumers, crops may be vastly improved as a result of TVA teaching and TVA phosphates, the whole region's standard of living may rise—from 1933 to 1939 it rose more than 70 per cent—but none of this counts with the utility companies. They want to control the sources of power, and now they see their big chance. They have been preparing for some years. More than a hundred big private electric-power companies have banded together as an association [National Association of Electric Companies], the top executive of which has just registered with Congress as a lobbyist. His salary, he has disclosed, is $650 thousand a year, which makes him the highest paid lobbyist in Washington. In addition to this direct pressure on Congress the association employs high-powered publicists to sell the people on the incomparable virtues of private ownership. The approach is national, using pages in color in *Life* and other slick magazines and network radio time, locally sponsored, of course. Local propaganda is not neglected by a long way. In every town and hamlet where private utilities have influence the private-power boys arrange speakers for luncheon meetings, buy local advertising, and spread the word against communism in general and the TVA in particular. Their henchmen operate in the legislatures of any state where public power is for sale or its development contemplated. In the far Northwest the private-power interests fight Bonneville with the same venom they show against TVA. They fight it even while they admit, as they did recently in the state of Washington, that only the national government can or will make the necessary investment to provide the additional power so badly needed. . . .

Certain private utilities would like to raise their rates now, but they think it would be politically dangerous to try it. If they did, municipalities would redouble their efforts to take over the systems and operate them under public ownership. The power boys reason that the way to stop that trend is to force existing public-power projects to sell all their power to private utilities, which will charge the consumer all the traffic will bear.

At least six bills have been introduced in Congress to check the expansion of public ownership. Some slash directly at the TVA. . . .

No farmer, worker or businessman wants to see these legislative hatchet men succeed. They know that the TVA is very much more than a generator of electric energy. It is a deep waterway 650 miles long for carrying all sorts of goods unimpeded by rapids or shallows or the snags of discriminatory freight rates. It is a chain of beautiful lakes where millions of persons can go fishing and boating. It is freedom from fear of floods, for the Tennessee is now a completely "engineered" river, controlled as a unit with every mile safeguarded. The TVA is industry, new industry—Valley-trained men and women work in factories which range in size from a two-man shop to the largest aluminum rolling mill in the world. Many small home-owner plants have come into being with the help of the TVA.

For the Valley people the TVA means more than a livelihood; it means almost a way of life. In former years the region was infested with malaria; in 1946, 9,300 examinations revealed only 28 positive cases. Farm living has become a new experience. Electricity eases the burdens of overworked women and helps the farmers with their heavy chores. The radio brings entertainment—music and news of the world. . . .

There is strength in the Valley to fight these threats to its future. The 138 municipally owned power companies and farmers' electrical cooperatives have been tempered in previous assaults upon the TVA. They will have the support of the newspapers and the chambers of commerce of the towns which have benefited from the Valley's development; and the growing trade-union movement is taking up its share of the load.

They will win—with the country's help—and the issue on which they will win is as real as the power bloc's talk of collectivism is phony.

THE PROPOSED COLUMBIA VALLEY
ADMINISTRATION

EDITOR'S INTRODUCTION

President Truman has given top priority to the Columbia Valley in legislation for new river basin authorities.

The problem is not, as in the Tennessee Valley, to give a lift to a poor region. The Columbia Valley, as Richard L. Neuberger points out in "CVA: Order on the Frontier," boasts of natural riches unsurpassed in the nation.

The main objectives of a CVA would be to develop these resources to keep pace with the rapid population and industrial growth of the Pacific Northwest, and to curb the extravagance with which they have too often been exploited in the past.

The Columbia's hydroelectric potential is the greatest in the United States. But the combined efforts of private utilities and of the Bonneville Power Administration, operating the huge Bonneville and Grand Coulee generating plants, have harnessed only about one tenth of this energy.

Private utilities and those associated with them assert that generating capacity is being increased as fast as the market can absorb the output. CVA's backers point, in reply, to an unemployment rate in the Pacific Northwest well above the national average. Expansion of existing industries and the location of new industries in a region of unrivaled facilities, they declare, awaits only the availability of more electric power.

Who shall do the job has been of greater concern to the Columbia Valley thus far than just what shall be done. The term "administration" in pending CVA bills is a sop to those who fear the implications of "authority."

37 BILLIONS TO REMAKE THE WEST [1]

Money from the federal Treasury is pouring into the West in record-breaking volume to help finance development of the region. An empire is gradually being built around vast water-resource projects.

In the year ending next June 30, the Treasury is to invest nearly $1.4 billion in the West, mostly for dams, power plants, irrigation, flood control and conservation. These capital improvements are to be the foundation for a new regional empire built largely at government expense.

United States investment in the seventeen western states, extending from the Dakotas to Texas and westward to the Pacific, is greater this year than the total spending on all public works in a typical New Deal year, 1939. Yet the 1950 investment is just an instalment on a program that already calls for expenditures of $37 billion over years ahead. Total costs will not stop there, with new ideas and projects appearing every year. . . .

The western empire that planners see is one in which an expanding population is supported by exploiting all resources in full. The official forecast is that population in the West will grow by 14 million between 1949 and 1975.

Big industries are to be pulled into the western spaces, away from the more crowded and vulnerable coastal areas. The deep West already is a haven for strategic industries including atomic-energy and aircraft plants. Oil shale, phosphate, coal and other minerals are to be tapped on a broader scale.

Around the raw materials, so the planning goes, metal-making and manufacturing industries will spring up. Centers of population and trade will follow.

New farms are to be created in large numbers, by irrigating deserts with river water. . . .

[1] From *United States News & World Report.* 27:17-20. December 2, 1949. Reprinted by permission from *U. S. News & World Report,* an independent weekly magazine on national and international affairs, published at Washington, D.C. Copyright 1949, United States News Publishing Corporation.

Western lands now under irrigation total 22 million acres. About 16 million more can be irrigated, on the basis of present ideas about costs and needs for new land. Changing conditions of the future may bring new decisions, planners say, decisions that much more land should be reclaimed—at higher cost, if necessary.

Around 5,650,000 acres will be irrigated as presently planned federal projects go through, during the next ten to fifteen years. Some 24,000 new family-size farms will be carved from the desert, and 65,000 other farms rescued from water shortages. After that, around 1960, at least 10,350,000 acres of reclaimable land would still be waiting for water.

Power plants are to rise along every major western river. Power-transmission systems will crisscross mountains and deserts, tying the whole West into one big power pool. . . .

Total federal power capacity of 3,374,224 kilowatts is operating now. Plants now under construction will add 2,697,000 kilowatts in years just ahead. Planned facilities will bring another 6,535,000 kilowatts into the system in the future. When that is achieved, total federal capacity will reach 12,606,224 kilowatts in the West.

No one doubts that blueprints for other projects will be available by that time. Experts see a potential of 37 million kilowatts of hydroelectric power in the western streams. Present United States electric power capacity, in all types of plants, is 73.3 million kilowatts.

Key to empire building in the West, the plans make clear, is capture, control and use of water from the rivers. Water itself is needed. Nearly all the areas of the Southwest are up against acute water shortages. Supplies are insufficient for present needs, to say nothing of future demands. And water is the main source for power today. Atomic installations planned for the West promise an abundant substitute, but only if and when the power of the atom can be applied.

In bringing water to the West, the Federal Government is embarking on the world's greatest reclamation programs, bar none. Mistakes and troubles in the effort are expected, and not lacking. . . .

Despite the problems, construction is going ahead faster year by year. The Bureau of Reclamation now spends more money in twelve months than it spent in its first thirty-five years —1902 to 1937. Local prosperity in many western areas depends in important degree on the flow of Treasury dollars from Washington.

Counting in the more ordinary federal public works with water projects, the West is getting a much larger share of federal aid than any other region. The seventeen western states, with 33.8 million people, are dividing up about 1.4 billion dollars' worth of federal public works this year. The thirty-one other states, with 115 million people, have only $1.6 billion for the things they need. . . .

Irrigation and power projects get the lion's share of federal building dollars in the West. Spending for these improvements will total $359 million this year [fiscal 1950] on Bureau of Reclamation projects alone. That is only half the sum the Reclamation planners wanted to spend, but it is five times the sum they spent in 1940. . . .

Flood control is to cost $192 million this year. Flood-protection activity is widespread, going forward in thirteen of the seventeen western states. In Texas, 32.7 million dollars' worth of work is scheduled, most of it on nine immense reservoirs, initial parts of the system that will some day control all the major rivers in the Arkansas, Oklahoma and Texas area.

North Dakota gets the next largest slice of flood-control funds, $28,221,000, almost all of it to be spent on the Garrison reservoir, a unit of the Missouri River control plan. In South Dakota, $23 million is set aside for the Fort Randall reservoir, another Missouri River unit.

Rivers and harbors improvements are confined to five states. Oregon projects receive more than half of the $53,328,000 allotted to the West for navigation improvements this year.

Power lines—transmitting and marketing systems—will be extended in the western states at a total federal investment of about $135 million. This includes an estimated $100 million for loans to farmers and cities by the Rural Electrification Administration for local power-distribution networks. Bonneville Power Administration is to spend around $30 million for lines from generating plants to consuming areas in the Pacific Northwest. Southwest Power Administration has around $5 million to spend on transmitting facilities in the Southwest as needed this year.

The West is in line for about $6.75 million for rural telephones under the program just approved by Congress. The telephone investment probably will skyrocket in years ahead.

Atomic-energy plants in the western area will be expanded at a cost of $197 million in fiscal year 1950. That is the price of buildings and equipment. Most of the money is to be spent at Hanford, Washington, and in New Mexico. But a beginning is to be made on the big new atomic-energy installation in Idaho.

Soil-conservation activities are to reach the hundred-million-dollar level in fiscal 1950. Federal payments to farmers who cooperate in conservation practices will total about $83 million on basis of tentative state allocations of funds. Technical advice by federal experts to farmers is valued at around $17 million.

Resource aids, such as forest protection, mining explorations and the like, will cost about $125 million in the current year. In this category are some of the most valuable programs of all, from the West's point of view. Experiments with oil shale have led to proposals for a ten-billion-dollar synthetic-oil industry, for example. Most of that industry would be located in the West, when set up.

All the more familiar types of federal public works will be going forward in the West as in other regions.

Highways will get $136,870,000 in federal aid for the present fiscal year.

Airports are down for $8,140,000 in United States funds. That will pay for part of the 146 airport projects in 11 Western States.

Veterans' hospitals and homes worth $45 million will be constructed in the West this year.

Public hospitals will be given $29,972,000 in federal funds. Congress has approved a total of $1.05 billion for financing up to two thirds of the cost on local hospitals in the United States.

Public-housing loans to local housing agencies already are approved amounting to nearly $4 million. That is to provide a start on 12,700 housing units in 28 western cities. United States housing loans may rise considerably in months ahead.

Other aids for the West include federal guarantee of private housing loans, Farmers Home Administration loans to farmers, Reconstruction Finance Corporation loans to businesses and communities.

Total federal investment in the West, or any other region, is seldom glimpsed as a whole, even in Washington, where spending plans are drawn. The very size of western developments, however, has been attracting the attention of other regions.

They see, from the West's example, that when government starts developing resources it tends to supply a ready and ever-rising flow of funds for a region's needs. Political parties feel obligated to keep the programs advancing.

The new-west plans, in fact, got their biggest boost after the 1948 election. President Truman promised western voters more dams, cheap power, irrigation. The voters reacted favorably. The Administration is making good on its promises now and proposing still larger programs for the future.

It all adds up to regional development on a scale never attempted before, anywhere in the world.

A TVA FOR THE COLUMBIA VALLEY [2]

President Truman's long-awaited bill to establish a Columbia Valley authority on the order of the Tennessee Valley Authority finally reached Congress on April 14 [1949]. It was presented by two Washington state representatives—Hugh B. Mitchell and Henry M. Jackson. It then went to the House Public Works Committee—and, despite Truman's help, that's probably where it's going to stay for a while.

[2] From news story. *Business Week.* p 19-23. April 23, 1949. Reprinted by permission.

In a special message to Congress, the President gave credit to existing federal agencies that have been developing the Northwest. But, he pointed out, there are "obvious limits" in trying to control the Columbia and other great river basins through federal interagency committees. "None of the representatives of the several departments and agencies concerned," he said, "is responsible for an over-all view of all the resources of the area."

Truman might have made a case in point had he wished. Only a few months ago he spanked the Army Engineers and the Bureau of Reclamation publicly, ordered them to quit squabbling over who will build what in the Columbia River basin.

Northwesterners see a case for unified control over the Columbia. They are only too aware of the river's rampages, particularly since the disastrous flood of last year. They are also irritated by the Northwest's chronic shortages of electric power.

Even so, public opinion in the region is by no means solid behind CVA. Labor unions, the National Grange, and the Farmers' Union are the only groups firmly backing the plan. Its enemies include the governors of Oregon, Washington, and Idaho; most of the region's press; the Farm Bureau; chambers of commerce; most businessmen. So CVA's more realistic backers are now planning a tub-thumping promotional program this year to work up grassroots sentiment for legislation in 1950. . . .

Though it is called an "administration" rather than an "authority," CVA resembles TVA in many ways.

Physically, a CVA would cover a bigger slice of territory than the TVA. Its bailiwick would include most of Washington, Oregon and Idaho; western Montana; the Snake River basin in northwestern Wyoming; and the upper reaches of the Owyhee River in northern Nevada. That's some 270 thousand square miles in all, as against the TVA's 40 thousand square miles, most of them in a single state.

As far as its powers go, CVA would have a narrower scope than TVA in some cases, wider in others.

CVA's chief functions are described in the bill as planning, construction, and operation of navigation, flood-control, reclamation and conservation projects; control over pollution; protection of fish and wildlife. But unlike TVA, it won't spread into land and mineral conservation. Thus, the Soil Conservation Service, Bureau of Mines, and state conservation bodies would continue their operations, though CVA would have statutory authority to look over their plans and programs.

CVA could go into business almost immediately after enactment of the bill, by virtue of the fact that it would absorb the plans, programs, and staffs of the Bureau of Reclamation, Bonneville Power Administration, and the Army Engineers in the region. (Only thing left to the Army would be channel and harbor improvement in tidal waters.)

The main thing that CVA's backers want to take over from TVA is its type of continuing fund for construction, which is fed both by (1) annual appropriations and (2) revenues from power and other sources. If CVA had to rely solely on annual congressional appropriations, it could do little more planning and construction than the federal agencies working along the Columbia have been able to do up to now.

But Bonneville Power Administration—which markets power from Grand Coulee and Bonneville—grossed nearly $25 million on its sales of power from these two projects alone in fiscal 1948. With more generators coming in soon at Coulee, McNary, the Dalles, Chief Joseph, and other dams, BPA's take on power will more than double in the next few years. This revenue—from power alone—would make a nice kitty for CVA construction jobs. In addition, CVA's funds would be swelled by payments for municipal water supply and for irrigation.

CVA's authority in the electric power field would be broad —much broader than that of TVA. The bill gives CVA the power:

To build "stand-by facilities" for any of its projects. This means that it could build steam-generating plants of the type for which TVA has been fighting for two years.

To string transmission lines. Major lines—not defined in the legislation—would be subject to congressional approval, as would all major water-control or electric-generating projects.

To set its own power rates, including a single "postage-stamp" rate for the entire area.

To buy existing privately owned electric utility systems, though not to condemn such property. It would sell these distribution facilities as rapidly as possible to public bodies or co-ops.

The bill forbids CVA to interfere with existing state water-rights laws. However, it could take over lands and water rights required for dams and other projects. Irrigation water would be distributed in accordance with statutes affecting the Reclamation Bureau, including the 160-acre land limitation on farms eligible for federal water.

If and when CVA becomes a reality, the odds-on favorite to head the three-man board of directors is Assistant Secretary of Interior C. Girard Davidson. He was part of the White House team that prepared the Mitchell-Jackson bill.

CVA—ORDER ON THE FRONTIER [3]

The Northwest has been a realm of legendary dimensions, always. Abundance is its trademark. It claims the swiftest rivers, the thickest forests, the most apples, the bulkiest mountains, the biggest salmon, the fiercest cougars, the heaviest elk, the greenest valleys. Superlatives govern everything from the width of glaciers to the length of beaches. . . .

But in 1949 A.D., nearly a century and a half after the white men came with the flag of freedom, resources are playing out. And the national government at last has a plan for the orderly and coordinated development of the country's final frontier.

This plan is CVA—a Columbia Valley Authority.

CVA would be built around the two great existing dams on the Columbia River—Grand Coulee and Bonneville. It would also include the McNary and the Chief Joseph Dams, to be added at a cost of approximately $475 million. All related resource activities in the region would come under CVA. . . .

Proponents of CVA estimate that the annual power revenues

[3] From an article by Richard L. Neuberger, Oregon State Senator, writer on affairs of the Pacific Northwest. *Survey.* 85:362-6. July 1949. Reprinted by permission.

of $60 million could eventually amortize the cost of the under-taking.

The idea of a Columbia Valley Authority is not new. In 1938 Senators Bone of Washington and Norris of Nebraska proposed such a project. However, it was lost when Secretary of the Interior Ickes suggested, as an alternative, a single administrator responsible to his department. Bone and Norris had advocated a three-man independent commission. A year later President Roosevelt advanced his "seven TVA's" extending across the nation. Naturally, CVA was included.

Then the proposal went on the shelf, as America prepared for defense and war. This type of social legislation was forgotten. CVA was not revived until President Truman made it a major issue of his second administration. . . .

In a region which had three times the national unemployment rate in May after a bad winter in the lumber industry, CVA has become a symbol of jobs to one faction and of socialism to another. The Columbia River carries to the sea nearly 35 million kilowatts of hydroelectricity. This is the Northwest's prime resource. Unlike timber, it does not face depletion from ax and fire. Unlike California's oil, it will not eventually trickle off into the shale. But only 3,244,049 of these kilowatts have been tapped under existing arrangements for expansion of the Northwest.

Arrangements are now incredibly hit-or-miss.

Competing agencies concerned with the same dam project report to different cabinet officers, to different congressional committees and get their funds through different budgets. At one dam, Bonneville, no fewer than four government bureaus are involved in operation. . . . These conflicting interests are never weighed on one pair of scales. . . .

Labor is for CVA because jobless lines are lengthening. The Northwest has been a one-industry area, and lumber cannot prop up an economy in which the number of able-bodied men has increased nearly 40 per cent in a few years. Because power can be generated more cheaply on the Columbia River than anywhere else in North America, trade unions believe manufacturing will follow the turbines. Leaders of the AFL and CIO are agreed that surplus kilowatts will mean new payrolls.

But now the Northwest confronts a desperate power shortage. Even as Governor Douglas McKay of conservative Oregon declared against CVA, the lights winked out in the capitol dome over his head. The state government had been ordered to save electricity in a region which contains 42 per cent of the nation's undeveloped water power.

The principal foes of CVA are the private utilities. Their "pocket nerves" tingle at the mere mention of President Truman's proposal. The dominant fear is that CVA will take after its exemplar, the Tennessee Valley Authority, in hastening public ownership of distribution facilities. A provision in the CVA bill provides that the authority can buy out power companies. But utilities are not popular in the Northwest. Portland pays the Pacific Power & Light Company $5.12 for 250 kilowatt hours of electricity, while the same amount of energy is sold by the municipal system in nearby Tacoma for $3.20.

Utility opposition to CVA is fairly well camouflaged. The principal organization resisting CVA is known as the Pacific Northwest Development Association. Peter Edison of *The Washington Daily News* lists these contributions to the association's war chest: Idaho Power Company, $1,855; Washington Power Company, $6,600; Pacific Power & Light Company, $5,600; Portland General Electric Company, $5,500; Northwestern Electric Company, $2,650.

Appearing before an Oregon legislative committee, when he was not under oath, the secretary of the development association declined to reveal the sources of these funds. The secretary was formerly with the Chicago, Milwaukee, St. Paul & Pacific, and some of the railroads are not especially happy about CVA either. Last year, 2.8 million tons of freight were hauled by barge on the Tennessee, as compared with a mere million tons on the Columbia, a far mightier river. A series of inland pools, encouraging river transportation all the way to Idaho, would drive down rail rates throughout the region.

The fight over CVA has long been rehearsed ideologically in the Missouri River Valley. . . . In the MVA region, the Army Engineers and the Bureau of Reclamation, those Siamese twins of vested bureaucracy, have combined in the Pick-Sloan plan. Two thousand miles westward, only the name is changed. In the Northwest it is the Weaver-Newell plan, Weaver being the army engineer and Newell the Reclamation delegate. The army alone proposes to spend $1.8 million under this scheme— and the object is hard to define except as something to circumvent CVA. . . .

The adversaries of CVA in the past have not been particularly gifted with prophecy. One of the organizations blanketing the Northwest with propaganda against the President's bill is E. Hofer & Sons, which issues a news letter, *Industrial News Review*, sustained in substantial measure by the utility industry. In 1939, shortly after Bonneville Dam was completed, the *News Review* gloated: "It becomes more and more apparent that Bonneville is an enormously costly white elephant. The great dam isn't selling enough power to keep even a small stand-by plant busy."

Since these words were written, the "white elephant" has collected operating revenues of approximately $85 million and sold 23.4 billion kilowatt hours of power. Indeed, equipment at Bonneville is overheated and strained to transmit energy to light-metal plants manufacturing half the nation's supply of aluminum. It also stokes the plutonium works at Hanford.

In the Northwest few federal undertakings have been synchronized with other federal moves. When an oil barge was impaled on rocks between Bonneville and Grand Coulee Dams, three days of negotiations among three government agencies were necessary to release sufficient water over the Coulee spillways to float the craft free. One of the most tragic gaps is the lack of unity between the offices which divert the Columbia downstream and those which guard the highlands. Forests nurture the great river; the worst floods occur where the trees have been stripped away indiscriminately.

CVA would tie together the loose ends. This is its role, which *The New York Times* claims "would be for the Columbia something like what unification is, or ought to be, in the national defense." It would compel the Army Engineers to consider aquatic life when they plan navigation. It would force the Reclamation Bureau to give thought to both power and irrigation. It would recognize a living relationship between a grassy slope at the Columbia's source and a $100 million power plant a thousand miles nearer the sea. It would even provide for storage dams in Canada to increase the river's power potential in the United States.

Under the CVA plan three directors would be appointed by the President with the approval of the Senate, each receiving $17,500 annually. Local advisory committees would represent labor, industry, and agriculture. Pacific Northwest headquarters of the Corps of Engineers, the Bureau of Reclamation, and the Bonneville Power Administration would be absorbed into the new regime. . . .

Headquarters of CVA would be in the Northwest, probably at Portland, Oregon, or Wenatchee, Washington. The bill requires that at least two of the three directors must be bona fide residents of the region. At present, ultimate control over the Columbia River projects is vested in the Chief of Engineers and the Secretary of the Interior. These men are three thousand miles away in the national capital. They seldom visit the Northwest. "CVA is home rule," contends . . . Congressman Hugh Mitchell of Seattle.

Ironic though it may seem, this shift of sovereignty to the region itself is condemned as "socialism" by most of the Northwest's newspapers. Among the large dailies in the states affected, only the *Oregonian* of Portland is uncommitted against CVA. It is neutral but has indicated probable support if the administration's bill receives amendment to insure more local autonomy. . . .

Chambers of commerce plead that "existing agencies" be permitted to do the job. The Bonneville administration is affectionately included among these bureaus. The chambers of commerce forget that when Bonneville was proposed to Congress in 1937, an imposing business delegation traveled to Washington to oppose it, and the plea was that "existing agencies" be allowed to do the job. At that time, "existing agencies" meant the Corps of Engineers. If some future President should suggest an improvement on CVA, the chambers of commerce of that era doubtless still would urge leaving the job to "existing agencies" even to CVA.

But CVA is more than a political issue. It is a national economic question, and the Columbia River is an economic asset of incalculable value. Long ago, Jefferson decided that the resources of the unknown West belonged to the country at large. This is more true than ever today, when the nation confronts a diminution of basic raw materials.

As long as snow melts in the Canadian Rockies and water flows downhill, the Columbia will be able to generate prodigious electric power. Yet last year America burned a million barrels of fuel oil to produce power. This oil has vanished in smoke, lacking the eternal qualities of tumbling glacial water. Economists believe a vast portion of the country's industry could expand into the Columbia Basin, using a fuel which will never be depleted.

But first the power must be extracted from the river. It is incongruous that a recent national conference of utility executives decided the country's worst power shortage existed in the region with the highest potential of hydroelectricity. All calculations in the Northwest have gone wrong. People believed those who said Bonneville was a "white elephant." Additional projects were not started. This is no delay to be made up between whistle stops. Four or five years are required to construct a dam which must be rooted into the floor of the continent's swiftest river. . . .

Despite the millions of idle kilowatts which the Columbia carries, Representative Horan of Spokane predicts the Northwest's power shortage will not be materially relieved before 1956. Trade unions wonder how their thousands of new members, migrants from the East and Middle West, can be kept at work by the forest products industry until that distant date. . . .

If mere expenditures would advance the Northwest, progress would have been speedy, for the Engineers have had a pipeline to the United States Treasury. But profligacy is no substitute for a program.

Where should the money be spent? Grand Coulee will pump water onto arid land. The first 87,000-acre tract will be ready for homesteads in the spring of 1952. Already a few ex-GI's and their families have settled on reclaimed desert near Pasco. Should pumps take precedence over transmission lines? Is the tentative Chief Joseph Dam, with a million kilowatts of power capacity, as immediately important as concrete canals crisscrossing land that will grow everything from alfalfa to artichokes when irrigated?

What does the Northwest need most urgently—power for industries and payrolls, or water for agricultural production? This touches the background, skills, and hopes of the migrants. Do they want to follow a plow or tend an assembly line? What is their training? Will the produce from irrigated farms cross the Cascades to Seattle or go down the river to Portland? Which first, navigation locks or railroad spurs?

Should the Reconstruction Finance Corporation lend money to the western railroads for eight thousand miles of trolley wires, so they can move locomotives with inexhaustible water power instead of dwindling reserves of diesel fuel? When will the Columbia generate the surplus power to operate trains from the Continental Divide to tidewater? Would electric engines in the West annually save 200 million gallons of diesel oil, as claimed by Dr. Pau Raver, Bonneville's administrator?

These are questions which only one agency can answer, an agency responsible for the Columbia from headwaters to the sea. This agency is CVA. Until it comes into existence, the Northwest will continue to stagger toward the end of the abundance on which its frontier prosperity has been based. . . .

PRESIDENT'S MESSAGE TO CONGRESS ON CVA [4]

I recommend that legislation be enacted reorganizing certain federal activities in the Columbia River Valley to the end that the Federal Government may play a more effective part in the

[4] From message of President Harry S. Truman on S. 1645, requesting establishment of a Columbia Valley Administration. *Congressional Record.* 95:4552-54, April 13, 1949.

development and conservation of the resources of the Pacific Northwest. . . .

In general, two main objectives should guide the organization of the government's resource activities. There should be unified treatment of the related resources within each natural area of the country—generally the watershed of a great river —and within the framework of sound nationwide policies. Furthermore, there should be the greatest possible decentralization of federal powers, and the greatest possible local participation in their exercise, without lessening the necessary accountability of federal officials to the President and to the Congress.

The traditional method of organizing the government's resource activities through departments and bureaus which carry on separate nationwide activities, does not itself provide for the unified consideration of each area's resources which is so necessary, nor does it easily lend itself to decentralization. It has long been apparent that some organizational adjustments are necessary.

We have not found—nor do I expect that we shall find— a single organizational pattern that will fit perfectly the resource problems in the many diverse areas of the country. . . .

The waters of the Columbia River system (among our rivers second only to the Mississippi in flow) are capable eventually of producing more than 30 million kilowatts of electric power, of which only a little more than 3 million kilowatts are now installed. There are possibilities of reclaiming many more acres of land by irrigation, as they may be needed, in addition to the 4 million acres now irrigated. More than 40 per cent of the nation's saw timber and many important minerals, including 60 per cent of our known phosphate reserves, are in the region. Properly developed and conserved, the resources of the Columbia Valley region can furnish enormous benefits to the people living there and to the nation as a whole.

The Pacific Northwest has been developing very rapidly in recent years. The population has jumped 37 per cent since 1940. The tonnage of agricultural production—not including livestock and livestock products—has risen about 25 per cent in Washington, Oregon, and Idaho between 1940 and 1947. Total income payments have increased 200 per cent since before the war in those three states, as compared to 150 per cent for the country as a whole. The per capita income is among the highest in the nation. These are signs of the progressive energy of the people of the region, and of the growth that can occur there.

However, this growth will not take place to the extent necessary to provide adequate employment for the growing population unless there is a steady program of investment in the development of basic resources in accordance with broadly conceived conservation and development plans.

The activities of the Federal Government have already been of great help. Bonneville and Grand Coulee Dams and the Bonneville power system, begun before the war, made possible the tremendous war and postwar expansion in population and industry. Industrial development in aluminum, electrochemical and electrometallurgical industries, atomic energy, phosphates, and other lines is going forward rapidly. Each of these requires large amounts of low-cost power, in the production of which the Columbia River and its tributaries offer greater possibilities than any other river system in the country. Continued industrial progress depends upon turning these hydroelectric-power potentialities into realities, since the present power supply is far short of the demand, and the region has no significant resources of coal or petroleum.

But far more than power is involved in the further development of the Columbia River for useful purposes. The disastrous flood of 1948 showed how much needs to be done, both in the river and on the land in the watershed, to reduce potential flood damage. The first irrigation water will soon be brought to the thirsty land in the Columbia basin project below Grand Coulee Dam, and other irrigation projects are possible. The important lower Columbia fisheries program, to adjust the salmon fishing industry to the dam construction program, needs to be pushed forward. The use of the river for low-cost transportation of bulk goods can be greatly expanded. . . .

It is obvious that federal activities and expenditures concerning land resources need to be planned in relation to those concerning water resources. Here again better organizational arrangements are needed than we now have.

I do not wish to minimize the substantial progress that has been made under the programs as they have been conducted in the past. However, we have now reached a point where the growing scope and complexity of the federal activities in the region require much greater integration and the full-time attention of top-level administrators if the tremendous potentialities of the region are to be wisely and rapidly developed.

I therefore recommend that the Congress enact legislation to provide a means for welding together the many federal activities concerned with the region's resources into a balanced, continuously developing program.

In doing so I recommend that certain federal activities in the region be consolidated into a single agency, called the Columbia Valley Administration. To that agency should be transferred the federal programs of constructing and operating physical facilities on the Columbia River and its tributaries for the multiple-purpose conservation and use of the water, including the generation and transmission of power. These programs are now carried on by the Bureau of Reclamation and the Bonneville Power Administration in the Department of the Interior, and by the Corps of Engineers in the Department of the Army. This consolidation will provide not only for a balanced program of constructing dams, irrigation works, power transmission lines, and other facilities, but also for a workable operating plan for using these facilities simultaneously for flood control, navigation, power generation and transmission, fish protection, and other purposes. It is plain common sense that the planning and operation of the system of river structures is a job for a single agency.

The Columbia Valley Administration would have the advantages of a sound foundation of basic planning already done, and a large construction program already under way. The bulk of its staff would be secured from the existing agencies in carrying on its construction work by contract so far as practicable. Under these circumstances, the establishment of the Columbia Valley Administration would result in no hesitation or delay in the development program. Instead, the Administration would carry forward the work already started in a more effective manner.

I do not recommend the consolidation of any other federal activities in the Columbia Valley Administration. I do recommend, however, that the Administration be given direct responsibility for preparing definite plans and programs for soil and forest conservation, mineral exploration and development, fish and wildlife conservation, and the other aspects of Federal resource activities in the region, and the means to see that those plans and programs move ahead in step. Such plans and programs would be worked out in cooperation with all interested groups—local, state, and federal, private and public.

In this way the activities of the Columbia Valley Administration and other federal agencies would be properly adjusted to each other and to the activities of state and local agencies, and the maximum degree of joint and cooperative action would result. In this way the activities of all agencies concerned with water, land, forest, mineral and fish and wildlife resources can be brought into a consistent pattern of conservation and development.

The Columbia River rises in Canada, and part of its watershed is in that country. Under long-standing treaties, the governments of Canada and the United States consult with each other on any development projects which affect international waters, including the Columbia River. The Columbia Valley Administration can work out, in cooperation with appropriate Canadian agencies and in accordance with our treaty obligations, practical means of developing the resources of the Columbia River region, on both sides of the international boundary, on an integrated basis. It is my hope that we will be able in this respect to demonstrate to the world new ways of achieving mutual benefit through international programs of resource development.

A further vital element in developing a better organization of federal resource activities in the Columbia Valley region is to bring about a larger degree of local participation. To this end I recommend that the Columbia Valley Administration be required to have its headquarters in the region, easily accessible to the people who live there. I recommend further that the Administration be required, with respect to all phases of its activities, to seek the advice, assistance, and participation of state and local governments, agriculture, labor and business groups, educational institutions and other representative groups concerned. This can best be done, as the Tennessee Valley Authority experience has shown, not through formalistic statutory machinery, but through the establishment by the Administration of a large number of advisory groups for its different activities and in different parts of the region, and through the use, wherever possible, of established local agencies to carry out the development program.

In these various ways the Columbia Valley Administration, while retaining its basic accountability to the President and the Congress, will be far more responsive to the needs and interests and desires of the people of the region than the present subordinate field establishments of the Government can be.

The Columbia Valley Administration should, of course, administer its activities in accordance with federal policies which apply to the whole country. In seeking decentralization of federal authority and the appropriate flexibility to meet the unique characteristics of the Pacific Northwest, we should not establish different national policies for that region than for the rest of the country.

For example, the Administration should be required, in accordance with long-established federal policy, to respect existing water rights and the water rights laws of the several states. The Administration should be required to follow the reclamation laws in contracting for the disposition of land or water in reclamation projects. It should be required to give the customary preferences and priorities to public agencies and cooperatives in disposing of electric energy. It should be required to demonstrate the economic soundness of the various projects it undertakes, and to repay reimbursable costs, in accordance with national policies. In short, its activities should harmonize, and not conflict, with federal policies concerning agriculture, commerce, labor, and the other broad areas of national interest.

Finally, the Columbia Valley Administration should be given, with respect to its revenue-producing activities, appropriate financial and operating flexibility under the business-type budgeting, accounting and auditing methods established by the Government Corporations Control Act. Without detracting from the necessary control of the Administration by the President and the Congress, this will permit more businesslike procedures and more steady and economical scheduling of construction and operations than are now possible.

These recommendations I regard as the fundamental elements of a better organization of federal resource activities in the Pacific Northwest. They involve no expansion of federal powers, no encroachment on the rights of states, communities or individuals. Instead they are designed to achieve a more sensible and unified organization of federal activities, which will result in a more effective program for resource development and more effective participation by the people of the region in shaping that program.

The enactment of legislation embodying these recommendations will bring government closer to the people—closer to the grass roots. This means government action that will be more responsive to the needs of the people.

A SENATORIAL ANALYSIS OF CVA [5]

The first major development in connection with the Columbia Valley was the Bonneville project, which was built by the Army Corps of Engineers to improve navigation, and for the additional purpose of generating electric power on the Columbia.

Sale of this electric power was placed under an administrator appointed by the Secretary of Interior. The Bonneville Act was followed by the Grand Coulee Dam or Columbia Basin Project Act, authorizing the Bureau of Reclamation, of the Department of Interior, to construct Grand Coulee Dam.

The sale of Grand Coulee electric power was also placed under the administrator of the Bonneville project.

[5] *A Study of the Reasons for and against a Proposed CVA.* Prepared by Senator Harry P. Cain for voters of the state of Washington, 1949. Mimeographed text supplied by the author. Reprinted by permission.

It was in 1940 that the first of what was to be a steady stream of legislative proposals were introduced in the Congress. At that time, in the second session of the Seventy-sixth Congress, Senator Bone and Congressmen Hill and Leavy, all of Washington State, introduced bills which would have set up a Columbia Power Administration. In the same Congress, Congressman Smith of Washington introduced a similar bill. No action was taken on any of them. In the following year, the same bills were reintroduced.

Senator Bone, and Congressmen Hill and Smith, then introduced bills which were entitled the Columbia Power Act of 1941. Two years later, thinking on this subject was marked by a broadened basis, and more of the so-called valley authority type bills were introduced for the Columbia River, even one by Congressman Rankin. His bill was followed by the introduction of the Columbia Valley Authority Act, which would have created the Authority, a Columbia Valley Advisory Council and a National River Basin Development Board. Later the same bill was reintroduced but with still a different version. The bills died in committee.

Congressman Walt Horan, of Wenatchee, after long study and consideration, introduced in the Seventy-ninth Congress a bill called The Columbia Valley Authority Act. It created a Cooperative Authority headed by a board of five directors and a Columbia Valley Advisory Council consisting of the regional governors.

The Authority was to formulate and present proposals to the President and Congress after submitting them to the Advisory Council for review. The proposals were to be effective unless affirmatively disapproved by Congress, by joint resolution within four legislative months. The rest of the provisions were, in the main, similar to the Columbia Valley Authority Act, but this bill also died, although more seriously considered than the others. Mr. Horan presently has another proposal which merits close study as he has lived all his life in the area involved.

The opening days of the last Congress saw the reintroduction by Congressman Rankin of the Conservation Authorities Act of 1945, providing for the establishment of eight conservation authorities, including one in the Columbia Valley. The bill received no action. This bill was followed further along in the first session by the Columbia Valley Authority Act, and was introduced by Senator Glen Taylor, of Idaho. The Senate Committee on Public Works submitted this bill to various government departments, such as the Treasury, War, Agriculture and so forth. Most of the departments suggested amendments; some were critical; the Federal Works Agency made a favorable report.

And now, here are, to the best of my ability, the two sides to the controversy over extending the valley authority idea to the Columbia River basin.

There are eleven general reasons in favor, and eleven reasons against, the establishment of a valley authority in the Columbia Basin.

First, we will take the side of the proponents of a Columbia Valley Authority. They contend, first: that a regional authority, such as a CVA, or TVA, has all the flexibility of action of a private corporation, and that such an authority is centralized and less subject to red tape and bureaucratic delay.

Two: Plans for a development of the Columbia basin, under a valley authority, possess the virtue of unity and every phase of development can be planned in its proper relation to the whole. Such planning is apt to be more balanced and unencumbered by traditional and possibly hampering procedures. Instead of a dozen agencies concerned with fragments of the problem, one agency, supposedly responsible to the people, can do a better total job.

Number three: Offices of the authority would be located in the area itself with all of the advantages which flow from that fact. Among these are more familiarity with the immediate circumstances of the problem, ability to render decisions on the spot and fix responsibility, and better cooperation with local agencies.

Four: Nothing is lost of the valuable assistance available from other government agencies, as most of the bills to create a Columbia Valley Authority provide that the Authority may call on other federal agencies for any information they may possess and for technical assistance.

Five: The TVA has been successful in accomplishing its original purpose, why should not other regions have the benefit of experience there?

Six: Those in favor of a CVA say that any authority established by Congress is still subject to its control. It is no absolutist, all-powerful agency but subject to any checks Congress may see fit to impose.

Seven: In using the corporate form, more businesslike management is possible with a probable actual money savings.

Eight: Development of the Columbia Valley in the past, by the many different government agencies, has not been as successful or beneficial as it might have been under a coordinated system such as has been so successful in the TVA region, it is argued by those who favor a CVA.

Nine: An authority will have the power to engage in activities, essential to a full development of the resources of a region, which are not now the concern of any agency at all. Among these are soil erosion control, topsoil rebuilding, provision of terminal facilities, development of new industries and the like.

Ten: Someone must decide the present conflict of interests between navigation and irrigation as well as power. An authority such as TVA can make these decisions for the benefit of the region as a whole.

And last: A Columbia Valley Authority might be self-liquidating. Power revenues might be sufficient to finance an entire comprehensive program, and based on experience in the TVA, there might be no loss of tax revenue. Payments in lieu of taxes, it is claimed, are provided in all bills thus far introduced.

Those who think that the establishment of a Columbia Valley Authority will hurt our state, the nation and its citizens have strong arguments. They argue like this:

First: It is contended that local governments stand to lose a large proportion of tax revenues as a result of any valley authority which withdraws from taxation large areas of land within the subdivision. The land already owned by the Federal Government in the Pacific Northwest, especially in Washington State, is alarming. Thirty-four per cent of our state's total land area is presently owned by the Federal Government and controlled in Washington, D.C.

Number two: Those against a CVA strongly contend that federally-controlled river basins, such as the Columbia and its tributaries, would divide the entire nation into many valley and other regional authorities, and then would render the State of Washington, and other states, as such, nearly obsolete. In other words, the Constitution would be circumvented and the rights of individual states would soon cease to exist and a point reached where states existed in name only.

Number three: Benefits to which the state of Washington is entitled, and benefits of other states, might be taken away and water and power transmitted in great quantities to California or elsewhere, while we in the Pacific Northwest, already faced with a shortage of power for years, might be made to suffer because of political power, exerted through a valley authority to send the electricity elsewhere.

Reason number four, advanced by opponents of a CVA, is that experience with the TVA would seem to justify the accusation that such authorities engage in activities which are in direct competition with private business and industry. "Government in business" is not a Constitutional activity of the Federal Government.

Five: Accent upon power revenues leads to the suspicion that regional authorities, based upon water resources, are only an excuse for the Federal Government to take over the power industry of the nation through subterfuge.

Six: Long established government agencies with fine records of achievement and specialized techniques can do a better job than new and inexperienced special authorities. A prime example of recognized good work is that of the Army Corps of Engineers.

Seven: Regional authorities constitute a new element in the structure of American government. The Constitution provides only for a national government and constituent states. If new elements are to be added it should be done through constitutional amendment. This is such an important consideration that it should not be determined indirectly by creating individual authorities by legislation.

Eight: Valley authorities' powers are constitutionally limited to the Federal Government's powers which in turn rest on the constitutional power to regulate commerce and navigation. Any powers beyond these are assumed at the expense of the states, and such assumption is unconstitutional.

Nine: A Columbia Valley Authority might well become a super-agency, above any control by anyone. The act creating such an authority would need to be carefully drawn lest the only check on its power be solely that of approval or disapproval of an already accomplished fact. Most of the bills so far introduced to establish valley authorities provide for a minimum of control by Congress.

Number ten in the list of general reasons against a CVA is that neither the TVA plan, nor any existing proposals for valley authorities, have provided for fusion of federal and state powers, nor for the means by which the powers of the state, and certain laws of the nation, are to be exercised over such an Authority.

And last, and number eleven: Plans for a Columbia Valley Authority possess the essence of state management and are so extreme that they border on communism.

Right, or wrong, these are the arguments, both for and against, used in the controversy over establishment of a Columbia Valley Authority in the state of Washington.

WHAT KIND OF CVA? [6]

The subject of tonight's discussion—What Kind of CVA?—is particularly intriguing to me because it presents a challenge as well as a reflection of openmindedness on the part of the people in the region. And now that the President's bill has been

[6] From an address by C. Girard Davidson, Assistant Secretary of the Interior, before the Junior Chamber of Commerce, Portland, Oregon. April 22, 1949. Mimeographed text supplied by the author. Reprinted by permission.

introduced in Congress, it is time to spell out in detail not only what kind of CVA, but what the *functions* of the CVA will be; what it is designed to accomplish.

First, any discussion of *functions* should be approached in the light of national need as well as regional need. Some people appear to forget that the Columbia basin is part of the United States. But anyone who looks at production, income and resources figures soon becomes aware that the Columbia River region has tremendous national significance.

To a nation which is losing hundreds of thousands of acres of productive farm land each year, in the face of a growing population, both at home and abroad, the irrigation potentials of the Columbia basin and its great store of phosphorous rock for fertilizer cannot be ignored. To a nation currently faced with a critical power shortage in most of its regions, the 30 million kilowatts of hydro capacity in the Columbia River system cannot be ignored. To a nation that requires a larger air force and at the same time has a shortage of at least 300 million pounds of aluminum production annually, the potentials of the Columbia assume a tremendous national security value.

This, in brief, is the national approach to CVA. This is the approach the 509 members of the Congress who do not come from the Pacific Northwest will have to take in considering a CVA.

There is also a regional approach which interests us as citizens of the Columbia basin because the Columbia basin is our home. To us in the region the question of full employment—of opportunity for individual initiative and enterprise to go constantly forward in developing our economy—is of paramount importance.

How this is to be accomplished places a great weight of responsibility upon those of us who believe that a CVA provides the means for securing these things for the Columbia River region.

Most of the confusion over the proposed Columbia Valley Administration can be quickly resolved by a simple, rational understanding of the Federal Government's responsibility in regional development.

Let me make clear here that the bill concerns itself with *federal* functions and *federal* functions *only*. It represents no encroachment upon states' rights, nor does it add any new powers to the work that is already being done by the Federal Government, and in this region there is but one single additional power granted by the bill. This has to do with the acquisition of utility systems, and severe restrictions are placed upon this single exception. Acquisition can only be accomplished through a willing seller and a willing buyer. The government is charged with the responsibility of divesting itself within the shortest possible time of any utility system acquired under the terms of the act. The Administration has no powers of condemnation in such acquisitions and it will not engage in the retail distribution of power. That remains a matter for local determination.

The work of the federal agencies responsible for development in the region has been unquestionably excellent, but what has been accomplished has been inadequate for the needs of the region—and far more costly than was necessary. . . . It has not been the fault of the individual agencies that this is so—rather it is the fault of the laws under which these agencies operate. Their individual responsibilities are not to any headquarters located right in the Northwest where they belong, but to offices in Washington, D.C., where sensibility to the region's needs is remote.

It is primarily because of this lack of organization that the Northwest is now confronted with problems that are in urgent need of solution. . . .

While more than four million acres of fertile but arid acres of land lie idle, thousands of people who might be usefully employed in turning those lands into productive farms, remain unemployed.

But let's touch on power for a moment. The Bonneville Power Administration, an agency of the Department of the Interior, is responsible for the transmission and wholesaling of power generated at federal projects; and yet it cannot possibly fulfill that responsibility without adequate high voltage transmission lines, nor without the power to send over those lines. Its program must be timed to coincide with the schedules of these other two developmental agencies [the Bureau of Reclamation and the Corps of Engineers]; yet there is no adequate provision of existing law which fully permits this.

As Congressman Horan put it just a few days ago:

Grand Coulee is one year behind on generating installations; Hungry Horse is three years behind in getting its first three generators installed; McNary is two years behind; Chief Joseph is four years behind; Detroit is three years behind; Ice Harbor is four years behind. At the rate we are going now, it will be 1958—nine years—before we catch up with the Northwest power shortage.

Here, in a region with the greatest power potential in the United States, we are actually starving for power that could mean new industry—as a matter of fact, during the past eighteen months, twenty separate industries which wanted to come into the region were unable to do so because of lack of power—and new industry means jobs. While the national average of unemployment is 6 per cent, the average for the Pacific Northwest is three times that average figure, yet with only 5 per cent of our tremendous power potential developed, there are people in the region today who ask, "What's wrong with the way we are doing now?"

What kind of CVA? The kind, of course, that will help solve just such problems by putting the government's business management in efficient working order and will help gain such things as these:

1. A correlated program of development which will permit private industry to bring at least two million more people into the Pacific Northwest by 1970.

2. Creation of at least 50 thousand new farms, at least 250 thousand new industrial jobs, and in all probability some 350 thousand new service jobs.

These goals are easily realized if we put our resources to work properly.

To business and industry that means new sources of income, new opportunities for free enterprise. That is why it sounds a little ridiculous when the critics of the Administration bill term it a socialistic or Marxian scheme.

The Columbia Valley Administration bill which has been introduced in Congress has been carefully worked out to fulfill these purposes, taking into account the rights and interests of the states concerned and making the Administration responsive to the desires of the people in the region. . . .

The bill establishes the Columbia Valley Administration as a federal corporation headed by a board of three directors serving staggered six-year terms. It requires that two of the directors be selected from bona fide residents of the Northwest, and the Administration have its headquarters in the region. It provides for the transfer of functions and property of the three river agencies with a minimum of delay after the directors are appointed, so that work on existing projects will be continued to speedy conclusion.

The measure makes it mandatory that the Columbia Valley Administration seek and rely upon the advice, assistance, and participation of the people of the region and their state and local governments and organizations. The Administration would be required to establish advisory boards and councils representative of all interests within the Columbia Valley affected by the Administration's activities. These boards would be permitted to report directly to the President and the Congress their findings on the Administration's operations through the medium of the Administration's annual reports.

For the benefit of those who claim that the CVA would eliminate home rule, I should like to ask what home rule provisions are enjoyed under present conditions? Where, for instance, is the Chief of Engineers, and where is the Commissioner of Reclamation?

The bill contains provisions protecting western water rights and applying existing reclamation laws. Among these is a clause stating that "no provision for works of irrigation in or under this Act shall be construed as affecting or intended to affect . . . the laws of any state relating to the control, appropriation, use or distribution of water . . . or any vested right acquired thereunder."

The proposed measure contains strong public power provisions similar to those existing in the Reclamation laws, the

Bonneville Project Act, and the Tennessee Valley Act. Preference in the sale of power to public agencies and cooperatives, and provisions for the acquisition of utility systems for resale to such public bodies are included.

There are specific restrictions in this bill upon the right of condemnation which may be exercised by the CVA, including a general limitation prohibiting the condemnation of any water right except as it may be appurtenant to land required for construction of dams, reservoirs and other works.

The CVA would be prohibited from using any political tests or qualifications for employment or promotion, which must be made on the basis of merit and efficiency. CVA employees would be protected in their jobs much as Federal Civil Service employees are protected.

Invariably, opposition propagandists point to the great difference between the Tennessee Valley and the Columbia Valley.

They are wrong on two counts:

1. Both of these areas have one thing in common: that is, a great river system which in the past in many ways has been a foe of progress and an instrument of destruction, but which, when harnessed and put to practical use, can prove to be the most important single natural resource in the region.

2. The President's proposal does not establish a "Tennessee-type" authority in the Columbia basin. The President's bill takes advantage of the TVA experience and tailors the application of that experience to the local needs of the Pacific Northwest.

When you have studied this bill, I think you will agree with President Truman's recent message on the CVA, in which he said:

> These recommendations . . . are designed to achieve a more sensible and unified program . . . for resource development and more effective participation by the people of the region in shaping that program.
>
> The enactment of legislation embodying these recommendations will bring the government closer to the people—closer to the grass roots. This means government action will be more responsive to the needs of the people.

WHY SENATOR MORSE OPPOSES THE CVA BILL [7]

I could not say honestly, Mr. President, that I am opposed to every provision of the bill, but I am opposed to enough of its provisions so that I cannot vote for it, and I want to mention just a few. I want to say, at the outset, that I have no objection to the statement of declaration of policy as set forth in section 2 of the bill, so long as that declaration of policy is limited to the interests of the Federal Government and the rights of the Federal Government in these projects and rivers. But, as one reads Senate bill 1645 he is quickly impressed by the fact that the Administration sponsoring the bill is overlooking the fact that the states and the local communities also have interests and rights in the rivers of the Pacific Northwest. This bill, so far as I am concerned, is primarily objectionable because it violates one of the tenets of constitutional liberalism for which I shall continue to fight, so long as I am in American politics. That tenet is simply this, that our democracy can never be any stronger than representative government at the local community, county, and state level, and that whenever we take steps which tend to diminish or take away from our people at the local level the responsibility for active participation in determining governmental policies relating to their daily lives, we are undermining the very strength of democracy itself. . . .

Section 3 provides:

To assist in carrying out the purposes of this act there is hereby created a body corporate with the name "Columbia Valley Administration" (referred to in this act as the "Administration"). The Administration shall be an instrumentality of the United States under the general supervision of the President.

Mr. President, I shall always be willing to give to the President of the United States or to sanction vesting in the President of the United States such powers as are essential to make our constitutional form of government work and such powers as are consistent with the clear check-and-balance theories of the Con-

[7] From remarks by Senator Wayne Morse of Oregon in the United States Senate, October 14, 1949. Congressional Record. 95:14869-905. October 14, 1949. Reprint supplied by the author.

stitution. But I reiterate tonight what I have said so many times, that I am opposed to vesting in the President of the United States any executive power that we do not need to vest in him in order to make our constitutional system of government work and in order to make our capitalistic system work for the benefit of all our people. . . .

"Oh," say the supporters of the CVA bill, "after all, Congress has a check. It has to confirm the three administrators, and, of course, the Committees on Appropriations have to approve the appropriation of the money." . . .

Every Senator here tonight knows that after the confirmation of an official of the executive branch, we practically from that time on lose any effective check over him. He goes his way. So, when some of the spokesmen for this particular CVA bill tell the people of my state, "Congress has control over this, it has to confirm the administrators," that is no effective check from the standpoint of determining or checking on the policy which those administrators can develop once they are confirmed. . . .

The people of the bureaus and departments of the government know very well that no Committee on Appropriations of the Congress has the facilities, the staff, or the time, really to go into questions of policy which are involved in the administration of the various government bureaus, departments, and administrative agencies, such as the proposed CVA. . . .

Let us take section 4, dealing with the Board of Directors. It provides:

The management of the Administration shall be vested in a board of three full-time Directors, who shall be appointed by the President, by and with the advice and consent of the Senate. The Chairman of the Board shall be designated by the President. At least two of the Directors shall be bona fide residents of the region at the time of appointment, and each Director shall maintain his residence in the region. The Board shall be responsible for policy, directive, and general supervisory functions. The Board shall appoint a chief executive officer who shall be responsible to the Board and shall perform such functions as the Board may determine. . . .

Mr. President, there are no limitations on the power of the board of directors, no provision that there shall be any local representation with voting power in determining policy. . . .

What has been done by those who framed the bill? Well, I think they have put a sop in it. They have put in a section which they think may lull the people of my section of the country into a false sense of security regarding the question of a voting voice in the determination of the policies respecting these projects. . . . Not one word in that section vests in the people of the Pacific Northwest any voting representation in determining the policies of these projects.

Mr. President, if that were my only objection to the bill it would be reason enough, so far as I am concerned, for the position I have taken that I would not vote for the bill in its present form. I will not vote for any legislation affecting the administration and the management of these projects that does not provide within its terms a cooperative arrangement between the local governments and the Federal Government which gives to the people and the local governments a representation in actually determining policy.

I feel that every representative of the Pacific Northwest in Congress ought to insist upon the formulation and development of some affirmative answer to the question, "What are you going to do about eliminating the waste, overlapping, and inefficiency which already characterize the federal agencies which are administering projects already built, and will undoubtedly continue in connection with the new projects if you do not enact some legislation which seeks to eliminate such waste and inefficiency?"

I am at work on an answer, and I shall propose it before my campaign is over. The problem is obviously a complex one, and the answers are not easy to work out. . . . I shall say tonight only that it is going to be along the lines of a cooperative state and federal corporation for administering these projects, which will give to the Federal Government and the state governments an active representative voice in determining policy. . . .

It will require at least three years to get legislation in perfected form which will be approved by the Congress. In the meantime there are some first steps which we can and should take if we are to avoid giving to three men the sweeping powers which section 6 of this bill gives to the commissioners. Listen to this:

Section 6. (a) The Administration shall have succession in its corporate name; may adopt and use a corporate seal which shall be judicially noticed; may adopt, amend, and repeal bylaws; may sue and be sued in its corporate name without regard to the provisions of title 28, United States Code, section 507; and may settle and adjust claims held by it against other parties or persons and by other parties or persons against it, for which purpose the Administration shall have, with respect to claims within the scope of title 28, United States Code, chapter 171, (Tort Claims Procedure), the functions assigned to the Attorney General by that chapter.

(b) Subject to the policies, conditions, and limitations stated in this act—

I have already pointed out that the limitations are inconsequential. The bill is characterized by its sweeping powers, not by its limitations.

Subject to the policies, conditions, and limitations stated in this act, the Administration is authorized and directed to construct, operate, and maintain projects (including stand-by facilities), and to carry out activities, necessary for the promotion of navigation (except for channel and harbor improvement work in tidal waters tributary to the Pacific Ocean); for the control and prevention of floods; for the conservation and reclamation of lands and land resources; for the development and conservation of forest, mineral, and fish and wildlife resources; for the generation, transmission, and disposition of electric energy; for the execution of such other responsibilities as are vested in the Administration by or pursuant to this act.

That is one of the clauses which lawyers refer to as a catch-all, a general clause, an omnibus clause. As the history of our Washington bureaus shows, there is always a creeping and growing tendency on the part of bureaucrats to read into such language more and more power, far beyond even the imagination of Congress at the time it enacts such legislation.

Returning again to section 6:

And, in connection with any of the foregoing, for the development and conservation of recreational resources and for the promotion of sanitation and pollution control: *Provided,* That in the location, design, and construction of any dam or other facility, or any series of dams or facilities, the Administration shall endeavor—

Note the language, Mr. President, "shall endeavor." It does not say that anything can be done about it if it does not do so. The language is "shall endeavor"—

to foster, protect, and facilitate the access of all anadromous fish to and from their spawning areas throughout the region.

(c) To the extent found necessary or appropriate in carrying out the foregoing subsection, or other provisions of law, but subject to the conditions and limitations herein stated, the Administration is authorized and shall have the power—

(1) to acquire real and personal property, including any interest therein, by purchase, lease, condemnation, exchange, transfer, donation, or otherwise, and to sell, lease, exchange, or otherwise dispose thereof, including donations incident to experimentation, demonstrations, or other similar uses (without regard to section 3709 of the Revised Statutes, as amended); and to obtain services by contract, donation, or otherwise; *Provided however,* That the Administration shall have no power to condemn any water right except as it may be appurtenant to land acquired incident to the construction of dams, reservoirs, or other projects or facilities.

That would be most of the water rights, Mr. President. Let me say to the farmers of my state vitally concerned with water rights in our streams that the exercise of the power in that section over water rights is a power which I think their representatives ought to have a voice in exercising. That power over water rights should not be limited, as the section which I have just read limits it, to three presidential appointees over whom those farmers would have no direct control, such as they would have in determining who should represent the local and state governments on the board of directors of a cooperative state and federal corporation. . . .

There are other broad powers. The section provides that these Presidential appointees shall have power—

(2) to make and carry out arrangements for the protection, alteration, reconstruction, relocation, replacement, or removal of railroad tracks,

highways, bridges, mills, ferries, electric-light plants, and any other properties, enterprises, and projects, which have been or are to be destroyed,
flooded, otherwise damaged, or endangered, as the result of any projects
or activities of the Administration. . . .

Mr. President, I stress again that we cannot safeguard the
principles of representative government in the Pacific Northwest unless the Federal Government and the states work out
together a cooperative program along the line of a cooperative
state and federal corporation, governmental in nature, for the
administration of these projects. That ought to be our ultimate
goal, but in the meantime let me say to all the people of my
state that the first two steps we should take are to proceed without delay to complete these projects, and to urge this administration to get the projects covered in the so-called Army Engineers-
Bureau of Reclamation Report No. 308, and as provided for in
Senate bill 2180, built at the earliest possible time, and as a
second step, proceed without delay as a Congress to put into
legislative form the recommendations of the Hoover Commission in respect to this general problem.

WHY A COLUMBIA VALLEY AUTHORITY? [8]

It will be recalled that President Truman, after his successful crossroads campaign for reelection and his own interpretation of that phenomenon, announced a long list of "liberal"
legislation which his administration proposed militantly to
support.

Major items were repeal of the Taft-Hartley Act, a civil
liberties program, enlargement of the farm support and social
security programs, socialized medicine, federal housing, federal education, and, among others of presumably dwindling importance, an extension of the regional authority idea to the
Columbia River basin.

Out in the Pacific Northwest there was at first only mild
uneasiness about the President's Columbia Valley Authority pro-

[8] From an article by Robert Ormond Case, author and journalist. *Nation's Business.* 37:34-6+. October, 1949. Reprinted by permission.

posal, even among the few but exceedingly vigilant observers of the national scene. . . .

Two events soon jolted the complacence of Northwest observers. The first came April 13, 1949, when President Truman sent a special message to Congress reiterating his demand for a CVA, a gesture which raised the issue to top rank among "must" legislation.

The second, and far more disturbing, indicated the extent to which the disciples of regimentation had gained the President's ear. For the first time known to our democratic processes—at least in so open a manner—the Chief Executive had instructed the heads of a department to "inform" the people of the "benefits" of legislation currently pending before Congress.

More specifically, permission had been given the Department of the Interior to use its propaganda resources—its many bureaus, its thousands of employees and the hidden weight of its multimillion-dollar budget in the Northwest—to influence the thinking of the people of the Columbia Valley, and their congressmen, toward the Administration's proposed CVA. Designated to mastermind this ideological blitz was C. Girard Davidson, Assistant Secretary of the Interior, formerly on the legal staff of the TVA under David Lilienthal, later chief counsel of the Bonneville Power Administration.

To grasp the impact of this latter development, it should be borne in mind that the Department of the Interior's budget and personnel today outranks those of many independent nations. Interior's Bonneville Power Administration exercises arbitrary control of more than half the hydroelectric power output of the Columbia basin, supplies Bonneville power to the area's largest private utilities on a year-to-year basis, and for a decade past has maintained a staff of consultants in the field "educating" the people as to the benefits of cheap public power.

These two developments—the President's special message and the unlimbering of Interior's heavy artillery—precipitated the current CVA battle raging in the Northwest. It is a showdown battle whose mounting uproar has as yet reached the national ear only as random echoes, but which will inevitably—when and if it emerges from committee to the floor of Congress—become an historic *cause célèbre*.

The reason is inherent in the bill itself. The administration-sponsored S. 1645 (together with the almost identical H.R. 4286 and 4287) is no mere ideological straw in the wind. It bluntly proposes that Congress should relinquish certain of its fundamental constitutional powers. As Harold Ickes himself phrased it in a committee hearing on a similar Missouri Valley Authority bill, its adoption would bring about "a basic reorganization of government as we have known it for the past 150 years."

A thumbnail outline of S. 1645 brings its ideological aims into sharp focus. Its sponsors claim its principal intent is the consolidation and coordination of existing federal bureaus in the Columbia basin. Much of the bill's wording is obviously designed to create that impression. Stripped of its benevolent and sometimes misleading verbiage S. 1645 proposes:

A. To create a new geographical unit of government neither federal nor state, comprising 255 thousand square miles, or some 9 per cent of the nation's land area. Included are all of Oregon (except the Klamath and Goose Lake basins), Washington and Idaho, and parts of Nevada, Utah, Montana and Wyoming.

B. To create a Columbia Valley "Administration" (known as an "Authority" in nineteen previous regional bills) comprised of three men appointed by the President (with the approval of Congress) for six-year staggered terms of office at salaries of $17,500 per year. Two must be "bona fide" residents of the Columbia Valley. The third, the chairman, may come from anywhere in the nation.

C. To this three-man board will be delegated enormous executive, legislative, appropriative and spending powers, including:

1. The power to spend all existing federal appropriations in the area (regardless of the purposes for which Congress made such appropriations) and all power revenues (a possible future total of $525 million at Bonneville's present wholesale rates) as the judgment of the board dictates.

2. All the powers and functions now possessed by the Bureau of Reclamation, the Corps of Engineers (except coastal installations) and the Bonneville Power Administration.

3. Regional planning powers which extend the authority of the three-man board to all other natural resource conservation and development agencies, federal or state.

4. The power to manage and even socialize the entire economy of the Columbia Valley through its authority, at its sole discretion, to condemn real and personal property; to condemn water rights; to sell electric power at retail; to buy and sell real estate; and to engage in any commercial or industrial activity, in competition with existing free enterprise, in the guise of "experiments" and "practical demonstrations" (called "pilot plants" in all previous CVA bills) which are unlimited as to type, cost and duration.

To the President's small but powerful group of advisers this channeling of authority from the President (and his advisers) to a three-man board immune to interference by the people of the region marks a liberal and enlightened step forward in the march of democracy.

To those of opposite opinion the bill creates an alien and dismaying superstructure of government. To citizens of the Columbia Valley who still believe in free enterprise, a free ballot and the ability of the people to govern themselves, the mere suggestion that such an "administration" should be created would be ludicrous except for the fact that S. 1645 actually has been written and introduced, and is being considered by Congress.

In the Northwest, at this writing, the battle lines are drawn sharply along party or pro-Administration lines. Six of the seven governors of the affected states (Oregon, Washington, Idaho, Nevada, Utah, Montana and Wyoming) are solidly against the proposed CVA. Below this level, the pro-CVA forces are spearheaded by Assistant Secretary of the Interior Davidson.

Backing up Davidson's campaign are the widespread shock troops of Interior's Bonneville Power Administration. Bonneville's staff of consultants precede or accompany Davidson in his successive swings through the region, manage his publicity and assist in organizing farmer-labor groups such as the League for CVA.

During the 1949 session of the Oregon Legislature two members—Senator Richard L. Neuberger and Representative Philip Dreyer—unsuccessfully attempted to force the adoption of a pro-CVA memorial to Congress. After the session it developed that Neuberger formerly had been on the Bonneville payroll, and Dreyer resigned his legislative post to assume "special duties" as a Bonneville consultant.

Principal public support for the CVA comes from farm-labor groups whose organization was either supervised or aided by Interior Department personnel. Farm opposition comes from the Oregon Farm Bureau Federation, the Idaho State Grange and leading livestock, reclamation and conservation associations in the affected states.

General across-the-board opposition comes from industrial, transport, engineering, commercial and mining associations, chambers of commerce, independent citizens' groups and approximately 82 per cent of the newspapers of the area. Two hundred and seven individual organizations in the Columbia Valley to date are on record as opposed to a CVA.

Prominent on this list is the five-state Pacific Northwest Development Association, or PNDA, a militant group organized in 1945 to oppose the first of the perennial CVA bills and which subsequently has kept its powder dry. Davidson has publicly labeled such citizens' groups as PNDA as "fronts" for that ghost of the Insull era, the "power trust."

The PNDA, in its turn, admits with a caustic "why not?" that power utilities are among its seven hundred odd supporting members, pointing out that these battle-scarred utilities are still members in good standing of the free enterprise system threatened by the CVA. Moreover, PNDA spokesmen insist, their organization's $30 thousand per year budget is puny indeed compared to that of their principal adversary, the Department of the Interior.

Specifically, PNDA spokesmen assert, Bonneville Power Administration has thus far failed to reveal how much of its multimillion-dollar revenues are being diverted to the CVA battle under such elastic budgetary devices as "public relations" and "administrative expense."

But these are only top-level maneuvers. The average man on the street, aware of the mounting CVA uproar, is befuddled when the implications of S. 1645 are explained to him. His almost invariable first reaction is the moot question: "Why a CVA?" It should be remembered, in this connection, that no measurable public demand for a CVA has ever come from the people of the Columbia Valley; the "demand," without exception, has been channeled direct from Washington.

Attempts of proponents to answer the moot question has resulted in some curious contradictions. Davidson's insistence, for example, that existing federal bureaus in the Columbia Valley are inefficient and outmoded is contradicted by the obvious fact that the region has done well in the matter of building and operating federal projects. Examples are the Bonneville Dam, the world's largest hydroelectric installation at tidewater; colossal Grand Coulee Dam, the world's largest power plant in any category; the million-acre Columbia basin irrigation project, already authorized and under construction; and scores of lesser reclamation, flood control and power plants in the blueprint stage and scheduled for construction as fast as Congress provides the necessary appropriations.

Currently before Congress, moreover, is the Corps of Engineers' long-range development plan for the Columbia basin—known technically as Revised Plan 308—together with the coordinated Bureau of Reclamation plan. This $3 billion blueprint was prepared at the direction of Congress. In it are included coordinated future plans and programs of existing agencies, and the heads of these agencies (including Secretary of the Interior Krug) formally approved it in a joint letter to the President dated April 11, 1949.

Since Revised Plan 308 also has received overwhelming public support in the Columbia Valley, as evidenced in public hearings, Davidson has been forced to some exceedingly nimble footwork to explain his attacks upon existing agencies, the alleged "demand" for a CVA, and the apparently opposing views of his own departmental superior, Interior Secretary Krug.

As a "selling argument," the Administration propaganda line has long since abandoned references to the "benefits" of the

TVA type of regional development. Opponents of CVA pointed out that Oregon, Washington and Idaho already boast of "benefits" greater than TVA can claim after fifteen years of operation.

Included in the list are the nation's lowest household and farm electric rates; the highest per capita use and the highest per capita farm electrification; some of the nation's most productive irrigated land and the highest living standard as reflected by the average wage scale, home ownership and motor vehicle ownership.

In other words, measured by unemotional economic yardsticks of which CVA opponents make constant use, no single region in the nation appears to be in less need of the benevolent theories which patently inspired the writing of S. 1645 to follow the TVA pattern.

The bill is before Congress, nevertheless, and the still moot question—"Why a CVA?"—is receiving its preliminary airing. Some of its proponents have conceded that the issue may not come to a test in the current session.

It will not die, however. If the present bill fails, a new crop will certainly follow, since the disciples of regimentation and "candy-coated state socialism" have been sampling exceedingly strong meat during the last decade and a half.

Meantime, if S. 1645 reaches the Senate floor, much will unquestionably be heard on the subject of the Department of the Interior's pro-CVA campaign in the Columbia Valley. Regardless of the outcome, future students of political science may well rank that unique spectacle—the people versus salaried employees of the people on an ideological issue—as a significant mutation, or perhaps throwback, in the evolution of representative self-government as heretofore known on this continent.

HOW NORTHWEST LEADERS FEEL ABOUT CVA [9]

I am unreservedly opposed to any regional authority operated by remote control from Washington. I am strongly com-

[9] From pamphlet distributed by the Pacific Northwest Development Association, 205 Multnomah Hotel. Portland, Oregon. 1949.

mitted to the proposition that a representative government should have those charged with high responsibility, such as are necessarily included in such an authority, directly responsible to the people themselves, and that can be gained only by election of such officials.—*Senator Guy Cordon of Oregon.*

As Governor of Wyoming, and now as Senator, I think I represent by far the majority sentiment of my state. The citizens of the state of Wyoming have on many occasions gone on record as opposed to all "authority" legislation and in favor of over-all development of our river basins by the Bureau of Reclamation, the Corps of Engineers and other federal and state agencies. We must protect the principle of state control of our water resources. —*Senator Lester C. Hunt of Wyoming.*

I think the regional representation issue is fundamental. I am not in favor of rushing a CVA bill through this session without adequate time for careful consideration. There are great differences in the social attitudes and economic needs of the people in the Columbia River region from those of the people in the Tennessee Valley.—*Senator Wayne Morse of Oregon.*

In the over-all, I believe that it is agreed that the TVA has done a splendid job.—*Senator James E. Murray of Montana, author of the MVA bill.*

I do not believe the TVA principles can be adequately applied to either the Columbia or the Missouri Valleys. Unless so-called valley authorities can be set up to place much of the direction, supervision and planning in the hands of the people living within areas involved, instead of being directed by a small group of men who would have almost unlimited authority, I shall be forced to oppose them.—*Senator Zales N. Ecton of Montana.*

I have some differences with the present operation of TVA which are borne out in my own Columbia interstate commission bill. Among them are lack of local control of the corporation, the refusal of the corporation to cooperate with specialized government agencies like the Soil Conservation Service, the lack of effective guarantees of labor rights to employees, inadequate accounting methods, lack of local representation on the governing board.—*Representative Walt Horan of Washington.*

More unified management of power, navigation, flood control and irrigation development will eliminate the confusion certain to result where the authority over these four purposes of river control is divided, as is presently the case. I am convinced, however, that in any boards or commissions created for a CVA, if we have a CVA, provision should be made requiring that the membership on such boards be confined to western men who know western conditions.—*Representative Russell V. Mack of Washington.*

I do not think that just because TVA has been successful in the South that a similar plan would be advantageous for the Pacific Northwest. Our people in the Pacific Northwest are different and our country is different. Flood control is a paramount issue on the Tennessee, while hydroelectric energy and irrigation are the important items on the Columbia, and their administrative direction is such that we do not assume the risk of having a bureaucratic commission to govern our policy.—*Representative Lowell Stockman of Oregon.*

I have opposed valley authorities and expect to do so, because to me they are contrary to our form of government. This concentration of political and economic power in the hands of a few is not, to my way of thinking, the best process for developing the resources of our great country.—*Representative Wesley D. D'Ewart of Montana.*

I think the overwhelming majority of people in TVA states and elsewhere are satisfied with TVA's operations, and I share that feeling. In applying the lessons of TVA to the Pacific Northwest, it does not follow that the "imprint of TVA" in the rigid sense, must necessarily be imposed. Certain differences in development and special regional problems must be taken into account. An objective and disinterested appraisal of TVA should prove helpful in enabling other valley authorities to avoid some of the pitfalls that TVA may have encountered.—*Representative Hugh Mitchell of Washington, author of CVA bills.*

I disagree with and disapprove of the whole philosophy upon which the CVA is based. I do not believe the administration bill or any other authority bill should be seriously considered by Congress until we first know why we need a bill and what kind of a bill, if any, is required.—*Representative Harris Ellsworth of Oregon.*

I am definitely opposed to any program that would place control in the hands of a few men who are non-residents of the Pacific Northwest and who would operate from Washington, and I likewise am opposed to granting broad economic powers over our region to a super-government agency.—*Representative Walter Norblad of Oregon.*

The question before us is not one of having a development program in the Pacific Northwest or of not having it. The question is whether we want the development of our region to be carried forward within the successful pattern of representative government, or taken over by a new device of government which is dangerously similar to the devices of the totalitarian state.—*Governor Douglas McKay of Oregon.*

What would be left of state and local government when such an agency gets into full swing? Is it not plain that the great state of Washington would revert to almost territorial status with all important government functions supervised by Federal officials?—*Governor Arthur B. Langlie of Washington.*

Idaho people generally fear the concentration of broad powers in a three-man board, as provided in authority proposals, because their appointment and their subsequent decisions could be based upon political considerations rather than upon the basis of sound economics. They fear the implications with respect to water rights and the jurisdiction of state courts concerning those water rights.—*Governor C. A. Robins of Idaho.*

The majority of the people living in the western states are not prepared, and never will be willing, to give up their rights under existing law for the control and use of water and subject themselves to the mandate of a three-man board not responsible to the people and clothed with authority which can properly, under the Constitution, only be vested in the Congress of the United States.—*Governor Vail Pittman of Nevada.*

DEATH SENTENCE FOR STATE GOVERNMENT [10]

A clear piece of evidence that the Truman Fair Deal is a far-reaching advance on the earlier series of reforms of the Roosevelt New Deal is in the proposal for a Columbia Valley Administration. This is a more autocratic setup than the Tennessee Valley Authority, and its scope is several times as large. The full text of Senate Bill 1645 should be read by those who would like to comprehend the extent to which the welfare state threatens our institutions. It is only possible in this space to hit the highlights.

Practically every Administration stalwart in the Senate appears as a cosponsor of the bill, which is being actively pressed by President Truman's Interior Department. It applies not only to the immense Columbia watershed, but to everything else in Washington and Oregon except the basins of the Klamath River and Goose Lake.

The proposal would set up a monopolistic government corporation, well protected from the reach of the governments of the four states of Washington, Oregon, Montana, and Idaho and, it should be added, practically independent of Congress. It specifies three directors with six-year tenure who would be utterly free of local control and who could only with great difficulty be removed by a new President. The appointments of their subordinates are specifically exempted from the Federal Civil Service. The magnitude of the Administration would ultimately bring a vast horde of employees to the region, with full voting rights and under the control of the directors.

Since the Columbia Valley is dependent on water and its uses for power, irrigation, navigation, and the maintenance of lumbering and wild life, the autocracy of the CVA would mean power of life or death for every economic, political, and financial activity. Through plenary governmental powers the CVA could and would become the owner of vast property and would be free to develop, distribute, lease, and dispose of that property without

[10] By Raymond Moley, contributing editor and columnist, *Newsweek*. *Newsweek*. 34:84. August 15, 1949. Reprinted by permission.

let or hindrance. It could at will rearrange highways, railways, bridges, mills, and electric-light plants, publicly or privately owned. It would make and distribute electric power and water without control by state or local regulation.

Since its huge properties would be removed from the reach of the taxing authorities of the state and local governments, those agencies, thus impoverished, would become mendicants dependent upon the CVA. In lieu of taxes, that administration would be authorized to dole out payments to such state and local units of government. It would have such great discretion in such doles that it is hard to see how state and local governments would retain a shred of independence. So that there could be no nonsense in the courts, the bill specifically says that "the determination by the . . . [CVA] of the necessity of making any payments and of the amounts thereof shall be final."

The CVA would determine the size of farm units that should be benefited by vital irrigation or flood protection. It would give or sell newly reclaimed land in such units as it might determine as "economic." We would have to go back some hundreds of years to find a parallel to such serfdom.

The CVA could operate with unlimited funds a wide variety of businesses exempt from the restraints that states have set up for the control of competition.

The CVA would start with a fund in the Treasury of the United States, appropriated without strings by Congress, and it could dip into that fund practically at its own discretion. But after a while it would be receiving huge sums from its own operations. It could literally play with hundreds of millions of dollars. And it could make its profitable power and irrigation business pay for almost any activity that might occur to the directors.

In the battle to come, the opponents of this plan will be smeared as tools of the power interests. The erstwhile important power interests have been left far behind in this drive for statism. It is not only private enterprise that is proscribed in the Columbia Valley Administration. It is the public's control of its own government.

THE PROPOSED MISSOURI VALLEY AUTHORITY

EDITOR'S INTRODUCTION

The Missouri is one of our most capricious rivers. Draining roughly one sixth of the area of the continental United States, which supplies something like half of our bread and food grains, the "Big Muddy" provides either too little water, or too much at one time and one place.

The Army Corps of Engineers and the Bureau of Reclamation have undertaken a tremendous job in the Missouri basin. Combining their efforts under the Pick-Sloan plan (named after Major General Lewis A. Pick, Army Corps of Engineers, and W. G. Sloan, Bureau of Reclamation), they had spent almost $1.3 billion up to the beginning of last year and were asking Congress for $6.5 billion more to carry out a six-year plan starting this year.

Meanwhile, a controversy rages throughout the Midwest and in Washington as to whether the Pick-Sloan partners have really coordinated their programs or are still pursuing the often conflicting courses they followed before the threat of a Missouri Valley Authority brought them hastily together. Is an MVA needed to take a unified view of the whole problem?

An example of the conflicts in the present set-up is the Engineers' project for a nine-foot navigation channel from the mouth of the Missouri up to Sioux City, Iowa. The Bureau of Reclamation insists that such a channel would require water that is needed for irrigation in the upper valley. No one has yet determined for a certainty whether the Missouri's flow is sufficient to sustain both projects.

State opposition to an MVA is strong. The Missouri Valley governors insist they are progressing satisfactorily by working through an advisory board with the two major agencies now tackling the job.

MVA: ORDER OUT OF CHAOS [1]

For the third time, Congress has before it a proposal to attack in a planned, effective fashion the major problems of that vast ten-state region—the Missouri Valley. These problems are the control of disastrous floods which plague some sections of the valley, and simultaneously the irrigation of other areas to counter dust-bowl potentialities. Integrated with these two efforts would go power development and also the safeguarding of the land from the erosion which, in flood time, washes away millions of tons of irreplaceable top soil.

There is a mounting demand in the Valley for such unified management of the Big Muddy and its tributaries. The demand is heightened by the acute danger of disastrous floods this month and next.

There were floods on the mainstream and tributaries in January, February and March. In the mountains at the western border of the basin a heavy snow lies white and serene and dangerous as a time bomb.

Warm rains or a chinook—a sudden warm wind blowing eastward out of the mountains—could rapidly melt the snow and flush the rivers far beyond their banks. It is the combination of melting snow and rain that causes the "June rise" in the Missouri, usually the worst flood of the year.

A Missouri Valley Authority, as envisaged in the bill introduced in the Eighty-first Congress by Senator James E. Murray of Montana and fifteen of his colleagues, would provide a unified management to take the place of the many conflicting "managements" of today. Modeled on TVA, it would have the form of a corporation. As such, it would avoid the red tape of ordinary government operations and could function with the initiative and flexibility of a well-run business. . . .

The initial thing MVA would have to do would be to make the first comprehensive study of the valley as a whole ever undertaken—the watershed, the river, and the tributaries of the

[1] From an article by Rufus Terral, editorial writer, *St. Louis Post-Dispatch.* *Survey.* 5:259-62. May 1949. Reprinted by permission.

river. MVA then could go to Congress with one big plan instead of a lot of little plans thrown together without regard to their relationship.

Here, on the face of it, is a reasonable, logical way to enlist and organize social-economic-engineering-scientific-administrative talent and wisdom and focus them on the creative management of water, soil, and power development. Set over against this the actualities of today—the extravagant, disorganized, and potentially dangerous handling of the waters of the Missouri Valley. Relatively few Americans seem to realize that there is rising in the West the most enormous engineering work on a river and its valley ever attempted in the history of the world.

Already $1.2 billion has been spent on it by the United States government. Its ultimate cost is put at $10.5 billion. That is five times the investment in TVA, five times the cost of the atomic bomb.

What is being done has been obscured in the public eye by the national debate over how it shall be done. For the Missouri Valley work is being performed before being planned. It is costing tens of millions of dollars more than it should, because the Army Engineers and the Reclamation Bureau leaped into it, inadequate and unready, to forestall a growing demand for a Missouri Valley Authority.

The Pick-Sloan "plan" is in fact a combination of two plans. One has navigation as a primary purpose, and therefore calls for a small number of large reservoirs. The other has irrigation as a primary purpose, and therefore calls for a large number of small reservoirs. . . . The two schemes, drawn from diametrically opposite viewpoints and for conflicting primary purposes, were pasted together and called the Pick-Sloan "plan."

There is no single head to manage the execution of the "plan." Instead, there are five heads, each independent of the others. There are the Army Engineers; the Department of the Interior, including the Reclamation Bureau, and seven other agencies; the Department of Agriculture, including the Soil Conservation Service, the Forest Service, the Rural Electrification Administration and seven other agencies; the Department of

Commerce, including four agencies; the Federal Power Commission.

No way exists for these five departments of government to function as a unit. No way exists for Congress to consider them as a whole or even in hearings by the same committees. The only way they have managed to get together to any degree is in what is known as the Missouri Basin Inter-Agency Committee. This committee is composed of representatives of all five agencies and the governors of five of the valley states. It has no legal authority whatever. Its decisions cannot be made binding on its members and therefore have been violated frequently. The committee meets almost every month at various cities in the valley. Each member has his retinue of technicians, sometimes several dozen of them. The apparatus is cumbersome, sporadic and impotent, and has succeeded chiefly in presenting as nearly united a front as possible for propaganda purposes. . . .

In consequence of this planless planning and unmanageable management, Pick-Sloan's navigation and irrigation work will require twice as much water as the Missouri River system is known to contain, so that still more tens of millions stand to be wasted in works built but left idle for want of water to operate them. In the greatest effort it or any other government ever made to bring natural resources into the service of the country, the United States is proceeding in a manner that assures its failure. Pick-Sloan has so thoroughly discredited itself in its four years of trial that support for it has steadily weakened, and today the demand for MVA is being renewed more insistently than ever before.

The reason preeminently is that MVA can do one thing the Pick-Sloan arrangement can never hope to do—it can supply a single management. It can do other things, too, such as bringing the plan from Washington into the region itself. The MVA directors, like the heads of the Army Engineers and the Reclamation Bureau, could act only within the limits set in advance by Congress. But in order to talk with the heads of the Army Engineers and the Reclamation Bureau and get their discussions on his problems within these limits the citizen must go to Washington. If he lacks the money or the time, the decisions are influenced, not by him, but by lobbies in Washington that do have the time and money. With MVA, the citizen who has to depend on himself to speak up for his interests would be within speaking distance of the responsible representatives of the government. Many people think that this closer communion between the citizen and his government is the finest thing TVA and MVA have to offer.

But the biggest advantage today would be to have a single central management for all the manifold phases of planning and operating the valley development.

For their part, the Army Engineers maintain that the Pick-Sloan plan will be complete as soon as all the departments have fitted their individual programs into it. They hold that the Inter-agency Committee is an effective means of coordinating the agencies. They make the further arguments that they should be allowed to remain in charge of river engineering work because (1) they always have been and because (2) they need the experience in peacetime in order to be able to perform their engineering functions with the army in time of war.

Not alone in the valley itself is the demand for MVA resurgent. MVA strength at Washington is enhanced in the Eighty-first Congress because that Congress was elected with a mandate from the voters for progressive legislation. Some of the ablest bearers of that mandate are fighting for MVA, among them Senators Humphrey of Minnesota, Douglas of Illinois, and Kefauver of Tennessee. . . .

Ranked against MVA are the two "front" organizations of the Army Engineers—the Mississippi Valley Association and the National Rivers and Harbors Congress, and the Reclamation Bureau's similar group, the National Reclamation Association. These organizations are supported by contractors, who profit from building the Army Engineers' dams. (TVA effected enormous savings by building its own dams, as would MVA.) They are supported by barge line operators, who look to the Army Engineers for their navigation channel. They are supported by electric power companies, which prefer Pick-Sloan to MVA because they think its competition would be less effective. They are supported by coal operators, who fear competition from low-cost electric power, although well-balanced power systems have steam as well as water power generating plants and TVA has increased the consumption of coal in its own valley. They are supported by members of Congress on powerful committees, whose potency at the polls is tied in with the pork-barrel system of rivers and harbors projects.

An almost constant series of reminders to do something about the Missouri Valley has been received by the Eighty-first Congress since the session's start in January [1949]. First the Department of the Interior, of which the Reclamation Bureau is a part, sent President Truman a memorandum saying it considered the valley authority method the best way of developing a region. This was in effect a rejection of the Pick-Sloan plan by one of its two prime movers. Next, President Truman came out for a Columbia Valley Authority. As exactly the same issue is involved in both regions, the parallel was obvious. Last year's disastrous floods in the Columbia Valley, and the subsequent revelation that feuds between the Army Engineers and the Reclamation Bureau had been holding up vital flood protection projects there, went far toward destroying the fiction that these two hostile agencies should be entrusted jointly with the future of any region.

Now the unkindest of all the cuts has come from a task force of the Hoover Commission on Organization of the Executive Department. It is in part an expression of the disillusionment of the Missouri Valley people themselves, for former Governor Leslie A. Miller of Wyoming is chairman and former Governor Ralph L. Carr of Colorado is one of its members. The task force, though it opposed a valley authority, thought so ill of the present arrangement that it recommended that the civil functions of the Army Engineers—such as those exercised in the Pick-Sloan setup—be merged with the Interior Department. . . .

Meanwhile, from Missouri to Montana and from Colorado to Iowa the Army Engineers and the Reclamation Bureau are building dams and levees, flood walls, hydroelectric power plants, irrigation ditches, tunnels and canals to divert water from one river into another. . . .

Since Pick-Sloan started, the Army Engineers have received $210 million from Congress, the Reclamation Bureau $175 million. All the agencies in the plan have received, including their appropriations for the same purposes, in the years before Pick-Sloan, a total of more than $1.2 billion. And what has been done by the Pick-Sloaners so far is a mere start on their plan. They mean, before they have finished, to build 123 dams, 20 hydroelectric generating plants, 1,500 miles of levees and flood walls, 150 irrigation projects covering nearly 5 million acres, and that 9-foot navigation channel.

From $661 million for the Army Engineers and $1,257,645,-000 for the Reclamation Bureau when the Pick-Sloan plan was announced four years ago, the two agencies have increased their askings to about $2 billion and $1.5 billion respectively. The increase is due to three things: adding to Pick-Sloan some projects that had been separate from it; expanding the projects already in Pick-Sloan; inflation. For all the agencies in Pick-Sloan the total estimated cost was $6.5 billion before the Department of Agriculture added $4 billion recently for its part of the work. Of the $10.5 billion grand total, therefore, the Army Engineers account for 19 per cent, the Reclamation Bureau for 14 per cent, the Department of Agriculture for 38 per cent, and the remaining 29 per cent is divided among the Department of Commerce agencies, the Federal Power Commission, the Public Health Service, and the Department of the Interior agencies other than the Reclamation Bureau.

It is interesting—and informative—to compare these percentages with the percentages of total appropriations that have been obtained by the same participants. Does the comparison bear out the contention of the Army Engineers that they are concerned with a well rounded program of development in which every phase will receive its proper emphasis? Or does it bear out the contention of MVA proponents that the Army Engineers have their eye on funds rather than on any effective plan?

The Army Engineers, with 19 per cent of the program, have obtained 41 per cent of the appropriations, or twice their share on a proportionate basis. The Reclamation Bureau, with

14 per cent of the program, has obtained 21 per cent of the appropriations, or one and one half times its share. All other participants, with 67 per cent of the program, have received 38 per cent of the appropriations, or less than two thirds of their proportionate share. In the Department of Agriculture two agencies—the Soil Conservation Service and the Forest Service—are down in the program for more than 9 per cent of the whole, but their share of the appropriations has been 1.6 per cent.

In short, the Army Engineers, having so far frozen out their superior competitor, MVA, are now engaged in freezing out their politically inferior allies.

How much more error can be built into two-hundred-foot-high concrete dams and into the hard steel of whirling turbines and into millions of acres of the nation's fertile land with billions of dollars of the nation's financial resources, before it is irretrievable? The national issue of MVA is not only vital but urgent. It is within the reach of this Congress to turn a fumbling failure in the valley of the Missouri into a model for the world.

PROVISIONS OF THE MVA BILL [2]

Mr. President, I have just introduced a bill providing for the control of the waters of the Missouri River and its tributaries and the development of the resources of the potentially rich land areas of that river basin. . . .

This legislation establishes a government corporate agency described as the Missouri Valley Authority. As a basic conception, it recognizes that much which now is being done by existing agencies in the area—local, state, and national—should continue to be done by these same agencies while they are fitted appropriately into a coordinated and unified plan designed to achieve the utmost economies, while at the same time carrying out the coordinated program of river control and regional resources development. Recognizing these facts, the bill proposes

[2] From remarks in the United States Senate by Senator James E. Murray of Montana. *Congressional Record.* 95:1740-4. March 2, 1949. Reprint supplied by the author.

that these existing agencies which have been engaged in the various activities in the area—reclamation, irrigation, flood control, soil erosion, forestation, wildlife, power development, and so forth—will be utilized in an integrated plan under the supervision of the Authority in carrying this program into effect. Under this unified and coordinated plan each of the existing agencies of the government which I have enumerated will be used to carry out the particular part of the program it is respectively equipped to perform.   That is a guiding principle upon which this proposed legislation has been built—in other words, to conserve all the efforts of a constructive character that now are being made, and at the same time to fix responsibility, so that waste and duplication are eliminated, and so that the engineering soundness and success of agreed-upon plans can be appraised and realized.

The headquarters of the MVA will be in the region itself. A head office and conveniently located regional offices will be there where the program is being carried out and where the people affected by it can reach those in charge readily and without great cost of time and money.   This decentralization of Federal Government activities is sound.   It seeks to achieve the great benefits of federal financing, planning, engineering, and high-grade administrative personnel, while making the work in the field subject to day-by-day scrutiny, participation, and evaluation of the people in the region, so they may have prompt contact with those supervising and carrying the program into effect.

The MVA will be administered by a board of directors of five American citizens, three of whom must have had a residence of at least five years in the Missouri basin before taking on their duties as directors.   They shall employ a general manager who will act under policies and plans approved by the board. Here is a well-tried and proven method of corporate administration by which our public and private business institutions have achieved outstanding and enviable success.

The MVA shall proceed immediately upon being established to develop and present to the President and the Congress as expeditiously as possible a comprehensive plan for the unified development of the Missouri Valley region in accordance with the purposes and policy of this act. No plan shall be effective, and no funds made available or works begun until the Congress shall have approved that plan in all its details and particulars.

Moreover, no plan can be presented to the President and the Congress until after it has had the careful examination and comment of an advisory board. That board will be composed of twelve citizens who represent in equal numbers the interests of agriculture, commerce and industry, labor, and wildlife and recreation in the Missouri Valley. In addition, it will have as members the principal officer of each of the following federal departments: Agriculture, Interior, Commerce, Justice, War, Labor, the Federal Power Commission, the Board of Governors of the Federal Reserve Bank, and the governor of each of the ten states in the Missouri basin. The governors shall also be constituted a special committee to advise and cooperate with the MVA on all matters involving federal state relationships.

Through this advisory committee, the states and localities and the diverse interests of the region will be fully aware of all proposals of program and policy, and be able to assist in their solution. Here is democracy in action.

I wish to stress the fact that no existing program, no flood control or other works already authorized and for which funds have been appropriated, will be delayed one day by the passage of the bill. For the bill provides that all such authorized projects shall go forward toward completion and be incorporated into any over-all plan developed by the MVA and approved by the Congress. . . .

Moreover, quarterly reports of progress are required of the MVA, so that at all times the Congress and the people to be benefited or affected will be acquainted with the proposed plans, the work under way, the accomplishments, and the progress of the program. Here is a decentralized, carefully planned, and efficient administrative policy designed to get a unified program of river development carried out without costly delay.

The bill specifically provides that the plans and projects shall be carried out in such manner as to protect the interests of the states in their watersheds and water rights. In this way, a considerable body of law in these western states, which has received the sanction of the courts since earliest statehood, and whose value in protecting the rights of citizens to this primary need of water has stood the test of time, will be recognized and continued in force and effect. . . .

The MVA bill recognizes the existence of an important body of law affecting the public lands, irrigation, reclamation, grazing, geological survey, national parks and monuments, mines and mineral holdings, and forest land that must not be affected in any manner. The bill expressly prescribes that these laws must be taken into full account in the plans and programs under the proposed legislation.

It is the intention of those sponsoring the measure that the existing government agencies shall be drawn upon to the fullest extent of their capacity. Consequently, the bill provides that they may be contracted with to perform that part of the program for which they have particular ability and experience. . . .

Lands to receive irrigation produced at taxpayers' expense in the Missouri basin are limited to the intent of the reclamation law which was put on the statute books during the administration of President Theodore Roosevelt in 1902. A single ownership can receive such irrigation water on 160 acres of irrigable land, plus not to exceed a minor fraction of a second 160 acres which may be required to round out the irrigated part of a family-operated farm. Of course, in addition thereto, the operator may own and use as much nonirrigated land as he sees fit.

This bill restricts the MVA to the wholesaling of electric power, with the exception that it can sell at retail to farms and rural communities which are not adequately served by existing utilities at reasonable rates.

All funds for carrying out the purpose of the proposed act must be authorized and appropriated by the Congress. Profits made from its operations must go into the United States Treasury. No sums from such profits can be used in further construction unless specifically so authorized by Congress. The business-like conduct of the MVA is further insured by provision that the General Accounting Office shall prescribe the exact forms of accounting to be followed and shall audit these accounts.

Of vital importance to the states and political subdivisions is the provision relating to removal by the MVA of taxable property from their rolls. In any such action, the local and state governments do not lose a single tax dollar. On the contrary, the greatly increased wealth created by the works of the MVA will add much taxable wealth to the tax rolls. And so far as the particular taxable property taken over by the MVA is concerned, the local and state governments will gain, also in that respect; for the bill provides that a sum not less than the revenue lost to the states and political subdivisions shall be paid upon their appraisal to the local taxing authorities. As MVA increases wealth and property values, so tax reappraisals of its property will result in larger revenues to the localities where the property is located.

Such are the main provisions of the bill. They have been developed as a result of the thorough testing and rigorous application of the legislative process, through several congressional hearings involving previous bills for this purpose. . . .

THE BATTLE OF THE RIVERS [3]

To that vast segment of the United States lying west of the Mississippi one of the most vital of all the problems facing Congress is the question of river valley development. The Southeast has its TVA; now the argument rages over whether or not there will be an MVA—Missouri Valley Authority—for a huge area between the Mississippi and the Rockies, and a CVA—Columbia Valley Authority—for the great Northwest.

Although each of these vast regions—and the many others susceptible to over-all development—has conditions peculiar to itself, innovations successful in one can serve as guideposts, if not blueprints, for the others. Thus in all the discussions over the future of the Columbia and the Missouri, it would be as foolish to ignore the success of the governmental approach in developing the valley of the Tennessee as to ignore the success

[3] Editorial. *New York Times.* 99:22. January 13, 1950. Reprinted by permission.

of the individualistic approach in the development of soil conservation districts throughout the nation.

Among the opponents of a federal authority for the Missouri similar to the TVA is an organization of business, industrial and financial interests known as the Mississippi Valley Association. This group is supporting instead the Pick-Sloan plan, a flood-control, navigation, power and irrigation program now being carried out by existing government agencies, notably the Army Corps of Engineers and the Bureau of Reclamation. The Missouri Valley Association may have some excellent reasons for opposing an MVA, but its argument about "socialization of river systems" is not very convincing. If it could be shown that TVA, for instance, had actually subverted democracy or destroyed individual initiative or undermined capitalism in the Southeast, then TVA could be justly viewed as a threat to American institutions. But we suspect that that particular valley authority has done just the opposite; and it stands as a magnificent project, not necessarily to be duplicated in every detail, but certainly not to be dismissed as "socialism."

What happens to the Missouri and the Columbia and all the other great river valleys of the nation is of surpassing importance to all of us, and it is essential that the national interest have overriding consideration in determining the course to be followed.

ANALYZING THE MVA BILL [4]

A super-government completely removed from control by the electorate will be fastened upon the people of the Missouri basin if the Missouri Valley Authority bill now in the United States Senate becomes law. . . .

It could and doubtless would create a new bureaucracy with officious powers transcending anything this region has yet seen. . . .

[4] From eight articles by Max Coffey, editor, *Omaha World-Herald*. *Omaha World-Herald*. April-May 1949. Published as a pamphlet by the Mississippi Valley Association, 511 Locust St. St. Louis, Missouri. 1949. Reprinted by permission.

There would be nothing the people could do about it, short of armed resistance, once this parade of superimposed power got under way.

The Missouri Valley Authority will be presented, in the arguments of its sponsors, as a centralized agency to carry out flood-control measures and develop water resources through irrigation, generation of power and improvement of recreational facilities.

But a reading of the bill introduced by Senator Murray of Montana reveals other purposes. The requests for authority go much further than water development—even into "such economic, social and cultural values as may be affected or furthered by the projects and activities."

What the MVA sponsors apparently have in mind is the imposition of the most paternalistic government-without-consent-of-the-governed since the Boston Tea Party.

That is a reasonable assumption, for it is reasonable to assume that the MVA sponsors are not asking for powers they do not intend to use.

The MVA bill provides for establishment of a government corporation

. . . to establish a Missouri Valley Authority to provide for unified water control and resource development on the Missouri River, its tributaries and watershed, to prevent floods, reclaim and irrigate lands, encourage agriculture, stimulate industrial expansion, develop low-cost hydroelectric power, protect wildlife, strengthen the national defense, and for other purposes.

There is nothing in that statement of aims that is not contained in the motives and principles of the Pick-Sloan plan, with the exception of the last four words, "and for other purposes."

These four words can contain the mailed fist in the soft glove as a further reading of the bill indicates.

The Murray bill for a Missouri Valley Authority provides that the Federal Government "shall establish and maintain a broad program of unified water control and resource development" for the Missouri River watershed.

It declares that administration shall be "entrusted" to a federal regional agency. This agency would be a government corporation.

The corporation would be "directed and controlled" by a board of five directors appointed by the President of the United States, "by and with the advice and consent of the Senate." . . .

The bill provides that "any member of the board may be removed by the President." There is no provision for any other method of removing a director from office, short of criminal action.

This board of five men would have complete control of water resources development in the Missouri basin.

The board would "be assisted" by an advisory committee. But the advisory committee would have virtually no specific powers and its advice would not have to be accepted. . . .

In a sweeping concession to the right of free speech, Mr. Murray's bill contains this provision: "The committee may make such comments to the corporation and to the President on the annual report as it sees fit to make." . . .

This figurehead advisory committee would comprise the governors of the ten Missouri basin states; "the principal officer or his designee" of the Federal Departments of Interior, Agriculture, Commerce, Justice, War, Labor, the Federal Power Commission, the Board of Governors of the Federal Reserve System and twelve residents of the Authority area appointed by the President. . . .

The committee thus would have thirty members, of whom only ten would be or represent the elected officials of the states. All the others, as well as all five of the corporation's board of governors, would be presidential appointees. . . .

The bill further emphasizes its contempt of the rights of the states.

It declares that

. . . the interests and rights of the states in determining the development of the watersheds within their borders and likewise their interests and rights in water utilization and control, as well as the preservation and protection of established and potential uses for all purposes, of the waters of the region's rivers, shall be recognized by such a regional agency to the fullest possible extent.

"The fullest possible extent" is a phrase subject to a variety of interpretations. But it is clear that the Board of the corporation would do the interpreting. Conceivably, it could at any time decide that "the fullest possible extent" meant precisely nothing.

There is nothing in this bill which compels a Missouri Valley Authority to accept any specific state limitation on its powers or compels it to bow to the will of the people of a state in the construction of any of its projects. . . .

The Missouri Valley Authority has no engineering plan.

The bill which would set up an MVA empowers the MVA Corporation to prepare a plan and present it to "the President and to the Congress." . . .

It is conceivable that an MVA board might decide that none of the work done on river development thus far is "practicable." Indeed, the bitter criticism that MVA sponsors have leveled at the Pick-Sloan plan would indicate that they would find little of it "practicable." . . .

With this background of extreme disagreement among the MVA'ers on the engineering phases, their scheme for getting an engineering plan approved is especially interesting.

The bill now in the Senate provides that the plan must be submitted to both Houses of Congress on the same day. Congress then has ninety days in which to disapprove it. If, after the plan has been before Congress for ninety consecutive days, it is not disapproved by both Houses by concurrent resolution, it becomes effective.

This constitutes a new wrinkle in the democratic process. It amounts in effect to an ultimatum from a bureaucratic corporation to Congress. . . .

And the corporation, once embarked, would be pretty sure of going unchecked. For written into the bill establishing an MVA is this language:

Subject only to the provisions of the Missouri Valley Authority Act, the corporation is authorized to make such expenditures and enter into such contracts, agreements and arrangements, upon such terms and conditions, and in such manner as it may deem necessary, including the final settlement of all claims and litigation by or against the corporation; and, notwithstanding the provisions of any other law governing the expenditure of public funds, the General Accounting Office, in the settlement of the accounts of the treasurer or other accountable officer of or employee of the corporation, shall not disallow credit for, nor withhold funds because of any expenditure, not tainted with fraud, which the board shall determine to have been necessary to carry out the provisions of said act.

The extent to which a Missouri Valley Authority board of five presidentially-appointed directors (removable only by the President) might reach into the daily lives of thousands of citizens is revealed by this paragraph of the bill which would establish an MVA:

> To insure the integrated and coordinated promotion of navigation, control and prevention of floods, safeguarding of navigable waters, reclamation of the public lands and protection of property of the United States, no dam, appurtenant works, sewer, dock, pier, wharf, bridge, trestle, landing, pipe, building, float, or other or different obstruction or polluter affecting navigation, the use of navigable waters, flood control and prevention, the public lands or property of the United States shall be constructed and thereafter operated or maintained over, across, along, in, or into the Missouri River, or any tributary stream of said river or any tributary of such stream, except in accordance with plans for such construction, operation, and maintenance approved by the local office of the Corporation.
>
> The Corporation shall draw up and make public rules and regulations under which incidental, temporary or minor construction, in the categories referred to in (the foregoing) paragraph, may be made by private citizens, corporate or public bodies without approval of the Corporation. Such structures of a semi-permanent or permanent character shall be listed with the Corporation.

A similar provision, in previous MVA bills, has been interpreted as meaning that a farmer building a pasture bridge would have to follow the dictates of the Authority or a hunter building a duck blind would have to follow the letter of the MVA regulations.

A continuing paragraph declares that "the Corporation may bring appropriate proceedings in a district court of the United States to enjoin any violation of this section . . ."—which apparently means that the common citizen would be under the constant surveillance of bureaucrats hired by the untouchable Board of Directors of the Corporation.

The board could hire as many employees as it wanted. The bill states:

> The board shall, without regard to the provisions of civil service laws applicable to officers and employees of the United States, employ a

general manager and such other managers, assistant managers, officers, employees, attorneys, agents and consultants as are necessary for the transaction of its business.

Further, the proposed law authorizes the Corporation

. . . to request the assistance and advice of any officer, agent or employee of any executive department or any independent office or agency of the United States, to enable the Corporation the better to carry out its powers successfully, and as far as practicable shall utilize the services of such officers, agents and employees and the President shall, if in his opinion the public interest, service or economy so require, direct that such assistance, advice and service be rendered to the Corporation, and any individual that may be by the President directed to render such assistance and service shall be thereafter subject to the orders, rules and regulations of the Board.

Which means, in the final analysis, that any employee of a federal agency in the Missouri basin might find himself working for the MVA.

The MVA Corporation, under terms of the bill now in Congress, is granted powers including, "but not by way of limitation":

[Powers] to acquire, construct, operate, maintain and improve dams, locks, reservoirs, levees, spillways, floodways, fishways, conduits, powerhouses, steam generating plants, transmission lines, rural electric lines and substations, canals, roads, roadways, docks, wharves, terminals, and recreation facilities, and facilities incidental thereto.

[And powers] to develop and provide such methods and conditions of water and land utilization as the Corporation deems necessary or appropriate to prevent and abate floods and drouths.

The Murray bill makes the MVA the overlord of irrigation. It provides for development of Federally-owned, irrigable lands into farm units, not exceeding 160 acres (or under certain conditions up to 240 acres), and resale to private ownership.

Federally-owned land could cover a considerable quantity, for under the eminent domain section of the act the MVA Corporation is empowered to condemn "such real and personal property and any interest therein . . . as in its judgment may be necessary in carrying out the purpose of this act."

The Corporation is empowered to sell irrigation water to private landowners. But it is forbidden to deliver water to any single landowner holding more than 160 acres of irrigable land until a public hearing has been held and the landowner given an opportunity to tell why he needs more than 160 acres of irrigable land. . . .

Any irrigable land above 160 acres or the adjusted acreage above 160 acres, as described in the preceding paragraph, is stated to be "excess land."

Now any farmer who owns such "excess land" cannot obtain delivery of water from the MVA for any amount of his land unless he first agrees to dispose of his "excess land" within a "reasonable time," which is defined as "not more than five years." And he must sell at an appraised value to be determined by the Corporation, or in case of disagreement, by an "impartial arbitrator."

Thus it is plain that a farmer who owns 320 acres of irrigable land could not irrigate even one acre of it with MVA water unless he proceeded to sell his "excess land" at a price set by the Corporation or some one else.

If an owner of irrigated land comes into possession of "excess land" through foreclosure or bequest he would be given three years to dispose of his "excess land." Alternative: no irrigation water from MVA.

But the MVA would not content itself with mere delivery of water. The Murray bill gives it authority also to contract with owners of land irrigated with MVA water

. . . to enter upon privately-owned lands . . . for the purpose of improving and developing said lands by land leveling and other soil improvement and conservancy devices, for the construction of farmstead buildings and improvements and for the development of ground waters for domestic purposes.

Thus it is apparent that the MVA would have power to muscle in on the Soil Conservation Service, public and private credit agencies. It would even dig your well.

The cost:

Reimbursable in full, with or without interest, within such period of years and upon such schedule of repayments as the Corporation may deem reasonable and proper.

The MVA board is authorized to sell power it generates to states, counties, municipalities, corporations, partnerships and individuals.

It is empowered to

. . . acquire, construct, operate, maintain and improve such electric transmission lines, rural electric lines, substations and other structures and facilities as it deems necessary or appropriate to bring electric energy available for sale from its projects to existing and potential markets, and to interconnect such projects with other public or private projects for the disposition or interchange of electric energy.

It is directed, to insure the disposition of the electric energy developed at a project for the benefit of the general public, and particularly of domestic and rural consumers, to give preference to

. . . states, districts, counties and municipalities . . . and to cooperative and other organizations not organized or administered for profit but primarily for the purpose of supplying electric energy to their members as nearly as possible at cost.

The Corporation is authorized to sell energy directly

. . . to farms and in rural communities which the Corporation finds are not adequately serviced with electric energy at reasonable rates.

The Board,

. . . in its discretion, is given power to acquire existing electric facilities in such farms and small villages.

The Murray bill provides that

. . . any contract for the sale of power may include such terms and conditions, including reasonable, nondiscriminatory resale rates, and provide for such rules and regulations as in the judgment of the Board may be necessary or desirable for carrying out the purpose of this act.

The difference between the MVA and the Pick-Sloan plan is well illustrated by the difference in their origins.

The MVA begins as a design for an authoritative administration to control people.

The Pick-Sloan plan began as an engineering design for the control of the natural forces which harass people.

The MVA has no engineering plan. It hasn't even an engineering survey. It is originated on the premise that authority and control must be established first. Then the Missouri basin can be remade to whatever design the authority desires.

The Pick-Sloan plan is slow on the administrative side. It is based on the premise that the business of first importance is to build the structures that can control floods, provide irrigation for arid areas and make the fullest multiple use of the resources inherent in Missouri River water.

It is based on the assumption that the people of the Missouri basin will have the intelligence and the fortitude to develop a plan of administration that will interfere the least with individualism.

Sponsors of the MVA deny, in effect, that the people of the Missouri basin have either. They see what they think are impossible barriers to the interstate cooperation that will be needed to make the Pick-Sloan plan work without a controlling superstate.

Yet there can be no denial that considerable progress has been made in the past three years in reconciling the viewpoints of states and creating within the Missouri basin a self-governing method of operating the Pick-Sloan plan.

Most of this progress has been due to the efforts of the Missouri Basin Inter-Agency Committee, comprising representatives of five federal agencies—the Army Engineers, the Bureau of Reclamation, the Federal Power Commission, the Department of Agriculture and the Department of Commerce—and five governors of states in the basin.

The governors have helped correlate activities of the Federal agencies, while safeguarding the prerogatives of the states. The Missouri Basin Inter-Agency Committee may be setting the pattern for the representative agency that will be required to correlate all activities when the Pick-Sloan plan reaches the operational stage.

In contrast to the blank-check, government-corporation method of developing the Missouri basin, the Pick-Sloan planners must go to Congress for separate appropriations on every project. They must clear with the governor of the state before they build a project.

The Pick-Sloan plan is based on the proposition that public approval must be obtained first.

The MVA works from the other end. It proceeds from the theory that if it can be pushed through Congress, in which the Missouri basin has a minority representation, then public approval so far as the Missouri basin is concerned can be ignored.

If this be not the case, the Missouri Valley Authority Bill is wasting a lot of legal verbiage making sure that it could be.

SHOULD THERE BE A MISSOURI VALLEY AUTHORITY? [5]

This commission [appointed by the Missouri State Legislature to report on the applicability of the TVA idea to the Missouri Valley] is not a planning agency but could not perform its function without a rational conception of the fundamental elements of the [Pick-Sloan] plan adopted by Congress for the control and utilization of water resources of the basin, and of the agencies charged by Congress with the duty of its consummation and administration.

Objectives of the plan:

(a) Flood Control: Protection for the Missouri Valley against a "probable" flood substantially exceeding in peak discharge any floods of record in that valley.

(b) Irrigation: The provision of water reserves adequate for the irrigation of an additional 4.75 million acres of arable land and for the supplementing of the supply for 500 thousand acres now irrigated but for which present available supplies are deficient.

(c) Navigation: Stabilization of channel and provision and maintenance of a nine foot minimum depth navigable channel throughout that reach of the river extending from Sioux City to St. Louis.

[5] From a statement by L. T. Berthe, conservation engineer and author of the majority report of a commission appointed by the Missouri State Legislature to inspect the Tennessee Valley Authority and report on its applicability to the Missouri Valley. 28p. Mississippi Valley Association. 511 Locust Street. St. Louis, Missouri. November 16, 1945. Reprinted by permission.

(d) Consumption Demands: Provision and maintenance of water reserves in the arid regions of the basin adequate for municipal, domestic and other beneficial and necessary consumptive uses.

(e) Power: Conversion of water power to pooled electric energy, to the extent consistent with conflicting water requirements, with a planned initial installed generating capacity in excess of one million kilowatts providing an estimated annual output, in excess of irrigation requirements, of nearly four billion kilowatt hours of firm power. . . .

In the Flood Control Act of 1944 and the Rivers and Harbors Act of 1945, Congress went further than adopting a plan and allotting to each agency its specific part in its construction and administration. It also provided that:

(a) The rights and interests of the states shall be recognized.

(b) The use of water arising west of the ninety-eighth meridian for navigation shall not conflict with its use for irrigation and other beneficial consumptive purposes.

(c) The plans of interested federal agencies shall be integrated.

(d) The states shall be consulted in the formulation of any plan by a federal agency for river basin development.

This statement of federal policy, now in the law, is known and often referred to as the "Water Bill of Rights." . . .

Just what is an "authority" as embodied in these river basin authority proposals? As defined by an eminent jurist, "It is a federal corporation, in the control of three men appointed by the President, clothed with the power of government."

It has all the flexibility of action of a private corporation without the legal restraints under which a private corporation must operate. The broad powers as set out in the respective bills proposed for establishment, and as conferred under the TVA Act, enable it, under the guise of river and water resource control, to ultimately "dominate the development, utilization and enjoyment of the natural resources within a region defined to include the whole or part of many states. . . . These powers are plenary (full, complete and unqualified) in their scope."

Senate Bill 555 (superseded by S.1160) for the establishment of a Missouri Valley Authority is even more liberal in the granting of widespread powers to be held and exercised by that Authority than is the TVA Act. It contains no restrictions which would prevent the Authority from branching into activities which would not only affect but might, if the Authority so desired, largely control the social and economic life of the people. There is hardly any line of business or activity in which it could not engage, if the Authority deemed it advisable.

I agree with Dr. A. E. Morgan, for many years chairman of TVA and the man chiefly responsible for its engineering achievements, that an "MVA would be a powerful instrument for bringing in a new social order." The question arises if that is the real purpose of its proponents. Would they be equally interested in a regional authority divested of powers not germane or essential to regional control of water resources? The general radical characteristics of those elements most vociferous in its support whom we encountered during our inspection of the basin area, impels one to believe otherwise.

Equally important is the fundamental question if the vast area of the Missouri basin with its widely separated interests, both in distances and in water use, is sufficiently integrated to adapt itself to regional control by a single "authority." The Tennessee River Basin is a compact area of unified interests, and the present chairman of TVA [David E. Lilienthal] has stated that "substantial additions to the territorial scope of the TVA would impair its effectiveness." . . .

The Missouri basin area is so vast, subject to such wide variance in climatic conditions and water use requirements that, despite the fact that it is drained by a common river system, it has little if any regional solidarity. Although basin-wide coordinated planning is an engineering prerequisite to river control, the water use factor automatically divides the basin into two or more definitely different economic and administrative regions.

In the arid areas of the upper basin, water is precious and water rights are more valuable than the land. Water for irrigation, municipal, industrial and domestic use is the main essential to the economic welfare of that region and its people. In Montana, Wyoming and Colorado water is real property. In some instances that legal status is written into the state constitutions. In Missouri, the same water coming down as floods is a public nuisance and its legal standing is that of a "common enemy." Next to flood control, it is interested in navigation. In both areas the generation of electric energy is considered as a desirable by-product always incidental and secondary to the fullest possible attainment of the primary objectives. . . .

By reason of his long experience as [first] chairman of TVA, Dr. Arthur E. Morgan is undoubtedly the world's greatest authority upon the requirements fundamental to the successful operation of regional authorities. . . In his article, "What About a Missouri Valley authority?" (*Waterways Magazine*, May 1945) he states:

> If social engineering is applied to the Missouri River, the resulting design will be very different from a duplication of the TVA. In my opinion it probably would provide for an over-all referee board to intervene and decide in cases of conflict of interest between the upper and lower river, or where there should be a sharing of burdens. Otherwise, I think probable that the interests of the two areas so widely separated in location and in interests should be administered separately . . . Probably the Reclamation Service should continue its irrigation interests and the Army should limit its control to the lower river.

That is precisely the administrative setup under which the adopted project is being operated, with the Inter-Agency Committee sitting in as "referee." The Inter-Agency Committee is functioning effectively, but it should be given a positive legal status, not as an "authority," but to assure that it shall continue to perform its present function as a coordinating referee and reviewing board to which the various parts of the basin and the respective states can bring their water planning problems to be passed upon. . . .

There is no such animal as one hundred per cent area flood protection. Flood waters must have either flowage or storage room, if flood crests are to be reduced or controlled and any considerable portion of the flood subject areas relieved from the flood menace. Whatever the final plan, it is reasonably certain that some sacrifice of farm areas is inevitable. No "authority" or planning or administrative agency can escape that fact.

The way to determine if advanced theories, however plausible or attractive, are sound, is to confront them with known fact. Thus, in this matter of the within-state reservoirs the theory has been advanced from some sources that major, or measurable flood control can be obtained through improved methods of land use and erosion prevention, thus obviating the need for reservoirs. Probably never again, even with the most advanced and efficient land conservation program, shall we ever approximate, much less exceed, the protective cover which obtained in the Missouri basin area in 1844. That was the year in which occurred the greatest Missouri River flood known.

Such methods and practices are constructive and desirable, but they are primarily necessary for the preservation of the land resources. They cannot substitute for flood control reservoirs and their control and extension is the province of and assignable to a land authority, not a river authority. Missouri will need some reservoirs on its tributaries. It may not need all of those proposed or of the precise capacity indicated, but what it must have can be determined by the suggested study and review. The governor can command the engineering advice of the state's technical staff, and he should be authorized by the General Assembly to retain outside consulting service, if he deems it essential to thorough analysis and presentation.

In any event, it seems obvious that the remedy lies in utilizing the existing agencies and not in the creation of a new agency. Certainly, judging by the Tennessee Valley experience, it does not lie in the direction of an "authority." Under the present plan, of the one and a half million acres in Missouri now subject to flood hazard (including both main and tributary valleys), 620 thousand acres are to be protected and relieved from that hazard. Of the remaining 880 thousand acres, 450 thousand acres will be subjected to reservoir flooding and 430 thousand acres along the non-reservoired tributaries will remain substantially as they are except for minor benefits from lowered backwater levels, or direct benefits accruing from channel rectification.

By contrast, under the planning and administration of the TVA, of the 666 thousand acres in the valley of that river and its tributaries originally subject to flood hazard, 600 thousand acres are now subject to either constant or occasional flooding and but 66 thousand acres have been relieved of and given protection against the flood hazard.

The following objections are made [by proponents of an MVA]:

(a) That there is no basin-wide authority established under the Pick-Sloan plan.

Conceded. It has already been shown that the basin is not adapted to single regional control. The administrative setup is that suggested by Dr. Arthur E. Morgan, first chairman of TVA and generally considered to be the best informed man on regional river "authorities" in America. The functional allotments to specific agencies assures the most experienced personnel available for the respective assignments.

(b) That the Inter-Agency Committee is without legal status, is merely advisory, exercises no real control or jurisdiction in the development and execution of the plan and could not do so even if given statutory standing.

It *is* functioning and doing it well. With the basin's congressional representation and its ten governors neither the Army or any other federal agency is likely to slap the basin in the face. The statement as to what it could not do, if given statutory standing, is pure conjecture. Its real job is that of a coordinating referee and it is doing that.

(c) The law "vests absolute and arbitrary control in the development and execution of said plan in two individuals—the Secretary of War and the Secretary of the Interior."

The powers are restricted, not plenary as proposed for the Directors of MVA. MVA would have three instead of two— but all three "strangers." Also, the departmental chiefs cannot bypass Congress as did TVA which was subject to direct Presidential domination—one-man rule.

(d) "Those directing the activities of each of the four agencies taking part in the development and execution of the so-called Pick-Sloan plan are not required to be residents of the Missouri Valley."

Granted, but in view of TVA experience where the real director of policy was the President, who didn't live in the Tennessee Valley, the "authority" alternative is not inviting. Also, the four governors on the Inter-Agency Committee live in the valley.

(e) The reservoirs in Missouri take too much fertile land; they may not be used to produce power; they are to be constructed "primarily" for development of river navigation; the plan fails to deal with soil erosion, etc.

All of which, except as to navigation and power, have already been discussed. The dams and reservoirs in Missouri are not to be used primarily for navigation benefits but for flood control. The very nature of the river and project assures that navigation demand upon these reservoirs will be nominal.

If the flood control objectives of the valley are to be attained, the power possibilities of the mid and lower reaches are nominal. Particularly, multi-purpose operation of the proposed tributary reservoirs in Missouri would be limited in scope by reason of the limited storage available and the absence of any sharp, well-defined line between flood and nonflood seasons which obtains in the Tennessee watershed area but does not obtain in the Missouri basin, and particularly not in the Missouri part of that basin. . . .

The cost of TVA power is no criterion of the cost of similarly generated power in any part of the Missouri basin. Power production costs are narrowly regional. In water power projects, that Providence which created and determined the type of the river and the character and distribution of the rainfall determines the actual cost of power production to a far greater degree than it can be controlled by any administrative authority or agency. The physical conditions control the cost of power production, not the "yardstick" theory or slogan of any "authority." The heavy storage available in the upper Missouri basin, and the heavy heads obtainable on its mountain tributaries, offer substantial power possibilities and the plan of the adopted project provides for or makes possible their development as rapidly as consumer demand develops; and that will probably be cheap power. . . .

Recommendations:

(1) Creation of a Missouri River Authority to supersede and supplant the existing agencies in charge of the control, de-

velopment and utilization of the water resources of the Missouri basin would result prejudicially to the interests of the people of the Missouri basin and particularly to the interests of the people of the state of Missouri.

(2) The Inter-Agency Committee should be given statutory standing in order that the people in the Missouri basin may be assured of the continuance of its present function as referee in matters of plan coordination and readjustment.

(3) Immediate steps should be taken to provide for a thorough review of the economic justification for, the location of and required capacities of the reservoirs planned under the adopted project to be constructed in the state of Missouri, and to have the construction of the Grand and Osage river reservoirs deferred until the completion of that study and review.

WHAT YOU CAN BELIEVE ABOUT MVA [6]

Proponents [of MVA] scoff at the superstate propoganda, and point to TVA. In seven TVA states, seven governors publicly affirm that freedom reigns, God bless America and the Tennessee Valley Authority.

The opposition hints darkly that the governors speak under compulsion; or, sure they're happy, they ride the gravy train; or, the freedom is illusory, because TVA chairman David Lilienthal [since succeeded by Gordon Clapp] is too foxy to exert all his despotic powers. Possibilities for coercion can be read into the TVA Act, but they don't emerge. TVA directors know well that they can be fired without ado, and TVA lacks the force essential to a superstate. It has no secret police, no private army, no courts of its own. It is the creature of Congress, which has amended the TVA Act five times.

On its face the authority system promises more democracy instead of less, because authority headquarters are in the home valley, instead of far-off Washington. Citizens who like to go gunning for bureaucrats can easily pot the ruffed authority species

[6] From an article by Wesley Price, associate editor, *Saturday Evening Post.* *Saturday Evening Post.* 29:22. June 19, 1946. Reprinted by permission.

from their doorsteps. The long-tailed Washington bureaucrat is out of range.

Federal manipulation of natural resources is directed from Washington by dozens of separate bureaus. They act under separate statutes, and beseech separate congressional committees for separate appropriations; and the separate committees can't easily detect overlaps of separate budgets and separate functions.

Washington bureau chiefs, burdened with forty-eight state duties, refer questions to their local men in the field. The field men refer important decisions back to the policy makers in Washington. . . .

An authority would make high policy decisions in, say Omaha, instead of Washington. It would supplant a multiplicity of federal agencies or unify their efforts in the region. One agency, the MVA, would have one plan to control the water and promote agriculture and industry in one river basin, and there would be only one budget to justify to Congress.

The CIO asserts that an MVA would make a hundred thousand jobs in construction of dams and related works, and fifty thousand jobs lasting five years in manufacture of electrical appliances for homes and farms.

It makes a case for MVA—until you recollect that Army dams and Reclamation dams will make jobs, too—quite as many as an MVA.

The emphasis given to huge multiple-purpose dams by the various Missouri-basin planners appalls soil conservationists. In their view, floods are mere symptoms of the valley's real illness, soil erosion. Loosened by careless farming and overgrazing, the good earth is being washed into the rivers and out to sea at a frightening rate. Each year the land is a little sicker, a little bonier.

It can't be cured by massive doses of concrete poured into main-stem dams. It needs careful doctoring to slow the water runoff and pin down the topsoil—terracing, contour plowing, new grass and trees, hundreds of thousands of farm ponds, and countless little dams in little brooks.

Unless conservationists are brought to the front by regional planners, the entire basin may someday be stripped of its topsoil.

It is feared that the big dams will be silted solid in about fifty years, at the present rate of erosion, although TVA studies indicate their reservoirs will be good for centuries. . . .

None of the plans for the Missouri Valley gives soil conservation a place comparable to that given flood control, navigation, power or irrigation. The Murray bill gives conservation enough mention to ensure authority control, and it is assumed that an MVA would emulate TVA's admirable land policy. . . .

Projected Army reservoirs will cover 900 thousand acres of fertile land, the farm association [Missouri Farmers' Association] estimates. Twenty thousand persons will be forced from their homes to make way for the water. State Auditor Forrest Smith [of Missouri] says fourteen counties will be financially ruined.

The acreage doomed to inundation is worth $18 million annually in farm income, by association figures, more than twice the average annual loss from flood damage. Floods are cheaper, the Missouri farmers argue, than Army schemes for controlling them. . . .

Army calculations minimize the predicted crop loss. Much land taken for reservoirs is rarely flooded. In ordinary years it is leased back to farmers. As for the acreage inside the levees, some of it wouldn't be there to quarrel about, if the Army hadn't made it by stabilizing the channel and halting bank erosion and cutoffs. And 1.8 million acres once subject to floods will be permanently protected. Solemn promise. . . .

All will not be lost, conservationwise, without an MVA. The farmers themselves, at popular elections, already have organized more than 220 soil-conservation districts, including some 300 thousand farms, in the Missouri Valley. However, the actual conservation work goes slowly. Really to nail down all the farm and rangeland in the country may take another fifty years, the way we're going. That's the estimate of Hugh H. Bennett, chief of the United States Soil Conservation Service.

The TVA has long been striking the tocsin of doom about soil erosion. Bennett hits the gong even harder. Somberly, he counts the acres on which our American civilization rests: 50 million acres of once-fertile cropland now gullied and destroyed; 100 million acres of cropland seriously damaged, with half the topsoil gone; another 100 million visibly slipping. There remain only 460 million acres of really good cropland, our national capital. All of it is subject to erosion, save 78 million acres.

"We couldn't live on 78 million acres," says Bennett. "We would cease to be a vigorous nation." . . .

An authority should improve the industrial climate in the Missouri Valley, but so should the Missouri Basin Inter-Agency Committee, properly administered. In any case, the Missouri Valley, thirteen times as large as the Tennessee, can't expect thirteen times as much hydroelectric power. It may get, in new installations, only half as much as TVA.

Rainfall and terrain make the Tennessee Valley a natural for power dams. The Missouri basin is not so well favored. TVA generated about 12 billion kilowatt-hours in fiscal 1945 [15,734,-764,000 in 1949]. The Federal Power Commission estimates a 10 billion kilowatt-hour potential for the Missouri basin. The Bureau of Reclamation sees no more than 3.8 billion. This may not be enough electricity to give the Missouri Valley an industrial boom, but it is more than enough to alarm the private power industry. . . .

The effort to impede government generation of power is mere skirmishing compared to the strife over who gets the government electricity, once it is produced. The private utilities want to buy it at the dam site, wholesale, feed it into their transmission lines and sell it at retail.

TVA built its own transmission lines and bought out existing networks. It can sell power to anyone, often sells to private utilities, and buys from them too. But TVA must give preference, under the act, to public and nonprofit agencies, such as municipally owned distribution systems, cooperatives, states and counties.

The Bureau of Reclamation, like the TVA, must give preference in power sales to municipalities and public bodies, under laws in effect since 1906. Unlike TVA, Reclamation frequently sells the entire output of a big dam to established private utilities. The power industry naturally favors Reclamation. If the Missouri Valley must be dammed, the utilities prefer to see it done by an Army-Reclamation team, not an MVA.

Under the Murray bill, MVA could run lines to villages or isolated farms any time the Authority decided they were paying too much for private power or getting inadequate service. A coarse interpretation of "inadequate service" or remorseless judgments of retail rates would permit an MVA to parallel every private power line from Cut Bank, Montana, to St. Louis, Missouri.

Such a policy would, of course, strangle private power in the Missouri Valley. Already the Government is producing 20 per cent of the nation's power, and planning to produce more. If authorities cover the forty-eight states, it is likely that government would have a monopoly on electric generation and the private power industry would no longer exist.

If the American people want to place the generation of power in government hands, it is their right to order that this be done, but they—and their representatives in Congress—should understand the issue clearly. There can be no sidestepping of this ultimate meaning of the move to blanket the country with TVA's. If carried out, it means the nationalization of electric power. It means, also, we shall be taking one step toward the socialization of American industry—a solid fact not to be confused with the "socialist plot" propaganda. . . .

In their calmer moments utility spokesmen call attention to advantages of cooperation between government and private power systems. The alternation of wet and dry seasons makes the output of hydroelectric dams erratic. The power flow can be firmed by cutting in steam plants—and private companies have the steam in plenty. They have, besides, big markets already wired and able to absorb the surges of government juice.

Private-power men hasten to add that any savings resulting from purchase of cheap government electricity should be passed along to the ultimate consumer *in toto*, under the supervision of state power commissions or other regulatory bodies. The industry subscribes to government regulation of business in the public interest, but protests, of course, against Government in business. . . .

Cheap and plentiful power is held out as a major inducement by MVA propagandists. If MVA sold power at TVA rates, they say, the people of the Missouri Valley would save more than $100 million a year on their electric bill. But there is disagreement over the Missouri Valley's power needs. Private companies report that their installed capacity in that area can generate more power than the market can take. . . .

At TVA's back door are the Alabama Power Company and the Georgia Power Company. They cried ruin when TVA set impossible rates a decade ago. Today these companies are flourishing despite taxes, interest payments and a rate schedule almost as low as TVA's. Volume is 'way up, of course. . . .

There is no doubt that an MVA would have great powers, affecting for good or ill the lives of 7 million people living in an area that is one sixth of the United States. Authority that is now scattered among a score of government bureaus towers menacingly when heaped up in one enormous pile, as it is in the Murray bill.

Top it off with a large measure of financial independence, a relaxation of congressional controls and a proviso that MVA can spread out of the Missouri Valley if its directors see fit. All that is in the Murray bill. It adds up to something tremendous. But it doesn't add up to a superstate, "Russian communistic," as it has been called, "relentlessly authoritarian . . . sinister . . . Fascist . . . despotic."

Superstates can defy peoples and legislatures. TVA can't, nor could an MVA. If an authority goes bad, Congress can dig it out of its valley much quicker than that big mistake, prohibition, was dug out of the Constitution.

The superstate skeleton has been rattled by seven state legislatures in the Missouri Valley in resolutions condemning the Murray bill. Eight of the ten governors are opposed to an MVA, professing fears that their state would atrophy under such an authority. . . .

Since 1944 the [Kansas City] *Star* has been smiting the authority idea without mercy.

Last summer the newspaper sent a writer to the Tennessee Valley to examine TVA at first hand, the *Star* being mighty partial to old-fashioned look-see reporting. The writer was not swept off his feet by TVA, but he was favorably impressed, and told why in a series of articles, which the authority-hating *Star* faithfully published. Presently the uncompromising tone of *Star* editorials softened.

From the concrete TVA experience one lesson is worth considering in the bills for all river valleys [said the *Star*]. The nub of the TVA success is its independent administration within the valley. The three board members are able to make decisions on the spot. It is free from the pulling and hauling and bumbling of bureaus back in Washington.

The *Star* threw out a suggestion: Let the President appoint a board representing industry, the Army Engineers and affected government bureaus, to carry out programs specifically authorized by Congress; within limits give the board authority to act, and money to spend at its own discretion.

The editorial was evidence of a shift in public opinion. Up the river from the *Star* is another influential newspaper, the *Omaha World-Herald*. It is firmly opposed to Murray's MVA, but it, too, recognizes that regional administration is a strong point in the case for an authority. What the valley probably needs, says the phrase-coining *World-Herald*, is an authority with a small *a*. . . .

An organization which was advertised last summer as bumbling, unwieldy and potentially quarrelsome—the Missouri Basin Inter-Agency Committee—is confounding its critics.

Fast working, it already has $250 million worth of projects ready for the bulldozers, as soon as Congress turns loose the money. It has planed down rough spots in the Pick-Sloan plan, and settled question after knotty question without once running to Washington. . . .

There's always that Thing, outside in the dark: MVA. Just standing there, it scares up a lot of action.

WHO ARE THE OPPONENTS OF MVA? [7]

The issue of a Missouri Valley Administration is not a sectional issue alone. The MVA is a vital program for the entire

[7] From remarks in the United States Senate by Senator Hubert H. Humphrey of Minnesota. *Congressional Record*. 95:1748-52. March 30, 1949.

nation. It is a national issue; it is a liberal issue. MVA will
mean more and cheaper production from more and cheaper electricity. It means more diversified agriculture, providing crops in
demand rather than crops in surplus. It means cheaper finished
products because it will bring cheaper transportation of raw materials out of the valley. MVA can make a great contribution to
food security for the world, because its soil-conservation provisions
will improve and extend the conservation practices of the basin.
MVA can strike a blow for free enterprise against monopoly in
such fields as light metals and fertilizer where big business controls supply and controls price. New business growing from
MVA's cheaper electric power can break the monopoly control. . . .

In the debate which has arisen over the Missouri Valley, the
same forces that have lined up in the other battles over liberal
legislation are lined up again. On the one hand we have high-
priced lobbyists for special interests, sniping constantly behind
the scenes, lobbyists who have beaten MVA for several years.
We have the large power companies, the railroads, the water
rights attorneys, and the general dissenters who want reaction at
any cost.

On the other hand there is a familiar line-up, too. First,
we have the inhabitants of the Valley itself, people who every
day are losing the wealth that can be created from the now
destructive Missouri. On this side we also have the consumers
of the whole country, looking always for cheaper and better
goods. And on this side of the picture we have the same spokesmen for the interests of the people who have constantly, throughout their long and statesmanlike service, represented honestly what
all the people want and deserve. . . .

Now let us look a little more closely at the line-up on this
bill. Let us look at the opposition, at those who are fighting
MVA.

First is the power lobby, whose rates in and near the Tennessee River were cut drastically by TVA.

Behind the power lobby comes a fake development association formed of the contractors to the Army and the Bureau of
Reclamation who now are engaged in a hodge-podge of contrary
maneuvers in the Missouri Valley today.

Next come the railroads, who no longer believe in the competitive system.

Last spring the Eightieth Congress eliminated any vestige of competitive action in the railroad industry with the Reed-Bulwinkle bill.   Now the railroads are out to prevent MVA from opening up the ways to healthy competition from river transportation.

Finally come the water-rights attorneys who stand to lose their constant, sterile litigation over ownership of the resources of all the people, namely, water.

Monopolists are holding their breath all over the country. They are fighting MVA because MVA would successfully fight them.   Besides the railroads and electric-power monopolies, MVA will challenge the Big Nine of the fertilizer industry and squeeze out monopoly profits and lower the price of fertilizer to our farmers.   Financiers whose capital is tied up in eastern industries have a big stake in keeping the Midwest from its most prosperous development—a development that would mean a higher standard of living for the entire nation.   Finally, light-metals industries could grow up around the new generators, to challenge the nearly complete one-firm monopoly in that field. . . .

HOW THE PICK-SLOAN PLAN FUNCTIONS [8]

There is a popular idea that the Missouri Basin Inter-Agency Committee was set up to accomplish the same thing as a board of directors for a corporation and because it does not take upon itself some of those duties which would ordinarily fall to such a board, there has been a studied effort on the part of some people to create the impression that it has many shortcomings.   The Inter-Agency Committee is a unique organization.   Nothing like it has existed in the world of internal resource development, and for that reason, it has been critically examined and studied by students of political economy and well-intentioned planners for the pur-

[8] From address by W. G. Sloan, engineer of the Bureau of Reclamation and joint author of the Pick-Sloan plan, delivered before the Mississippi Valley Association, St. Louis, Missouri, February 7, 1950.   Mimeographed text supplied by the author.   Reprinted by permission.

pose of searching out its flaws and in seeking a conclusion as to its workability in other sections of the United States. Having been a member of the Committee for about four years and its chairman for the past year, I believe I can speak with some assurance concerning the workings of the Committee. . . .

Early in the year 1943 a voluntary federal Inter-Agency Committee was formed in Washington for the purpose of bringing about better cooperation among the various federal departments in Washington having to do with resource development in the United States. On March 29, 1945 this federal Inter-Agency Committee passed a resolution which states in part:

In order to facilitate progress on the multiple-purpose development program authorized by the Congress for the Missouri River Basin, there is established a Missouri Basin Inter-Agency Committee. The purpose of this committee is to implement the policies and purposes of the federal Inter-Agency River Basin Committee established under the federal Inter-Agency Agreement dated 29 December 1943 by providing a means through which the field representatives of the participating federal agencies may effectively interchange information and coordinate their activities among themselves and with those of the states in the preparation of reports and in the planning and execution of works for the control and use of the waters of the Missouri River basin. The establishment of this committee should not be interpreted as related to or in any way affecting the consideration now being given by the President and the Congress to the possible creation of a Missouri Valley Authority, or any other administrative device.

Note that the principal purpose for which the Missouri Basin Inter-Agency Committee was established was to provide a means through which field representatives of federal agencies may *interchange information* and *coordinate activities* among themselves and with the states in preparation of reports and planning and execution of works.

The Committee has no authority in the administration of the public works within the Missouri basin nor has it responsibility for execution of the works. It is simply a voluntary coordinating body. . . .

Three departments, Army, Interior, and Agriculture, carry the bulk of action work in the Missouri basin development, but as a necessary complement to the work of those agencies, the Department of Commerce is represented on the Committee for the purpose of channeling the vast amount of statistical information which it gathers and its knowledge of business enterprises and opportunities to the over-all study of basin development being pursued by the Inter-Agency Committee. The Weather Bureau and Coast and Geodetic Survey are important agencies of Commerce with active participation in the basin work. The present representative of Commerce on the Committee is the Regional Director of the Branch of Foreign and Domestic Commerce. . . .

Since the Committee is a voluntary organization it receives no appropriations as an entity of the federal government, nor does it receive any contributions from any of the states involved. The salary and expenses of each of the federal members are paid by the respective departments of the government. The expenses of state personnel are provided by the respective states. Expenses of the monthly meetings are usually provided by the community in which the meeting is held. . . .

When problems of coordination arise they usually involve only one or two of the agencies. It has been the practice of the Committee to advise these agencies to work out their problems among themselves and bring the matter before the full Committee only if they have been unable to reach an agreement.

In the development of the Missouri River basin the plan envisions development of all of the natural resources of the basin. In the beginning, major emphasis was placed upon control and use of the water resources but, in authorizing the development, the Congress stated the principle of broad development of all of its resources and thus enlarged to a great extent upon the original conception. Consequently, any interpretation of the concept of broad resource development involved many other things besides the use of the water flowing in the streams. Thus minerals, fish and wildlife, recreation, industrial and all the activities which make up the basic, natural, renewable, and processed resources of the basin were brought into the picture. No single agency of the federal government has been functioning or has jurisdiction over all of such activities. It became of paramount importance, therefore, that there should be a central body to view the basin development as a whole and to coordinate all of the individual activities for the purpose of achieving the final goal in resource development. Each of the government agencies is expert along particular lines. Each of them has built up organizations to fulfill its specific functions and each of them receives annual appropriations for the purpose of carrying out the mandates of Congress. The voluntary Inter-Agency Committee is endeavoring to bring about this coordination without compulsion, without authority and with only the will and desire to work together toward a common end. . . .

The first step in coordination of the programs of the agencies was taken at the very first meeting of the Committee. Each agency representative presented a statement of the interests of his department in the program. Soon thereafter a compilation was made of all of these programs for the information and guidance of the Committee. From that date to the present there has been a studied effort by the Committee to thoroughly inform not only the members of the Committee but also the attending press and public, of the myriad details of the program, progress which is being made and the problems which are continually arising in coordination and accomplishment.

In the beginning there appeared to be a reluctance on the part of state members to voice in public questions concerning the advisability of constructing this part or that part of the project, its effect upon conditions in their own state or the need for some of the work which had been programed. But as time went on and a better understanding and better acquaintance was acquired this reluctance changed to an eagerness and willingness to lay their cards on the table and work the problems out in public. The mere presentation of the programs of the various agencies has tended to make them conscious of the need of coordinating their work and producing effective results which will stand up in the spotlight of a public meeting.

Responsible administrators of the various agencies have become acquainted with each other. The breakdown of a specialist's viewpoint to that of a broader, more civic-minded attitude has become increasingly apparent as the meetings have followed one after the other. It is in this educational aspect of the Committee's work that the most effective results can be seen.

The average attendance by those registered at the meetings throughout the years has been as follows: 1945: 44; 1946: 61; 1947: 57; 1948: 69; and, 1949: 83.

At the present time agenda and minutes of the meetings are distributed to approximately 450 individuals and government agencies.

All members of the Committee take back to their own agencies and to their states an understanding of the over-all problems and progress which could be obtained in no other way. Early activities of the Committee were toward probing the interrelated activities of the agencies and a groping to understand the relationship of each of the programs with others.

As of today most of the important or key structures in the development plan are either contracted for or have been initiated. A new stage is approaching wherein the attention of the Committee is being devoted more and more to operational programs, the conflicts between state and federal jurisdiction and the methods and means of continuing harmonious cooperation beyond the construction stage into the operational stage.

In addition to the activities of the Federal Government in a broad program such as this, each of the individual states is carrying on many activities complementary to or related to and affected by the activities of the Federal agencies. The Inter-Agency Committee offers and accepts the opportunities to enable each of the state agencies to understand and realize the relationship of the individual states to the federal program. Thus there is brought about a meeting of the minds of those in charge of state activities with those in charge of federal activities. . . . So much for the makeup and workings of the Inter-Agency Committee.

There appears to be a growing recognition of its role in this great development. Its effectiveness must be measured by the unanimity of the support it receives from the people in the basin.

There are some honest critics of the Missouri basin program but, in the main, no adverse criticism stems from the well-informed. Therein lies the strength of the Inter-Agency Committee—to inform the people—critics and supporters alike. To be well informed on the many complex facets of the program is to support the development. There has always been opposition to the program since it was first proposed and authorized, but this opposition originates largely from interests outside the Missouri River basin. Charges have been made that the government bureaus operating under the program are wasting federal funds, that they are torn by rivalry and have refused to work together. Panaceas have been proposed to demolish the straw men they have constructed. Lately there has been a new rush of criticism and some of it has come from within the Missouri basin itself. . . .

Perhaps the criticism which has been made has received its greatest impetus from a document which was incorporated in the Task Force Report of the Hoover Commission on Natural Resources. This Task Force Report has often been erroneously referred to as a part of the Hoover Report. It is not. Apparently the Commission felt that a case study of the Missouri basin development would yield basic information to assist their Commission in formulating recommendations as to reorganization of the Federal Government for greater efficiency. They, therefore, employed a young professor of geography from the University of Chicago to make such a case study for them. He had never before had any experience in resource development planning, nor had he ever visited the Missouri River basin. His case study was based upon such reports, newspaper articles, etc., as he was able to find in libraries and with the aid of conversations with various executives in Washington. Neither the findings nor the recommendations of this case study were quoted by the Commission in its final report. The prestige given to his report is a natural result of its incorporation within the Task Force Report on Natural Resources and, therefore, deserves serious consideration in any study of the advantages or disadvantages in carrying out a basin-wide development on such a big scale as is proceeding in the Missouri basin.

The report occupies some thirty printed pages and is accompanied by a bibliography setting forth the publications used as a basis for the study. The author apparently did not realize that the development has now been proceeding for five years and that there is already under way at least 40 per cent of the work contemplated in the development. Such a conclusion can be drawn from the opening statement of his report, which is as follows:

> For many years Missouri River basin development has been the subject of an intermittent but fierce struggle between seemingly irreconcilable groups in the United States.

Such a statement might have been true five years ago. It certainly has not been true at any time since the development program was authorized by the Congress in December of 1944. Whatever differences of opinion there might have been prior to that time and however bitter the controversies might have been, all were resolved upon the passage of the authorizing act, and from that day to this opponents have been searching in vain for evidences of non-cooperation, competition and waste.

You people in the lower part of the Missouri basin are well aware of the struggles in the basin and in the Congress over the plans of development, before the whole problem was aired within the committees of Congress. You are also aware that since that time there has been such a unanimity of opinion in all parts of the basin that the Congress has appropriated increasing amounts from year to year to carry out the work with very little argument or controversy.

In the summary of the case study to which I am referring, there is a prelude to those findings. The statement is made that while the Missouri basin will benefit greatly from the works to be constructed and other federal activities in the area, the procedure is not recommended as a pattern for similar development in other areas. Seven conclusions are listed to support this statement. Let me make it clear that those of us who are engaged in this development program do not consider ourselves missionaries to other parts of the United States nor do we contend categorically that what is being accomplished here can be used again in other parts of the country. Each area of the United States has its own peculiar problems and in outlining a program for other basins, the problems peculiar to each should dictate the nature of administration required and the manner in which the work should be executed. We do contend, however, that within the Missouri basin the job is being accomplished as expeditiously as the funds made available will permit, with a minimum of friction and with a greater degree of cooperation by the various federal agencies than has ever been attained in the history of the country.

TEAMWORK IN RIVER BASIN DEVELOPMENT [9]

The theme of my remarks here today is one of federal and state teamwork on the nation's greatest river basin development in the valley of the Missouri. . . .

However, this particular meeting of the Mississippi Valley Association is undoubtedly one of the most portentous in its entire history. For the past several years now, confusing and conflicting information has been circulated about the country on this business of river development, which has certainly been deliberate in its objective as it has been purposeful in its propaganda. I use the word "propaganda" advisedly as it has reached a crescendo of late. From my own particular experiences . . . I have become cognizant of it and, like a lot of other people these days, pretty well able to recognize it whenever I see it or hear it. . . .

So today we people out on the job who are in the construction business, the Bureau of Reclamation, and the Corps of Engineers can laugh at the ridiculousness of this propaganda, but the real hurt is against the people at home—the people who have had the faith and loyalty through the years *in* those established agencies of the Federal Government to whom the work has been entrusted for as much as 125 years. In my talk today, therefore, I am going first to give you a short factual report on the progress of the work in the Missouri basin; and then I am going to touch upon a few aspects of the work of the Corps of Engineers in developing the Pick-Sloan plan on the Missouri in relation to work throughout the rest of this great Mississippi Valley. . . .

Now, with this background, I am going to discuss the first of my two objectives—the *progress* to date on the Missouri River development. Initially let me say that more than 40 per cent of the work authorized by Congress in the Missouri basin under the

[9] From a speech by Brigadier General S. D. Sturgis, Jr., Corps of Engineers, before the Mississippi Valley Association, St. Louis, Missouri, February 7, 1950. Mimeographed text supplied by the author. Reprinted by permission.

Flood Control Act of 1944 is under construction today. This represents work, the total estimated cost of which is nearly $2 billion. For those self-appointed but irresponsible experts who are constantly referring to the crumbling of our agencies and dissension in the Missouri Valley—even implying that we have not yet gotten together on a plan—the Bureau, the Corps and the states of the basin have done a pretty good job, I think, in getting 40 per cent of such a tremendous program under construction within four years of the time of the initial appropriations by Congress.

The projects now being built or completed constitute the backbone of the basin plan for the Four Horsemen of Prosperity—flood control, irrigation, power, and navigation. This project is in an advanced construction stage, which, within four or five years will be ready to produce major benefits for the people of the Missouri Valley.

Construction strides this year make it possible to anticipate that two of the largest multiple-purpose projects being built by the Corps of Engineers on the Missouri River will be substantially completed and ready for initial operation in four or five years. These are the Garrison Dam in North Dakota and the Fort Randall Dam in South Dakota.

You may be interested to know that Garrison Dam near Bismarck, North Dakota is now 26 per cent complete. This largest rolled-earth fill dam in the world will create the greatest single storage reservoir in the entire basin plan. Consider the potential human benefits in the storage of 23 million acre-feet of water and you grasp something of what this will mean to the people of our valley.

By the close of 1949, the Corps of Engineers had under construction 73 per cent of its authorized projects for Missouri River flood control and multiple-purpose development. Construction contracts in force at the close of the year totaled $160 million on *its* part of the comprehensive valley program. This is in addition to Corps of Engineers contracts in the amount of $47 million which were completed in 1949, and previous contracts on work accomplished in prior years.

At the close of four years of construction, we have virtually completed the Cherry Creek flood control dam, initiated in 1946, and it now is ready to function to protect the City of Denver against floods on Cherry Creek. The Kanopolis flood control dam on the Smoky Hill River near Salina, Kansas, was completed in 1948 and is functioning very effectively. Fort Randall Dam near Yankton, South Dakota, another major project which will exercise important controls on the main river, is 23 per cent complete; and initial work is under way on the Oahe Dam near Pierre, South Dakota, also a key main river project in that state. Harlan County Dam on the Republican River in Nebraska, now 54 per cent complete, is expected to go into operation by 1952.

We have built or are building 160 miles of agricultural levees along the Missouri River below Sioux City, Iowa, a system which eventually will extend all the way downriver to the mouth near St. Louis.

Construction of fifty-three miles of dike and revetment structures in the main river was accomplished in the 1949 working season as part of the authorized nine-foot navigation project on the Missouri River.

This leads me, in conclusion, to the charge made by certain critics of our river basin development programs, that there is nothing but conflict between the federal agencies charged with the work. By this means, they apparently hope to create confusion and dissension.

There are conflicts in laws and differences of opinion among local interests; and sometimes but less frequently, there are honest differences of opinion on technical matters between the agencies. But these conflicts in laws, and local interests and differences in engineering opinions are healthy and typical of a democratic approach. They have been, or are being, reconciled by cooperative actions of all concerned, under the able guidance of the Inter-Agency Committee.

Only through the give and take method around the conference table, such as marks the program in the Missouri basin, can a truly sound and democratic solution be found for the problems to which any such vast undertaking as this is bound to give rise. Fundamental divergences among local interests exist in *every* river basin development. In a sense, they spring from the same fundamental causes that, as I have shown, existed in antiquity. A mere shift of organizational approach to these problems offers no solution. The suggestion that changing organization charts will solve the natural conflicts of irrigation and navigation is, to say the least, naive.

Any new organization adopted in this country and charged with river development would be confronted with exactly the same conflicts in laws and local interests as those that exist today. Similarly it would be faced with the same necessity of solving those problems *in a democratic rather than arbitrary way* on a basis of cooperation with the people, just as we are doing now.

In the Missouri basin, there are no serious points of conflict between the federal agencies on the one hand, or the federal agencies and the states on the other. There are problems as between the basin states, but no insurmountable obstacles exist which prevent complete coordination on the state as well as the federal level.

The answer to every coordination problem has been found in teamwork; teamwork of federal and state agencies whose first concern is public service, and who have learned in the Missouri basin how to get along and work together. So far, both at the state and federal level this approach has been remarkably non-partisan and nonpolitical and the several governors, past and present members of the Missouri Basin Inter-Agency Committee, deserve great credit to date for keeping our problems on the statesman's level in the long-range interest of the basin as a whole.

As the development of the whole great Mississippi system proceeds, the same principle of give and take, in my opinion, should exist throughout the *entire* valley. The lower river can't ignore the Missouri basin's reservoir requirements and their capacity to affect Mississippi floods. The Missouri and other tributaries can't expect to build reservoirs on smaller tributaries with no capacity to help navigation, pollution, and floods in the lower reaches of those tributaries, as well as the lower Mississippi. The rivers where navigation is well established should not advo-cate proposals that are adverse or of dubious value to the development of commerce on less advanced tributaries. We must avoid lip service and stretch our dimensions to include the good of the whole valley if we expect to develop its economy to the maximum.

The Mississippi Valley Association performs a valuable service to the people of this entire valley. It provides a forum to which valley problems may be taken and conflicts reconciled in a democratic rather than an arbitrary way. It represents the best interests of all the people of this valley. You can change our federal organization charts ad infinitum, but that will not change the people or solve their problems. In the final analysis it is an association such as this that can effect tremendous progress in this respect.

DEFICIENCIES OF THE COMPROMISE PLAN [10]

Mr. President, I am very happy indeed to be associated with the able Senator from Montana [James E. Murray] . . . and with the other cosponsors of the bill [to establish a Missouri Valley Authority]. . . .

On August 22, 1944, I introduced a bill in the second session of the Seventy-eighth Congress to create a Missouri Valley Administration.

It was apparent then, as it is increasingly apparent today, that it is imperative that we have a single planning and administrative agency dealing with the Missouri River. . . .

In spite of the emphasis that has been given this movement in the Federal Government, out in the Missouri basin the agencies of the Federal Government have been going exactly in the opposite direction. Out there, the Army engineers, the Bureau of Reclamation, the Departments of Agriculture and Commerce, the Federal Power Commission and at least a score of their lesser agencies, have created a supercouncil of bureaus, designed to protect the powers, prerogatives and perquisites of each in the basin, instead of following the sound sort of merger and realign-

[10] From remarks in the United States Senate by Senator Guy M. Gillette of Iowa. *Congressional Record.* 95:1744-48. March 30, 1949.

ment of authorities and responsibilities which is going on everywhere else in the Government.

Let me give my colleagues a little history of this supercouncil
of the bureaus.

Following the floods of 1943, the Army engineers rushed
together a plan for the lower Missouri River and presented it to
the Seventy-eighth Congress. The *Washington Post,* in a recent
story concerning General Lewis A. Pick, said that General Pick
developed the plan in ninety days. It was not quite that speedy.
As a matter of fact, the Army engineers had done years of work
on the lower Missouri, charting its channel and studying its
behavior—and hauling gravel back and forth—so the claim that
the general did this stupendous job in just ninety days is about
as exaggerated as the premature report of Mark Twain's death.

However, there were those, including the Bureau of Reclamation, who apparently thought the plan reflected only about ninety
days' study. When the Pick plan was submitted to Congress,
the Bureau of Reclamation attacked it vigorously. W. Glenn
Sloan told a committee of the Senate, as spokesman for the
Bureau, that the gigantic Garrison Dam in North Dakota

. . . is unnecessary in any plan for developing navigation or any other
purpose. We recommend the elmination of Garrison Dam because we
think it is unnecessary and not worth the expenditure.

That dam was then estimated to cost around $130 million.
The estimates run around $200 million today.

Sloan also testified, still for the Bureau of Reclamation, that
the $15 million Gavins Point Dam

. . . is a very expensive dam for the benefits to be derived from it. As
a power proposition, the cost per kilowatt hour for the development there
is 30 to 40 times the cost of power at any of these other dams.

Mr. Sloan had been assigned the task of developing a
Missouri River plan for the Bureau of Reclamation. It was
apparent to the Bureau that the Pick plan for a flowing navigation
channel would require all the river's water, and that there would
be none left for irrigation if the Army got priority. So they
opposed the Army before Congress and offered their own Sloan
plan.

We were told at the time that the Sloan plan would not work, that some of the projects proposed were fantastic and un-economic. We were told that the giant Souris irrigation project in North Dakota would cost many times what farmers could afford to pay, and that it was an engineering fantasy. We were told that the James River irrigation project in South Dakota was not needed—that the area had plenty of water except two or three years out of ten.

It was at about this time that both the distinguished Senator from Montana [Mr. Murray] and I introduced bills to create a Missouri Valley Authority.

The effect on these two bickering, battling agencies was almost electric. Within sixty days after our bills were introduced—on October 16 and 17, 1944—the Army and the Bureau of Reclamation held a joint meeting in Omaha, Nebraska, and in those two days claimed that they had completely integrated their conflicting plans. . . .

Mr. President, the tragic deficiencies of the Pick-Sloan plan are now recognized in every quarter. The deficiencies of the superagency which was set up to follow up the Omaha compromise are just as marked.

The superagency was officially known as the Missouri Basin Inter-Agency Committee. It included Army engineers and the Bureau of Reclamation as the principal participants, but with the Federal Power Commission and the Departments of Agriculture and Commerce, representing all their subordinate bureaus, holding memberships. . . .

Someone has suggested that the Missouri Basin Inter-Agency Committee should be renamed the Missouri Basin Adding and Subtracting Society.

Seriously, that is not a bad description of the way this group operated after their first few meetings. Under the arrangements which grew up, the various agencies now come into the meetings and report the projects they plan to undertake, give an estimate of their cost, and the amount needed each year from Congress. There are no arguments, no discussion of conflicts, feasibility, or the manner in which each project fits into an over-all development and operating plan. . . . When every agency has put in its

Washington to subtract the grand total from Congress and the sums, the group adds them up and they all come down here to Treasury.

A careful examination of the meetings and the operations of that group will show that that is the total real limit of its functioning. It has served the participants as a public front. It has met at a different state capital each month, hearing speeches from the various agencies about what they are doing, and adding up totals to be subtracted from the public till.

As the Hoover Commission has pointed out, this Inter-Agency Committee has never yet tackled the real problem of allocation to various uses of the supply of water actually in the Missouri basin. It has never tackled the elimination of conflicts in plans and the development of an ultimate, over-all water-operation plan which will give the Missouri basin the most of irrigation, of electric power, of navigation and flood control. . . .

The Pick-Sloan plan, in its total concept, is but a fraction of a total basin plan. It deals with the river. It does not deal with the problems of the land, of soil conservation, of the development of land and mineral resources, and of the human resources of the valley. It has no plan for stopping the loss of 300 million tons of topsoil annually. It does not provide for the development of the plant-food resources on the western rim of the Missouri watershed, to make conservation practices economic for farmers, who would then help to stop erosion and floods back on the land. It does not contain any forestry plans, to help stop floods as well as protect and restore our forests and our soil.

The Pick-Sloan plan does not include the coordination of power and navigation developments with the establishment of new industries, which are so greatly needed.

The Pick-Sloan plan does not include any plans for development of basin-wide recreational facilities for preservation or increase of wildlife, for industrial research and stimulation, for the development of other facilities which make life for people in the Missouri watershed richer and better.

The Pick-Sloan plan is only a fraction of the total basin development—in all its phases—which is needed in our great watershed. We need an over-all agency which will relate the problems of the land and the water, and then the problems of the people to those of developing the land and water, so that the basin may become the source of strength to the nation which it should be. . . .

PIECEMEAL PLANNING [11]

The impractability of piecemeal river-basin planning has been demonstrated in the Missouri basin.

First plan for development of that stream was General Lewis A. Pick's proposed flowing navigation channel in the lower river (Sioux City to the mouth). Next, the Bureau of Reclamation's W. G. Sloan proposed extensive irrigation projects to be watered out of the main stream just above Pick's channel. At that point in planning, the Hoover Commission warned that there are "grave doubts" about the adequacy of water in the river for both the Pick and Sloan schemes.

Recently the Department of Agriculture has filed a third Missouri basin plan, for extensive soil and forest conservation and water-stabilization structures back at the heads of creeks. The Bureau of Reclamation, alarmed, has protested against too great acceleration of conservation and the proposed construction of 407 thousand farm ponds intended to help conserve the pastures and range lands. They might "seriously jeopardize" water supply for works already planned, said Sloan, Reclamation Commissioner Straus and [former] Interior Secretary Krug.

This is a confession and a blunder, said Ben Stong of the Regional Committee for MVA.

Previously, Interior and the Army have been brazening out the water shortage, refusing to admit it. Now they have confessed, and they have blundered by saying that the farmers should eat at second table, if any. Western farmers do not surrender their scarce water that easily.

Meantime, the Federal Power Commission has come forward with a sane way out of the dilemma. The FPC argues, in effect, that if the agricultural program could be advanced enough materially to reduce silt in the lower Missouri River, a series of

[11] Editorial. *New Republic.* 121:8. October 24, 1949. Reprinted by permission.

low-head dams could be built which would provide slack-water navigation plus 12.5 billion kilowatt hours of electric power annually. Unlike Pick's flowing navigation channel, the slack-water channel would not require any of the West's precious water.[12]

Moral of the story: Rivers should be planned all at once, for multiple purposes. Result of the story: Senator James E. Murray (Democrat, Montana) will probably make another effort to get an MVA, asking for a preliminary commission to study the present planning mess.

MISSOURI VALLEY TASK FORCE [13]

Since the experts reporting to the Hoover Commission on Organization of the Executive Branch of the Government have tackled so many ramifications and published such voluminous reports, some of their most striking findings are likely to remain buried. This is particularly the case with such normally uncontroversial topics as Natural Resources (Appendix L). And such considerations as the Hoover men raise about development of the vast Missouri Valley deserve to come to light—indeed, one sixth of the land area of the whole United States is involved.

The 2,460-mile Missouri Valley presents a complex problem because of its periodically recurring serious droughts and floods and the diversity of interests and needs between the upper and the lower reaches of the Valley. Nearer the source—in the Great Plains area of Montana, Wyoming, Colorado, the Dakotas and western Nebraska—the big need is irrigation; in the lower valley—east Nebraska, Kansas, Iowa and Missouri—it is flood control. Advocates of a Missouri Valley Authority have long contended that these and other major regional needs could best be met, in the interests of all, by an integrated, coordinated

[12] It is pointed out by Rufus Terral in *The Missouri Valley—Land of Drought, Flood and Promise* (p 121) that Army engineers, studying the possibility of a slack-water channel, concluded that the cost of dredging out silt accumulating at the rate of 140 million tons annually would be excessive.—Ed.

[13] By Edward S. Skillin, editor of *Commonweal. Commonweal,* 6:145-6. May 20, 1949. Reprinted by permission.

program directed by an over-all authority. Furthermore, they have accused the Army Engineers and the Reclamation Bureau of the Federal Department of the Interior of reaching the compromise Pick-Sloan plan, which is now actually under way, only in order to forestall the creation of the long-sought Missouri Valley Authority. Fear that an MVA might be created is assuredly the most plausible reason that the Engineers and the Bureau have, for the moment, compromised their long-standing differences. . . .

If a group of men is on the lookout for inefficiencies, the Pick-Sloan irrigation, navigation, water-power and flood control program presents plenty of openings. The Hoover "Task Force" in the Missouri Valley not unsurprisingly found the plan embodies what "is essentially an hydraulic engineering approach" and points out that "no means are provided for an integrated dynamic view of the region as a whole." . . . At another juncture the task force states: "Successful regulation of the Missouri and its tributaries for the development of irrigation, navigation and water power can only be managed on a basin-wide scale."

Moreover, the report goes further and says that the Pick-Sloan forces, by starting with big dams, have gone at the whole thing "backward." This has afforded great satisfaction to adherents of a Missouri Valley Authority patterned on the TVA. For these latter had hardly expected so much ammunition from a conservative source.

On the other hand the task force readily admits that the construction of dams, development of new sources of hydroelectric power, the strengthening of the levees on the lower Missouri and other aspects of the Pick-Sloan program inevitably will benefit the people of the Great Plains and the lower valley. The Hoover investigators criticize its inefficiencies more than its objectives, indicating how it is wasteful, and suggest ways in which the potentialities of this great river valley, heavily endowed with mineral, forest and agricultural resources, could be more adequately realized.

There are two specific points in the report which may considerably revise the ideas of those who advocate the TVA type of river valley authority for the nation's major streams. For such projects tend to include coordinated developments in every direction: irrigation, hydroelectric power, flood control, navigation and the like. The object is to build up the economy of the whole area, and of all elements in the area encompassed by the valley.

But on the Missouri River, it seems, navigation is a questionable objective. Periods of drought tend to be of several years' duration to begin with. As a result there are doubts whether a navigable channel can be maintained consistently enough to serve as a regular means of low-cost transportation.

The present channel below Sioux City is but six feet deep and the plan is to increase it to nine feet—to provide a waterway for something more than skiffs and barges. With the reservoirs already operating or in prospect on the upper streams, it would be possible to maintain this new nine-foot channel even in most bad years. Yet by the time the channel is completed, the Mississippi itself, into which the Missouri flows at St. Louis, is to have a new twelve-foot channel. Apparently any practicable Missouri River navigation would have to be able to handle boats from the Father of Waters. And it is clearly not feasible for this vast tributary to store up enough water to maintain a twelve-foot channel of its own during recurring dry spells.

This would seem to throw the idea of developing river traffic on the Missouri into a cocked hat; it throws into serious question the wisdom of expenditures for such facilities at all. But the Hoover men do not find this in the least disturbing. As they now present it, the only purpose of river traffic—no matter how picturesque—is to provide competition with the railroads, and surely there must be other, uncostly means of reducing the excessive freight rates in the area.

The other question raised about over-all development has to do with irrigation. In the great majority of years, which are adequately moist, the farmers on the Great Plains show little interest in irrigation—perhaps they are too busy expanding their plantings and the cropping of their herds. Whatever the reason, the task force found surprisingly limited popular interest in any extensive expansion of irrigation there.

Moreover, it is hardly in the public interest to expend vast sums for increasing the agricultural production of an area which has a greater and more basic need of realizing its great industrial potential.   Such expansion of farm production is particularly questionable now in a period of huge commodity surpluses, from the viewpoint either of the region itself or of the United States as a whole.   Indeed the only way to set a long-needed economic upturn in motion in this depressed area is to establish a good balance between farming and industry.

So that if an over-all authority, such as MVA, were eventually to replace the Pick-Sloan makeshift, and supplant the purely advisory Missouri Basin Inter-Agency Committee as well, its program might be more restricted than has generally been supposed.

If it were able to give due proportion both to the vital interests of the region and those of the nation as a whole, the new authority might very conceivably curtail the billion a year American taxpayers are to pay out annually for Missouri Valley projects for the next six years.

Such savings would be indeed a surprising result of attempting a major development of the Missouri basin as a whole. These savings could then be added, for a genuine appraisal, to the increase in local and national wealth resulting from intelligent regional development.   At the same time the revised program would also provide an effective check to the major droughts and equally destructive floods which have so periodically scourged the vast Missouri Valley.

THE PROPOSED ST. LAWRENCE
SEAWAY

EDITOR'S INTRODUCTION

The St. Lawrence Seaway project is unique among river development plans in the United States in that it envisages an international authority to supervise construction of (1) a canal by-passing three rapids in the St. Lawrence river, and (2) hydroelectric plants along the St. Lawrence and Niagara Rivers.

Under an agreement with Canada ratified (except for certain provisions) by the United States Senate in 1947, the international authority would collect tolls for use of the canal to liquidate its cost and provide for its maintenance. The canal would be the final link in a deep-water navigation channel linking Duluth, Minnesota, with the Atlantic Ocean via the Great Lakes, the Erie Canal, and the St. Lawrence River.

The "certain provisions" still unratified relate to ownership and operation of the power-generating facilities. All but one of the proposals placed before Congress during the thirty-four years over which the St. Lawrence project has been a subject of debate have contemplated turning over the generating plants to the province of Ontario and the state of New York; the cost of construction and operation would be met by revenue from the sale of electricity. One bill, however, provides for federal operation of the power facilities on the American side to provide electricity not only for New York but for Northern New England; this bill has been opposed by the legislature of the state of New York and generally by the state's representatives in Congress.

FOR THE ST. LAWRENCE SEAWAY PROJECT [1]

Mr. President, the purpose of Senate Joint Resolution 111 [to approve an agreement between the United States and Canada

[1] From remarks in the United States Senate by Senator Alexander R. Wiley of Wisconsin. *Congressional Record.* 94:531-543. January 26, 1948.

relating to the Great Lakes-St. Lawrence Basin] is to authorize the construction of the St. Lawrence seaway and power project. The reasons for the affirmative recommendation by an overwhelming majority of the Foreign Relations Committee are spread in the voluminous records of the committee, which held extensive hearings on this subject in 1933, 1946 and 1947.

Before this debate is concluded, the following facts will be amply proved:

First. The St. Lawrence seaway is a needed navigation facility which will relieve recurrent shortages of transportation and eliminate the economic wastage that results from the inability of the railroads to carry the peak traffic in the summer months.

Second. The St. Lawrence seaway will reduce transportation costs in an area which contains more than 50 million people, an area which has become not only the arsenal of democracy for war but also the hope of the world in the revitalization of human and material welfare in food production and in manufactured and mineral products.

Third. The St. Lawrence power project, which is a by-product of this undertaking, will supply 2.2 million horsepower of electricity to Canada and the United States in an area which has been suffering from the beginning of World War II with recurrent power shortages. This power is cheaper than any alternative source now available in the northeastern part of the United States.

Fourth. The St. Lawrence project as herein presented will be an addition to our national defense potential by virtue of the additional and much-needed navigation and power facilities which it will make available for necessary industrial mobilization in a time of emergency.

Fifth. The St. Lawrence project will be self-liquidating, returning to the government and the people, the taxpayers of this nation, the capital investment and interest upon that investment, as well as all operating costs. It will be self-liquidating in its navigation aspects as well as in the sale of power.

Sixth. It will be amply demonstrated that the opposition to the St. Lawrence project seems mainly centered in certain small economic and financial groups in the East who seem anxious to maintain their hold on transportation from the Middle West to the seacoast and their hold upon the power supply for the northeastern area.

It will be demonstrated that no economic harm is actually threatened to those interests but that their position seems motivated principally by their desire to maintain their hold upon the future growth of this whole territory.

The St. Lawrence project now before Congress has two purposes: First, it will make it possible for ocean-going, deep-draft vessels to travel directly from the Atlantic Ocean into the Great Lakes. It will make seaports of such great cities as Buffalo, Cleveland, Toledo, Detroit, Chicago, Milwaukee and Duluth. It will bring the great agricultural and industrial productive capacity of the Middle West into direct communication by cheap water transportation with the rest of the world and with the Atlantic, Gulf and Pacific coasts of the United States.

As a navigation project, it is as important to our country as the Suez Canal is to Europe, as the Dardanelles is to Russia, as the Panama Canal is to the east and west coasts of the Western Hemisphere.

In building the necessary dams and canals on the St. Lawrence River, there will be a large by-product of cheap hydroelectric power in northern New York. The capacity of this single powerhouse will be 2.2 million horsepower, the largest power capacity of a single project with the exception of Grand Coulee. This will be three times as large as the Dneiper Dam, the pride of Russia. The annual output of electricity will be larger than all the power produced by the Tennessee Valley Authority in 1944. It is cheap power, costing one and two-thirds mills per kilowatt hour of average output at the station, one quarter as expensive as the cheapest source of steam power in that area.

The power will be divided equally with Canada. The American share will be available for distribution as far south as New York City, and throughout the New England states. Cheap waterpower in that area of 20 million people means lower monthly electric bills, more industries, more jobs, greater sales of electric appliances, more farms electrified.

This is not a new project, but a bid for final completion of a waterway that has been in the process of construction for forty years. The Great Lakes now provide deep-water navigation throughout their length and breadth. . . .

The eastern end of the St. Lawrence River is navigable for ocean ships for a thousand miles from the Atlantic Ocean to Montreal, Canada. . . .

The only impediment that prevents through navigation is the presence of some rapids in the St. Lawrence River between Ogdensburg, New York, on the upper St. Lawrence, and Montreal on the lower St. Lawrence. Over this distance of 119 miles, the water level drops some 223 feet in three series of rapids. The project now before Congress contemplates the construction of the necessary dams, canals, and locks by Canada and the United States to complete this work, with a huge by-product of cheap water power. We can join the Great Lakes and the Atlantic together for ocean navigation by helping to knock away the rocks in the St. Lawrence rapids through congressional approval of Senate Joint Resolution 111.

AGAINST THE ST LAWRENCE SEAWAY PROJECT [2]

First, the seasonal factor: No discussion of any aspect or phase of the St. Lawrence seaway is possible without taking into account the fact that the seaway, or the "iceway" as it may more appropriately be called, is closed for approximately 40 per cent of the year to traffic of any kind. This raises great problems, such as the adjustment of cargo schedules to the navigation season, the interrelationship between the seaway type of transportation and other existing land and air transportation and port facilities, the problem of scheduling projected shipbuilding and ship-repair activities with this short season, the problem of overhead and other personnel and many other allied questions.

[2] From remarks in the United States Senate, by Senator Henry Cabot Lodge, Jr., of Massachusetts. *Congressional Record.* 94:531-43. January 26, 1948.

Secondly, the vulnerability of the Great Lakes-St. Lawrence area: The uncontradicted testimony is that this seaway would traverse the most vulnerable area, from a defense point of view, of the United States.

Third, the manpower problem: The seaway is an added defense commitment, in the words of the Secretary of the Army, of such magnitude that it would require an uncalculated amount of additional men and material for its defense. The present depleted condition of our armed forces makes it virtually impossible to assure that such men and material would be available.

Fourth, the actual defense of the seaway: It has been pointed out by several military experts in the field of air defense that the seaway simply could not be defended at all from a determined air attack.

Fifth, special vulnerability to bombing, sabotage, and accident: Almost every witness called attention to the ease with which a lock-structured canal of this type is open to air attack. It has recently come to be acknowledged that even the Panama Canal is, because of its structure, dangerously sensitive to this type of attack. An attractive and remunerative objective is set up for fifth-column activity, either by way of sabotage to the locks themselves or to ship-scuttling, or even accident.

Sixth, navigational and other hazards: Attention has been drawn to the fact that not only is the St. Lawrence a peculiarly hazardous route because of numerous locks, narrow, treacherous and dangerous channels, through islands and reefs of granite rock with currents and frequent fogs and mists, but it is also an easy and remunerative target for attack by submarine or aircraft because of the very nature of the channel itself and the difficulty for taking proper evasive tactics.

Seventh, the distance and time factors: I have pointed out that while there is a slight distance advantage, this factor is of little consequence and that the important thing, from a national defense point of view, is that as much time as possible be saved in order to speed up shipments and in order to reduce the period of exposure to hostile attack. It has been conclusively shown that insofar as this vital time factor is concerned, the St. Lawrence seaway offers no advantage whatsoever; indeed it is at a disadvantage compared with existing routes.

Eighth, types of ships which could use the seaway: American shipping lines could not operate through the proposed seaway because of the limited draft. The twenty-seven-foot canals and channels mean that vessels can operate only with a draft of about twenty-four feet. Ninety per cent of United States cargo vessels operate with a loaded draft substantially in excess of that, and most of the ships built under our wartime program for cargo carriers exceed this draft. This utterly eliminates the usefulness of the seaway as an alternate or reserve route in time of war. This unquestionably means that substantially all the traffic which might move via the proposed waterway would be in foreign bottoms. Recollection of the sad state in which we found our merchant marine at the outset of the war and of the most unhealthy consequences of such a condition ought to be sufficient to prevent our deliberately contributing to the reestablishment of that situation.

Ninth, shipbuilding and ship-repairing facilities: No convincing justification has been advanced for changing the pattern of our shipbuilding and ship repair industry. It served us well in the last war, and there is nothing to indicate that the foreseeable war of the future demands any such drastic change as is contemplated here. Not only is there no justification, but the situation itself, because of other factors involved, would make such an undertaking very questionable indeed.

Tenth, the iron ore situation: Testimony from experienced and expert witnesses indicates that the often-reported depletion of iron ore reserves in the Lake Superior region is distorted. The development of the St. Lawrence seaway would be a very important step in the direction of making this country dependent upon importation from foreign countries for iron ore, one of our most vital raw materials. We still remember with regret our dependence at the beginning of World War II upon foreign countries for rubber and certain other vital raw material. Our policy in connection with material as vital to our safety and economy as iron ore should be farsighted and not shortsighted. The farsighted policy in this case certainly calls for development of our resources of iron ore, and the Federal Government should certainly refrain from placing obstacles in the way of pursuing such a course.

Eleventh, the amount of easement on railroads and port facilities: It has been clearly demonstrated, using even the most favorable and optimistic estimates of proposed new tonnage over the seaway, that the amount by which the seaway would ease the wartime strain on other means of transportation is wholly negligible and cannot be taken into account when dealing with this problem.

Twelfth, the Army's attitude: The Secretary of the Army has testified that the St. Lawrence seaway is not vital to our national defense. The best he could say for it was that it was helpful.

ST. LAWRENCE POWER [3]

Since the United States and Canada in 1941 agreed formally to carry out the St. Lawrence Seaway and Power Project more than twenty bills in approval have been introduced in Congress. All stipulated that the hydroelectric power plant to be constructed was to be turned over to the state of New York, provided the state paid its share of the cost. Now comes Representative Blatnik of Minnesota with a resolution that flies in the face of state ownership and calls for federalization. His is the first bill that repudiates a federal-state accord which has been endorsed by every president and by every government of the state since 1933, as well as by the Corps of Engineers, the Federal Power Commission, the State Department and every other federal agency concerned with the development of the St. Lawrence.

If a St. Lawrence hydroelectric plant generated an excess of power that could be utilized in New England a case for federalization might be made out. But there has long been a shortage of electric power in upper New York. Even in the New York City area the demand for electric power exceeded the assured supply in 1947. Such is the demand for power that the public

[3] Editorial. *New York Times.* 98:26. February 23, 1949. Reprinted by permission.

utility companies of the state are prepared to install new generating capacity of 280 thousand kilowatts in the New York City area alone and 354 thousand kilowatts elsewhere. If we now had both St. Lawrence hydroelectric and the planned public utility steam power the state could utilize it all.

Since the American portion of the St. Lawrence plant will lie within the boundaries of the state and since the state needs all the power that it can obtain there is no need of federalization. Representative Blatnik's bill can serve no other purpose than that of granting the Federal Government rights for which it has never asked and for which there is no justification.

THE AUTHORITY IDEA IN
PERSPECTIVE

EDITOR'S INTRODUCTION

Although the CVA and MVA bills are the only ones now under active consideration in Congress, at least eleven measures have been introduced to extend the TVA principle to other river basins. One bill would create nine more TVA's.

All but one of these bills would set up federal corporations. Although the multiplicity of government corporations that have sprung up (forty-six in the first five years of the New Deal) take many forms, those proposed for river basin authorities have distinguishing marks:

They start out with capital funds provided by Congress and obtain their annual appropriations directly from Congress, rather than through cabinet departments. Their directors are responsible only to the President and Congress, and in general they require specific congressional approval for each of their projects.

Numerous government corporations are operating in the fields of flood control, irrigation, navigation, and power generation without the broad powers embodied in valley authority legislation. Among these are the Bonneville Power Administration in Washington, the Central Valley Project in California, and others in Texas, Utah, Arizona, Colorado, Montana, Wyoming, etc.

David E. Lilienthal sees in valley authorities an alternative to overcentralized "Big Government." The Hoover Commission sees certain advantages in our traditional departmental organization for administering national resources. Howard Bloomfield tells how a private utility company does the job for one of our lesser river valleys. R. H. S. Crossman regards the TVA idea as a key to economic cooperation for peace throughout the world.

These and other provocative suggestions are presented on the following pages.

PROPOSED "VALLEY AUTHORITY"
LEGISLATION [1]

Ten bills proposing the establishment of "valley authorities" comparable in some degree to the Tennessee Valley Authority are now [1946] before the Seventy-ninth Congress [which did not take final action on any of them]. An eleventh bill, introduced by Representative J. Percy Priest of Tennessee, would enlarge the area over which the TVA has jurisdiction by including the Cumberland Valley.

The chief issues are, of course, whether any more valley authorities shall be established, and, if so, where. The range of thought on these issues is underlined by the diversity of the proposals. Two of the bills which are identical—S. 555 and H.R. 2203—provide for the establishment of a Missouri Valley Authority. Four more—S. 460, H.R. 2923, and two more identical bills, S. 1716 and H.R. 5083—would set up a Columbia River Authority. H.R. 2540 would establish an Ohio Valley Authority, and S. 737 would provide a Savannah Valley Authority. H.R. 1824, titled "The Conservation Authorities Act [introduced January 29, 1945, by Representative John E. Rankin of Mississippi] would apportion the entire country among nine "conservation authorities" by enlarging the area over which the TVA has jurisdiction and by setting up eight new authorities—an Atlantic Seaboard Authority, a Great Lakes-Ohio Valley Authority, and Missouri Valley, Arkansas Valley, Southwestern, Columbia, California, and Colorado Authorities. A tenth bill, formulated by the Department of the Interior, and presented to the Congress at hearings before the Senate Commerce Committee, would establish a Missouri Valley Authority and would facilitate the establishment of other regional authorities. . . .

These proposals raise numerous collateral issues, many of which hinge on the question of the degree to which the proposed authorities should be modeled on the Tennessee Valley Authority. This is true not only as to the powers proposed to be granted, but

[1] From an article by Wesley C. Clark, professor of political science, Syracuse University, and formerly assistant to the Secretary of the Interior. *American Political Science Review*. 50:62-69. February 1946. Reprinted by permission.

also in respect to the administrative mechanisms through which such powers would be exercised. The law . . . provides . . . that the Tennessee Valley Authority shall be a corporation. The ten proposals now before Congress are in agreement on the proposition that future valley authorities shall be established as federal corporations.

The TVA Act provides . . . that the corporation be administered by a board of directors, appointed for nine years by the President with the advice and consent of the Senate. The chairman is designated by the President, and the board of directors reports the activities of the corporation directly to the President. The directors are paid $10,000 a year and are enjoined from engaging in other businesses and from having an interest in the fertilizer or power industries. They are also required to profess a belief in the wisdom and feasibility of the act. The only part of this section of the TVA Act to which all the new proposals generally subscribe is that pertaining to the directors' financial interests and belief in the act.

Whether these regional corporations shall be advised by "councils" composed of residents of the regions affected is one of the immediate issues confronting Congress. The TVA Act contains no provision establishing such a council. . . . But it is perhaps significant that eight of the ten bills provide for the establishment of advisory councils composed of people in the regions covered by the proposed authority or authorities. . . .

That there may be a problem in coordinating the programs and activities of the proposed authorities in the national interest is anticipated by three of the ten proposals. The rest follow the pattern of the Tennessee Valley Act, which, since it established the first and only valley authority in the country, contained no reference to the problem of coordinating the work of the TVA with that of other authorities. H.R. 1824, the bill which would blanket the country with river authorities, provides . . . that the President shall supervise the integration and coordination of the authorities which would be established. To aid him, the President might consult with a "council" composed of one director from each authority, the director of the Bureau of the

Budget, and the chairman of the National Resources Committee. . . .

With two exceptions (H.R. 2540 and H.R. 1824), the bills recognize the fact that regional authorities are arms of the Federal Government and exempt from local taxation, and take notice of the possibility that the operations of the proposed authorities might be of such magnitude as to disrupt the tax structure of the regions in which it is proposed to locate them. In this the bills follow the general pattern laid down in the TVA Act. . . .

Different concepts of the degree of accountability owed by an authority to Congress are contained in the proposals. All of the bills require that each authority submit to an annual audit by the Comptroller General of the United States, the watchdog set up by the legislative branch of the government. . . .

But the fact that procedures are established by which the recommendations of the various authorities may be approved by Congress does not necessarily provide the funds whereby these recommendations may be put into effect. The proposal whose financial provisions bear the closest resemblance to the TVA Act is S. 737, which provides . . . that the corporation, after deducting the cost of doing business and an amount deemed by the board to be necessary to withhold as operating capital, shall turn over its net proceeds to the United States Treasury. . . .

The TVA Act (Sec. 26) provides for a continuing fund of $1,000,000 for emergency expenses, and also provides that the corporation may keep what it deems necessary for operating expenses. The rest of its proceeds are turned over to the Treasury. The TVA has had several authorizations to issue bonds in specific amounts and for specific purposes. . . .

Like the TVA, seven of the bills would require the proposed authorities to conform to the uniform system of accounting for public utilities prescribed by the Federal Power Commission. . . .

In general, the proposals would give the authorities power to cope with problems of flood control, navigation, water power, reclamation, stream pollution, conservation, soil erosion, and agriculture. . . . Four of the bills, S. 555 and H.R. 2203, H.R. 2540 and the Interior Department proposal, would authorize the authorities to integrate the disposal and use of surplus war plants into over-all recommendations in connection with valley development.

So far as the disposition of electric power is concerned, there are four points of variance: (1) whether an authority should have the power to sell electricity at wholesale and retail; (2) whether the authority should have the power to assist purchasers, actual or potential, in acquiring or operating distribution systems; (3) whether any limits should be placed on the authorities' power to take over local distribution systems; and (4) what kind of limitations should be placed on the rates at which electric power produced by an authority might be sold. Eight of the proposals authorize the authorities to sell power at wholesale or retail. . . .

The Interior Department proposal provides that power shall be sold only at wholesale. H.R. 1824 is the only bill which does not authorize the authorities to assist actual or potential purchasers in the operation or acquisition of distributing systems. H.R. 2923 is the only proposal which would forbid the authorities to take over local systems if the local authorities object. S. 555 and H.R. 2203, S. 460, and S. 737 contain no specific provisions that power bought at wholesale from the authorities be sold at reasonable and nondiscriminatory rates to the ultimate consumer.

The largest difference between the original TVA Act and the proposals now before Congress is the emphasis in the new proposals upon the use of water, not for the generation of electric power, but for reclamation and irrigation.

The emphasis in this article on points of difference should not be permitted to cloud the fact that in many areas the proposals for new valley authorities follow the TVA pattern with a great deal of fidelity. For instance, the provisions regarding employees of the proposed corporations are taken almost word for word from the provisions of the TVA Act. These provide that persons may be employed without reference to the United States Civil Service Act, but that the corporation may set up its own civil service system if it wishes.

In summary, it may be said that the proposals indicate that there are questions which still remain open despite the success of TVA. These would seem to include: (1) Should the proposed authorities be administered by a single administrator or by a multiple-member board?; (2) Should the activities of the various authorities be coordinated and supervised, and, if so, by whom? (3) To what degree, if any, should the proposed authorities be compelled to consult and advise with "local" advisory councils?; (4) Should the authorities make payments in lieu of taxes to the states and the local divisions of government and, if so, to whom and how much?; (5) To what extent shall the proposed authorities be accountable to Congress?; (6) To what extent shall the proposed authorities be financially independent of Congress?; and (7) Should the authorities engage in the retail distribution and sale of power?

MORE AUTHORITIES FOR RIVER VALLEYS? [2]

Yes!

Congress set up the Tennessee Valley Authority in 1933 to develop the resources of that region, and to help raise the standard of living in an area of general economic poverty. The "authority" was a frank experiment in *regional* planning and *regional* government. Flood control and soil conservation were desperately needed.

Because no one state could work out a successful program by itself, Congress took over the job, creating a new, unified, planning agency. It seems the plainest common sense to extend this pattern now to other river valleys in similar need of large-scale development.

The Missouri River basin, spanning one sixth of the continental United States, is an excellent case in point. When rains flood the Missouri Valley, they strike at the heart of America's "bread basket." One hundred million tons of irreplaceable topsoil wash away through the Missouri every year.

Yet what is being done about it? Downstream states are worried about flood control; the dry upstream states want better

[2] By Carol L. Thompson, associate executive editor, *Current History*. Reprinted from *Senior Scholastic*. 54:6-7. May 4, 1949. Copyright 1949. By permission of the editors.

irrigation. All Missouri Valley states suffer from the conflict of control between the Bureau of Reclamation and the Army Corps of Engineers, under flood control legislation passed by Congress in 1944. These two agencies, dividing the valley between them, have limited interests which do not extend to matters like conservation and power production.

Similar problems arise in the Columbia River Valley, which faces an acute electric power shortage every year. There dozens of agencies are at work driving toward useful goals—but not in a united, efficient, far-seeing manner. There must be, says Mr. Truman, "unified treatment of the related resources within each natural area of the country," accompanied by "the greatest possible local participation." Hundreds of millions of dollars of federal funds are now being spent each year in reclamation and other projects in the Columbia basin. It is unintelligent not to coordinate these expenditures under a single authority.

Thus we see, on the one hand, state governments incapable of handling regional problems by themselves and federal agencies in frequent conflict when dealing with such problems. On the other hand, there is the TVA—in shining contrast.

The basic principle of the TVA is to work for "decentralized industry, family-sized farms and thriving small towns." As far as possible the TVA works through state and local agencies. TVA control remains within the region, centered in the Authority's three-man board. Its operations are not bound by red tape to government officials in Washington.

Today the success of the TVA is recognized by the majority of the people in the states it serves. The state and municipal governments, as well as many business organizations in the region, have taken advantage of its benefits and have approved its policies. Thousands of trees have been planted to hold the water on the land. The value of Tennessee Valley farm products has multiplied, and eighteen hundred new industrial plants have been opened.

The most widely discussed phase of the TVA has been the production and use of cheap electric power. The low rates charged by TVA have greatly increased the use of electricity in the valley in industry, farms, and homes. Sales of home electrical equipment have jumped.

Public utility corporations object to government production of electric power. They complain that they are heavily taxed, while TVA facilities are exempt from taxation. They claim that the lower TVA rates are not fairly calculated, but are actually subsidized by all taxpayers. Nevertheless some private utilities have adopted some of TVA's methods and have been able to reduce their competitive rates. And it is estimated that the taxpayers' heavy initial investment in TVA power facilities will be repaid by consumers within the TVA region within the next forty years.

The creation of further regional valley authorities will not set up any new "superstates." They will provide the means to deal with critical regional problems, with the help and for the benefit of the people of these regions.

No!

Those who are ready to set up gigantic regional authorities in every major river valley overlook the inner heart of our tremendously successful economic system and democratic government.

Through the TVA the Federal Government has gone into business on a grand scale. It competes with private enterprise at numerous points. Extension of valley authorities and federal electric power production will inevitably drive every public utility company in the nation out of business. We will have taken long strides toward a system of socialism. In the TVA area already, the Commonwealth and Southern Company, unable to operate at a profit in competition with tax-subsidized TVA power, was compelled to sell its property outright to TVA.

State and local initiative also suffers under the steamroller impact of regional authority. Planning and inspiration in the TVA area has rested largely with TVA officials, and states and communities have come to lean on them as on a crutch. The vitality and effectiveness of local government is threatened, and with it, the core of our democratic system.

The most unfair feature of regional authorities is the use of money from the federal treasury for the benefit of a special group. How can TVA *fail* to work, with the taxes of 150 million Americans going to support it? This problem does not arise in cases where the states themselves undertake these projects, or where the Federal Government supplies a proportional share of funds (as for highways or hospitals, for instance) to every state. An extension of the TVA plan to other areas would simply increase the tax burdens of citizens living outside these areas.

Looking at the problems of the Tennessee Valley and the solutions worked out by TVA, too many people assume that the pattern can be applied elsewhere. No notion could be more deceiving. The TVA went to work in a downtrodden, underdeveloped area. The Tennessee Valley has no major irrigation need—one of the severest problems to be solved elsewhere. In the Columbia and Missouri basins, plans for irrigation conflict with plans for flood control and navigable channels.

There is no crying need for all-around emergency help in the Columbia Valley, for instance, as there was in the Tennessee Valley. The Pacific Northwest is one of the most progressive and prosperous regions in the nation. It has the highest per capita income in the United States, while TVA states have only 60 per cent of the national average—even after fifteen years of TVA. Despite TVA's "cheap" power, private companies in the northwest charge lower rates than those charged by TVA.

Arrayed against a CVA are the seven governors of the region, business interests, and many other influential groups. Governor Douglas McKay of Oregon asked recently:

> What's the matter with the way we are doing now? That is the American system. We do not need to delegate authority to a board or a commission to regulate the economy of the northwestern states.

Republican Senator Wayne Morse or Oregon, who supports Federal aid in many other fields, says:

> I am anything but convinced that we in the Pacific Northwest want any Government agencies in control of our rivers. . . . Our economy is entirely different, and our people are strong believers in a maximum of self-government.

There are, indeed, many critical problems in our river valleys, but these problems can be solved by the close cooperation of the states. Little-known waterway compacts now operate in many states, smoothing the rough spots in interstate differences. The Colorado River compact, in which seven states cooperate, is a successful model. Today more than eighty-seven such compacts, approved by Congress, cover a wide range of subjects from ocean fishing to recreation and parks. If there is a fault to be found in the solution of regional problems, more vital and alert state governments are the remedy.

Let us always be wary of attempts to enlarge the size and authority of governments. The American democratic system takes its strength from active participation of all citizens in state and local government, with a minimum of dependence on regional or national government.

THE REGIONAL AUTHORITY ISSUE [3]

It is easy to say complacently "It can't happen here." The fact is that a form of socialism has happened in the Tennessee Valley. The only reason why the public is not fully aware of the consequences is that the men who direct the TVA know that they must still tread warily. They have only one hitch around a part of the economic life of the nation. They want to tie in eight more hitches before they give us the works. . . .

If this principle of government by superstates were adopted, it would mean that the economic, political and social life of more than 130 million people would be subject to the dictatorial whims of a small group of twenty-seven men, not elected by the people, but hand-picked by the man occupying the White House at the time of their appointment

The powers of these men would by-pass all of the constitutional restrictions of this democracy, override the rights of sovereign states and, as is provided in the Mitchell [CVA] and Mur-

[3] From address by Lachlan Macleay, president, Mississippi Valley Association, before the Flood Control Committee of the Peoria (Illinois) Association of Commerce, March 14, 1946. Published by the Mississippi Valley Association. 511 Locust Street. St. Louis, Missouri. 1946. Reprinted by permission.

ray [MVA] bills, which are admitted by the CIO, which appears to be their chief sponsor, to be the model for regional authorities, their powers would supersede in many ways the powers of Congress.

The proponents of TVA are silent on the broad and autocratic powers which that Authority possesses. In addition to the right to acquire land, to dictate power rates, to displace families and whole communities, the Authority has the power to construct and operate any project and conduct any activity which it deems necessary in the promotion of anything that three men say is the proper way of life. Many of the activities now conducted by TVA are only remotely connected with the purposes for which the Authority was supposedly created. The threat of such far-reaching powers to private enterprise and to individual initiative, the qualities which helped make America the greatest industrial nation in the world, is too obvious to need emphasis.

If the TVA and its administrators were infallible—which they are not—and its policies always above reproach—which they have not been—such vast power and supervision over the lives of American citizens is not consistent with the American heritage of freedom and the rights guaranteed under our Constitution.

I am not predicting that we shall ever have in this country communism as it is known in Russia, or fascism as it existed in Germany and Italy, but if we are not alert to the danger that faces us, we shall wake up some day to find that the American people have become the servants of the state instead of the state being the servant of the people.

If this philosophy of government, which is so vigorously supported by the CIO, spreads, it is inevitable that it will grow in political as well as economic power. The time is sure to come when candidates for Congress who hope to be elected from any Authority area will have to bow to the will of the Authority. When that day arrives, we will have gone a long way down the dangerous road toward dictatorship in the United States.

This philosophy of government, expounded by these ism-addicts is not, with all deference to the chairman of TVA, "Democracy on the March." In reality, it is "Democracy in Retreat"—a retreat from which there may be no recovery. This is not my opinion alone, nor merely the sober judgment of the Association I represent. Let me cite the warning of the Senate Committee on Irrigation and Reclamation in the report on the Murray Bill. After hearing the evidence of both sides, the committee declared:

> The creation of an MVA would amount to the welding of economic and political powers resulting in nothing short of autocracy. It would mean the substitution of arbitrary power for democratic processes. It would mean the creation of a superstate—neither federal nor state—and not contemplated by our Constitution. It would subject the social, cultural and economic welfare of the Missouri basin to the dictates and whims of a three-man board, not responsible to the people and largely irresponsible to Congress itself. It would constitute a virtual abdication by the Congress in favor of government by federal corporations, wielding autocratic powers. It would challenge state sovereignty and destroy systems of laws, both state and federal, under which western agriculture has grown and prospered. It would throttle in the West the reclamation program which has been prosecuted through the years by an experienced agency and which has met with the approval of Congress and of the people directly affected. It would permit a three-man board to avail itself of trust funds created for reclamation. It would be an excursion into an uncharted field of vast expenditures of public funds and of experimentation under a board unencumbered by the restraints that a democracy should erect against agencies of government. . . .

Under the free enterprise system the United States in 150 years has became the most powerful nation in the world. Are we going to change our form of government to give more power to the Political Action Committee of the CIO which is seeking, through the Missouri Valley Authority bill and other similar legislation, to impose totalitarian government on the people of this country?

Representatives of the CIO, in hearings before the Irrigation and Reclamation Committee held recently in Washington, demanded the passage of the Missouri Valley Authority bill, and they used the word "demand." They went further and said that they intended to have authorities in every regional basin in the United States, and legislation to provide for that is now pending in Washington in the Rankin Bill which would set up nine autonomous authorities—only Mr. Rankin's bill provides for only one administrator for each authority instead of three.

Under our present system Congress controls the development of all of our river basins. If the people in any basin want changes in the plan or the program they can go to Congress and Congress will act as the people direct.

In our opinion these regional authority bills are the most outrageous socialistic legislation ever offered in the Congress of the United States. They would be the opening wedge to the complete economic and political control of the United States by any organized minority. That is what ruined Germany, Italy and Japan.

We are old-fashioned enough to believe in the old-time religion of democracy in America, of initiative and private enterprise, and in the will of the people prevailing. We believe, too, that if the people of this country are fully aware of the danger that confronts them in this phony ideology, which masks its true objectives under the disguise of public welfare, the American people will make it impossible for dictatorship to gain a foothold here.

We would like to remind you that freedom is never entirely won. Each generation must fight to preserve its freedom. That is our job now so that we may in turn pass on this priceless heritage of freedom from political dictatorship to our children to aid and inspire them in building a better America and a better world.

ADVANTAGES OF DEPARTMENTAL
ORGANIZATION [4]

The committee is of the opinion that the functions of the TVA should not be consolidated with other natural resource development functions at least at this time. TVA was established as an experiment. The development of the Tennessee River basin is not yet completed, and the committee therefore recommends that TVA be continued. The committee is, however, also opposed to the extension of the valley authority type of organiza-

[4] From *Task Force Report on Natural Resources.* p95-7. (Appendix L). [Hoover] Commission on Organization of the Executive Branch of the Government. Supt. of Docs. Washington, D.C. January 1949.

tion to other river basins at this time. It believes that the functions of the national government with respect to water resource development should be entrusted to regular departments of the government, provided drastic reorganizations are effected.

There are important values in the traditional vertical bureau and departmental type of organization that make it desirable to administer natural resource development functions through that means.

a. It provides greater assurance of similar treatment of similar resource problems throughout the nation than would a regional type of organization.

b. It makes possible the utilization of central services which cannot be afforded in each regional area.

c. It makes possible the development of standards by which similar programs in many river basins can be measured.

d. It operates as a restraint on sectional tendencies which might influence a regional authority to develop regional resources in a manner detrimental to the best national interests.

The committee is keenly aware of the dangers of extreme centralization, and its recommendations take full account of the desirability of decentralized administration. It recognizes further the validity of river basin areas as proper units for the decentralized administration of the natural resource functions of the national government. At the same time, it cannot overlook the fact that there are overriding national interests in the development of our water and other resources. The development of the potentialities of one region cannot be considered without careful regard to its effects on the economies of other regions, and that of the nation as a whole. Irrigation and land drainage, power development, and navigation improvements, for example, need to be examined in the light of their effects on the total economy, not merely on that of a particular river basin. The committee is concerned that the undesirable effects of establishing a series of regional authorities would lie not merely in the increasing friction that might develop among these authorities, but in a growing disregard of the national interest in resource development.

It has been suggested that the resolution of interregional conflicts and the protection of national interests could be left to

Congress. Within limits, it is true that sectional and regional conflicts of interest always have to be adjusted by Congress, whatever the form of administrative organization. It should not be overlooked, however, that the successful resolution of sectional or regional conflicts, and the harmonizing of regional and national interests, can be greatly facilitated by proper administrative organization. The committee has noted that one reason for the unsatisfactory state of national water policies is the absence of a proper organization of national functions in this area. It is idle to expect Congress to formulate initially a detailed national water resource development program. The Congress unquestionably will, and ought to, have the last word. The only way in which it can be expected to arrive at soundly conceived policies, however, is for it to have adequate assistance from the administrative branch in bringing before it the facts and viewpoints which are most significant, and in formulating suggested policies. Such assistance can be provided most effectively by an agency with nationwide responsibility.

The committee wishes to make clear that in stressing the values of the traditional departmental form of organization it does not mean to imply that these values are actually being realized at the present time. The contrary is true. Under the existing system local interests, rarely even harmonized on a regional basis, too often predominate. The logrolling method of distributing federal funds is certainly not unknown in this area. Authority for development is divided in an uneconomic and inefficient manner. Responsibility to the Executive exists in name only. In fact, the situation has been and is so bad that sooner or later a strong movement for valley authorities is bound to be revived unless drastic changes are put into effect. Properly organized, the ordinary departmental system can incorporate the desirable features of regional organization, at the same time avoiding its undesirable features. The essentials of sound departmental organization in this area may be summarized as follows:

a. Some agency must be granted fairly broad responsibility to integrate at least the major federal water development functions in given river basins. The scope of its functions need not be as broad as that of TVA, but it must be broad enough to enable the agency to formulate a program of water use and control taking into consideration the purposes of navigation, flood control, irrigation, power development, pollution control, recreation, domestic and industrial water consumption, etc.

b. The jurisdiction of the agency with full responsibility for water resource development in a river basin must be coextensive with the boundaries of that basin. It makes no sense to divide responsibility between two water development agencies operating in the same basin.

c. The agency with responsibility for water resource development within a river basin must make provision for adequate decentralization so that basic resource decisions will be made in the light of conditions in the areas they affect. The advantages of "grass roots" administration should be preserved.

d. Similarly, if other bureaus and departments with related functions are to share in this development they will need to modify their programs to make possible more effective coordination than is now possible. This means a greater degree of decentralization along river basin lines; greater uniformity in regional and field office headquarters; more even delegations of authority; and a policy of adapting national departmental programs to the pace of regional water resource development.

e. Adoption of a mechanism for interagency review and coordination on a national and regional scale, with strong presidential support.

f. Adoption of uniform legislative and administrative standards for estimating costs and benefits, determining over-all economic and engineering feasibility, requiring repayment of costs, making authorizations and appropriations for multiple-purpose projects and the several features thereof.

The strongest argument for valley authorities has been that reform in the directions indicated above has proceeded at a geologic pace, as one observer has characterized it. The committee believes that if the consolidations it has recommended are not carried into action and if the present competition among federal resource agencies continues, the establishment of regional authorities will in all probability become necessary.

THESE GOVERNMENT CORPORATIONS [5]

If we in the United States are to use the public corporation wisely and dodge the pitfalls that accompany it, we should be well aware that the form with which we are most familiar here is not the only one.

There are three principal varieties of the public corporation:

1. The *mixed enterprise*, in which both public and private ownership combine to form a corporate partnership;

2. The *public utility trust*, in which ownership is private, profits are limited by charter, and management is provided by the government; and

3. The *government-owned corporation*, where both ownership and management are public.

Which of these forms takes hold in any given country seems to be largely the result of chance. An experiment is tried, it seems to work, it is repeated, and presently the original experience has become a precedent. Certainly there is little logic in the fact that France has tended to prefer the mixed enterprise, Britain the public utility trust, and Germany the government-owned corporation, whereas, here in the United States, although our social tradition resembles those of England and France more than that of Germany, we have used the government-owned corporation almost exclusively. It all goes back to our first American experiment in the field, over forty years ago: the United States government's purchase of the capital stock of the Panama Railroad Company, back in 1904. . . .

In consequence of its early success, it became an example for other American ventures in public business.

These have fallen into six main groups: transportation, represented by the Panama Railroad Company and the Inland Waterways Corporation; banking, of which the Export-Import Bank and the Federal Deposit Insurance Corporation are examples; industrial credit, a field occupied by the Reconstruction Finance Corporation and a half-dozen wartime subsidiaries which pur-

[5] From an article by Marshall E. Dimock, former professor of political science, Northwestern University. *Harper's Magazine.* 190:569-79. May 1945. Reprinted by permission.

chase and produce essential commodities and finance manufacturing plants; housing, including the Defense Homes Corporation, the United States Housing Corporation, and the Home Owner's Loan Corporation (its three billions of outlay now in process of liquidation); and regional development and power, represented, of course, by the Tennessee Valley Authority. . . .

Here in the United States, as already noted, we have stuck to the government-owned corporation, following the original Panama experiment, which was blessed with autonomy, a real board of directors, and self-contained financing. Generally speaking, the corporations which the government set up during World War I—such as the Emergency Fleet Corporation and the United States Grain Corporation—followed the legitimate corporate pattern. On the other hand, the Inland Waterways Corporation, which was established in 1924, has drifted away from original corporate traditions. It has not been entirely self-financed and throughout most of its history has been officer-dominated rather than guided by a representative board of directors with real powers. And by 1932, when the RFC was created, the corporate model began to lose many of its most important business characteristics. One might have thought that the pattern would have become set by that time, and that the underlying principles might have become ingrained in official thinking. This did not happen.

In two thousand years of corporate history, the term "corporation" has never possessed any kind of innate magic. There is nothing about corporate characteristics that cannot be changed or lost. Romancers such as Blackstone became eloquent about personality, perpetuity, limited liability, and other so-called innate traits, but experience has proved that all of these are subject to loss or profound modification. There is nothing in a device that can keep men from changing it if they will. The only real safeguard is a comprehension of concept and principle by the community.

The really important features of corporations are their freedoms and unities—their autonomy of management and finance. Since 1932, federal corporations in this country have steadily lost sight of these guiding principles. If we are to continue to use the public corporation we had better relearn some of the important things we have forgotten.

The public corporations created in recent years, for example, have generally been run by their officers. In some cases they are a one-man show, with an officer of cabinet rank voting the government's stock and making all the important decisions. . . . Under such circumstances the administration of a corporation does not greatly differ from the administration of a department.

The first great problem which faces us, therefore, is what is going to happen to the independent board of directors. This is equally important in the case of private corporations, where the trend is also away from directorships chosen from outside the business. The arguments for officer control are that managers know the business more intimately than outsiders; that officers give all of their time to the job, as outsiders do not; and that hence there is an economy of time and explanation.

Over against these, however, are considerations which would seem to carry more weight. Ownership requires independent representation if it is to exercise any degree of control. Concentration of power inevitably leads to its abuse. Outside viewpoints help to offset bureaucracy and grooving. Corporations must adjust themselves to larger social forces and hence need the experience of men in larger fields; public attitudes are better judged by nonofficer directors; and last and perhaps most important, the public will have more confidence in an enterprise, and be less inclined to interfere with it, if the traditional separation is continued between layman boards and professional management. History is replete with object lessons demonstrating the force of these principles. Let American businessmen profit by the trusteeship principle incorporated into public utility trusts. Let federal bureaucrats ponder the loss of corporate identity if representative boards are not reinstated.

Congress has consistently favored the corporate structure. It produces speedy action when time is scarce. But Congress does not seem to comprehend an essential feature of the corporation, namely, that the board of directors performs the role of a "little legislature." If the corporation is to discharge important functions of government and if autonomy is to be safeguarded, a representative group of men acting on behalf of the sovereign legislature must constitute an essential part of its organization. Congress cannot possibly supervise these enterprises itelf—they are too many and their operations are far too complex. Yet supervision on behalf of the public is something they emphatically need, lest they be used for personal, political, or even corrupt purposes. Therefore Congress should provide the inner controls through incorporation, and then delegate future policy decisions and the direction of management to the board of directors. This requires an independent board, a separation between the making and execution of policy. A corporation is no stronger than its board of directors. If Congress does not see fit to revitalize this function, the corporation will lose ground in public confidence.

The second great requirement of the successful public corporation is self-contained financing. Ideally, the public corporation should have the right to use subscribed capital; to raise new capital by the issuance of bonds or other evidences of indebtedness; to utilize operating revenues to defray operating expenses, provide working capital, or finance expansions; to build up reserves out of earned income or other revenue; to introduce commercial accounting methods; and to carry on purchasing with ordinary business freedom. In recent years, however, Congress has sometimes insisted upon appropriating funds for public corporations when they could just as well have been borrowed, and has required that net earnings be turned over to the general treasury even when they were needed at once for the ensuing year's operations. If Congress will not treat the public corporation's finances as business operations, then the public corporation cannot expect to deserve business respect.

There has also been an invasion of personnel freedoms in the management of the public corporation. This type of enterprise differs from ordinary government in that, until recently, it was free from civil service laws. But since 1938, under pressure from the standardizers-at-all-costs in Washington, Congress has almost completely undermined this necessary requirement of business management. Congress should reconsider. The British are under no illusion as to the disadvantages of grafting the "civil service mentality" onto a corporate enterprise. In this country the Commission of Inquiry on Public Service Personnel laid down the sound rule in 1935 that "Utility undertakings should be excluded from the normal civil service personnel system. . . . The personnel problem can be better handled in such cases as a part of management than as a part of government." Said Senator Wadsworth at the time when a corporation was being considered for the Muscle Shoals project, "You may apply civil service rules . . . if you please; but do not expect profits."

If public corporations are to be usefully employed in vital areas of our national economy, we must, therefore, follow certain time-tested principles. These may be summarized as follows:

1. *The corporate device should be used for business purposes only.* Unless sales and profit-and-loss are intrinsic, the government would do better to use the departmental method. The public corporation will lose its virtue if a business operation is combined with nonbusiness programs and the combination is treated as a self-financing unit. (Here something akin to Gresham's Law seems to apply.)

2. *Financial self-sufficiency is necessary to business success.* This is the crux of the matter.

3. *A representative board of directors, chosen for demonstrated ability and attachment to the public interest, should be relied upon to secure public responsibility.* Except for granting the charter and modifying it if need be, Congress should keep hands off and let the board of directors do its proper job. The appropriate cabinet officer should be a member of the board *but should have no more power than his colleagues.*

4. *Business enterprises should develop their own personnel systems free from civil service rules and regulations.*

5. *There should be no exceptions to the rule that public corporations may sue and be sued.*

Congress should move without further delay to enact a model incorporation law for public corporations, setting forth the major principles and the measures of accountability which control corporate functioning. Simultaneously steps should be taken to repair the breaches in corporate practice which now threaten to reduce this type of enterprise to a hollow symbol. Otherwise we may discover too late that we as a people have delivered huge power into the hands of men who are unable to wield it responsibly and effectively.

AN ALTERNATIVE TO BIG GOVERNMENT [6]

Experts in administration are trying to persuade the American people that centralized Big Government is inevitable. We are told that, because of the complexities of modern living, swift communication and transportation, virtually every problem has become a national problem and that therefore every phase of our lives must be administered from Washington.

It is obvious many problems that could once be dealt with as a matter of local and state policy now do require a national policy. The central government, in such cases, through congressional action, must enunciate such a national policy and authorize the expenditure of federal funds.

But it does not follow that the administration of that policy must be on a nationwide basis. We must rid ourselves of the notion that a new staff, with every member paid out of the federal treasury, has to administer every detail of each new federal law or regulation.

The alternative to Big Government is administration of national policies by state and local units of government. Our problem is to divorce the two ideas of *authority* and *administration of authority.* The distinction is one the apologists for Big Government persistently overlook.

The Tennessee Valley Authority is practical proof that despite the interrelation of our vast country, despite the need for national policy on many matters heretofore local, the actual carrying out of those policies can effectively be placed in the hands of local agencies.

The TVA is an agency of the Federal Government. Its activities, however, are directed not from Washington but from the Tennessee Valley. It is not incorporated within any Wash-

⁶ By David E. Lilienthal, former chairman, Tennessee Valley Authority. *Reader's Digest.* 50:75-8. May 1947. Reprinted by permission.

ington bureau or department. Furthermore, by persistent effort the TVA has delegated its functions so that most of them are carried out by local and state personnel. This is effected by contracts setting up joint two-way partnerships with cities, towns, counties, state boards of health, state conservation commissions, city power boards, farmers' cooperatives, county extension services and state agricultural colleges.

The TVA was charged with a responsibility for the development of the land of the Tennessee Valley, embracing parts of seven states. It was essential that there be extensive practical demonstrations of the value of new phosphate fertilizers we were developing in the Muscle Shoals laboratories. To do this TVA did not set up a large central staff. It did not send federal employees onto the farms. We entered into a joint program with existing agencies. The state colleges of agriculture, the state extension services, the county agents undertook to carry forward the actual demonstration program. The TVA reimburses the local agencies for the salaries and expenses of local experts who are carrying out a national policy and responsibility.

Another illustration is afforded by the TVA's power system. Through a system of more than twenty dams on the Tennessee River and its tributaries, huge amounts of electricity are generated. Congress directed that this electricity be sold. The TVA operates the generating plants and six thousand miles of transmission lines that carry the electricity over an area nearly as large as that of Great Britain. But distribution of the electricity is decentralized; 141 locally owned, locally managed, locally financed distribution agencies carry it to the ultimate consumers from the city gates where TVA delivers it wholesale. Thus again an alternative to centralized administration was found.

The United States Agricultural Extension Service, organized in 1914 to carry on the educational activities of the Department of Agriculture, is another successful example of decentralized administration. Contracts are made with state land-grant universities to administer teaching, research, and demonstration. County agents are selected by state and local boards. The Federal Government contributes to the support of the program but cannot dictate local policies.

Since 1918, state educational systems have efficiently administered federal funds granted for training in vocational agriculture. National aid to public health began in 1919. Conforming to certain policies and standards set by the Federal Government, state and local health units have carried on their relentless campaigns against disease and their constructive programs of improvement in sanitation and health protection in every community in the land.

The TVA encountered plenty of resistance to decentralized methods: so will any other federal agency. The plea for centralized control by a specialized bureau rests on a double assumption: that *uniformity* is desirable *as an end in itself*; and that similar practices can be obtained only by direct supervisory control. Neither assumption is self-evident.

Overcentralization has a special appeal to the administrator who quite conscientiously fears the complexity of his job in a coast-to-coast responsibility. The simplifications, the uniform rules and regulations which centralization encourages are convenient for him, however inconvenient they may be for the public.

Again, there are managers who honestly doubt whether they can discharge their own vast responsibilities for nationwide programs if they must rely upon units of governments over which they do not have authority.

But the risks involved in delegations to and agreements with local agencies seem clearly preferable to the folly of centralized administration. Indeed, these risks are implicit in our democratic faith. Nor should we overlook the deeper question of how we can help our state and local governments gain in competence and capacity. Surely we should not encourage local government to escape its duties or abdicate its responsibilities to Big Government, for this process merely perpetuates the local weaknesses.

If we turn administration of localized problems over to Washington on the ground, as some assert, that we thus escape the inefficiencies and political shenanigans of local communities, we are fooling no one but ourselves. We merely transfer the political pressures in administrative matters from local to federal political channels.

The fundamental solution is to crowd more, not less responsibility into the community. Only as the consequences of administrative errors become more localized can we expect citizens to clean up their own local inadequacies. It is folly to concentrate more and more power in the national capital, so distant from the everyday life of the ordinary people as to wither and deaden the average citizen's sense of participation in government affairs. For in this citizen participation lies the very vitality of a democracy.

Alive to this challenge, the states through their Council of State Governments, have recently declared their intention to work vigorously for decentralized administration. State officials plan to survey all federal grants-in-aid services, with a view to better local administration.

Centralization always glorifies the importance of paper work. As men and organizations acquire a preoccupation with papers, they become less understanding, less perceptive of the reality of those matters with which they should be dealing; actual people and problems in real America—highways, wheat, drought, floods, back yards, blast furnaces.

More disastrous still, we are threatened with the loss of the people's confidence, the very foundation of democratic government. Fear or ridicule of the capriciousness of some government officials takes the place of pride. Democracy cannot thrive long in an atmosphere of scorn or fear. One of two things ultimately happens: either distrustful citizens refuse to yield to the national government the powers which it should have, or an arrogant central government imposes its will by force. In either case the substance of democracy has perished.

Big Government will get bigger and more highly centralized unless there is a conscious, continuous, creative administrative effort to reverse the trend. So prone are we to accept Big Government, to take the easy way out by handing our local problems over piecemeal to one remote agency after another, that the federal administrator who suggests an alternative course is hailed as the exception to the rule. I cite one newsworthy illustration.

Speaking in the Northwest recently, the [former] Secretary of the Interior, J. A. Krug, urged with forceful words the creation of a regional agency, decentralized and autonomous, to aid in the unified development of the Columbia River Valley. In explaining the decentralizing consequences of this proposal, Secretary Krug said:

> Final decisions would be made here in the Northwest, instead of in my department in Washington. Contrary to the charges which are frequently made against federal officials, I desire this. I would like to give up some of my power and authority exercised at Washington and see it exercised here.

In such a spirit of self-imposed restraint lies true democratic statesmanship, and the road to a workable alternative to Big Government.

THE GOVERNMENT DIDN'T HAVE TO DO IT [7]

Clint Spurr is a blunt, hard-boiled businessman, president of the Monongahela Power Company, Fairmont, West Virginia. He says his company is in business to make money but adds, "How can you sell power to a farmer who isn't prosperous enough to buy it?" Spurr helps his farmer customers to be prosperous.

What has been going on in this neck of the woods can be illustrated by the case of Cameron Stalnaker, a tall, blue-eyed man who dug coal for fourteen years with an abiding determination to be his own boss and work "upstairs" in the sun. No longer would a strike-call reach for the food on the table where he sat with his wife and four children. Cameron and his wife, Icie, saved something every payday. Six years ago they bought 256 acres at Mill Creek, West Virginia. Four years ago he quit the mines.

When Stalnaker began farming, he milked his cows under a tree. Thinking of that makes him prouder of his 30-cow cement-block barn and 156-ton silo he built in 1948 and the milkhouse he added in 1949. The run-down farmhouse has been repaired,

[7] By Howard Bloomfield, former editor of *Adventure Magazine* and writer on agricultural subjects. *Reader's Digest*. 56:73-5. April 1950. Condensed from "The Farmer Must Make Money—First." *Country Gentleman*. 120:21+. February 1950. Reprinted by permission.

the pump on the back porch is gone. There's running hot water, an electric range and refrigerator.

"Bob Templeton here," said Stalnaker, "helped me get plans for the barn and we worked together laying out the milkhouse. I didn't know much about farming, but a man gets a wonderful lot of help nowadays."

Templeton is one of the crew that makes the "Farming for Better Living" program tick in twenty-five counties. The crew is made up of former county agents and extension specialists who help farmers set up books, get soil tests, put a cow in touch with an "artificial bull," survey wood lots, organize milk-production committees—and then raise prize money for good farming competitions. Instead of being paid out of taxes, the salaries and expenses are paid by the Monongahela Power Company.

Before Clint Spurr took over the presidency of the Monongahela Power Company in 1935, he had been running street railways and knew little about power. But he believed that business and community progress should go hand in hand. A New Deal committee had been studying the territory with a view to setting up a kind of TVA. Its survey showed that farm cash income in the ten counties was the lowest in the United States—$389—and that the 21 per cent of the population who were farmers received only 3 per cent of the region's income. The report was pigeonholed, however, with the recommendation that the private power company be given an opportunity to see what it could do about developing the region.

Spurr responded by carrying the challenge to the newspaper editors of his territory. The outcome was that the Upper Monongahela Valley Association was formed, sponsored by the newspapers and power company, to treat the social and economic ills of the region.

To help UMVA, Spurr started his Territorial Development Department. Here are employed the five ex-county agents and vocational agricultural teachers who direct the Farming for Better Living program; also a conservationist, a farm-management counselor and a forester. None of these people sells electricity. They sell only better farming. "We're trying to make ourselves so important in the solution of the people's problems that they never think of looking to Washington for help," Spurr says.

West Virginia is a natural for grazing and for poultry, but the state had to import dairy products, millions of pounds of poultry and millions of dozens of eggs. It imported 800 thousand bushels of potatoes even though it has some splendid potato land.

UMVA and the Extension Service sent out a sound-movie truck which traveled 190 thousand miles and showed good-farming films to 200 thousand persons. UMVA promoted a co-operative which marketed potatoes in uniform brand-name sacks. Growers found a ready market at better prices than they had ever received before. The buckwheat-flour mills were likewise joined to market their produce uniformly.

UMVA bought two purebred Jersey bulls which were lent to farm groups in return for one bull calf a year. This dairy-herd improvement plan was enlarged to twelve Jersey and six Holstein bulls, then was superseded by the more modern system of artificial insemination, operating from a bull farm which is probably unique in that it was started by a chamber of commerce. The program, begun in 1946 with 403 members in 5 counties, now has 4,200 members in 39 counties.

Annual ham and bacon shows are promoted. So are cattle and sheep breed shows, dairy-cattle, feeder-calf and beef-cattle shows. And a successful cauliflower-growing-and-marketing program was launched.

Once these special projects were well under way, UMVA, the Extension Service and the power company came up with the Farming for Better Living program, which runs a prize contest in each county and then combines counties for regional prizes. About two thousand families participated in 1949, all working to keep their farms on the upgrade.

The prizes, awarded for progressive improvement of farm and home, include paints, tool kits, baby chicks, brooders, savings bonds and purebred heifer calves. They are donated by many businesses as well as by the power company.

Each year regional books are published giving photographs of regional and county winners and a one-page account of the achievements of each family. The power company is only briefly mentioned.

Clint Spurr says, "Help push and get the job done and don't worry about the credit. The customer has to make money before we do. So working for our communities is good business for all concerned."

Some idea of the results he has achieved can be gained from the statement of a newspaper editor in the territory who campaigned for years for government ownership of power: "The reason I switched to private ownership is the job the power company is doing developing our communities. It's a better job than the government can do, and much cheaper on us taxpayers."

TVA'S FOR WORLD PEACE [8]

What the world needs is not merely American dollars, food and machinery. We need an American idea as well. Without that idea American loans will be dollars down the drain.

So far, that idea has not been forthcoming. The defense of free enterprise and the ideological war against communism, which seemed to be the substance of the Truman doctrine, are not creative ideas for building a sane world, but slogans of political propaganda, almost as sterile as class war or world revolution. They may or may not be useful for uniting the American people behind the foreign policy of the Administration—that is an internal matter of no concern to an Englishman—but they are certainly not principles on which a positive and constructive American policy can be built. . . .

Americans have one great advantage over Englishmen in handling world politics. They have grown up in the political climate of a federal state, whereas we have only the experience of a centralized democracy; and our commonwealth consists not of a federation, but of completely autonomous dominions, like Canada, or completely dependent colonies. Our British idea of international cooperation is always of a confederation devoid of

[8] From an article by R. H. S. Crossman, Labour Member of Parliament. *New York Times Magazine.* 94:12+. August 24, 1947. Reprinted by permission.

central authority, whereas an American, accustomed to the healthy friction between federal and states' rights, envisages world order also in federal terms.

What is therefore needed today is a projection on a world scale of the American concept of the division of sovereignty. In Western Europe and the Middle East, national sovereignty must be subjected to supranational authorities capable of carrying out economic reconstruction across national frontiers. But on the other hand national self-determination must be safeguarded against central despotism. We need to argue out on a European scale the battle which has been the central issue of American domestic politics since the War of Independence.

But now this central issue can no longer be expressed in purely political terms. All talk of a United States of Europe, or even of Western Europe, is wishful thinking. The international anarchy of Europe will not be superseded by a federal state on the pattern of the United States of America. National sovereignty must be integrated into a series of emergency plans for economic reconstruction. Both in the planning and in the execution of these plans, America could play a decisive role. . . .

Despite the fierce political controversies which preceded its establishment and which still surround it, the Tennessee Valley Authority is now admitted even by its critics to be the outstanding achievement of the New Deal. It accomplished for an area and a population bigger than those of many European countries a revolution in the standard of life. It developed economic potentialities previously unperceived. It successfully challenged traditional vested interests in order to improve the standard of living of the common man.

When we think of the American way of life, we think of the skyscraper and of TVA. They symbolize for us American engineering—colossal, but without the blind ruthlessness of Russian communism. Is the TVA Socialist or capitalist? The question seems irrelevant. It is a typical American reaction to a social problem which has made the old argument between socialism and free enterprise an anachronism. It is revolutionary, but no one can accuse it of being un-American.

Is it possible, then, that the creative American idea for which the world is looking can be found here? At least it is well worth thinking over. . . . Instead of asking how much each nation requires to avoid bankruptcy, the statesmen should ask:

"What natural resources have we Europeans? How, forgetting frontiers and tariffs and national rivalries, can we best develop these natural resources and reconstruct their derivative industries? Forget for a few moments which nations own the Alps and consider them solely as a source of hydroelectric power which, if developed, can be of benefit to France, Italy, Austria and Yugoslavia. Forget in whose territory the coal and iron of Western Europe is found and work out a plan for developing them for the good of all. Instead of political intrigue, let us turn our attention to social engineering."

A plan worked out in this way is something which the American people could regard as a long-term business investment. The dollars would not be charitable relief for Britain or France or Germany, but the capital for the development of Western European iron and steel and Alpine hydroelectric power.

The same principles can be applied in the Middle East. Here the analogy with TVA is even closer. . . . If the statesmen could forget politics and prepare plans for the scientific use of the waters of the Jordan and Mount Hermon in order to irrigate the stony mountains and the sandy plains of Palestine and Trans-Jordan, they would be offering to the American people a sound field for business investment.

In ancient times the Euphrates Valley maintained a population of 20,000,000. Now 2,225,000 poverty-stricken, diseased and illiterate peasants eke out an existence in its waterless wastes. A Euphrates Valley Authority, under supranational control, is a practical business proposition which would pay dividends in the long run.

Let us take two test cases and see how the idea would work out in practice in the rehabilitation of the Ruhr and in the use of the waters of the Jordan for increasing the cultivable area of Palestine. In both Western Germany and in Palestine, relatively straightforward economic tasks are bedabbled by politics.

From an industrial point of view, granted a free flow of food and raw material, there is nothing intrinsically difficult in the job of raising the level of the Ruhr steel production as long as it is agreed first to insure that by reconstructing this center of German heavy industry we shall not inadvertently give a basis for the revival of German militarism. Second, find some method of providing the colossal finance which will be tolerable to a British control authority already under fire from irate British taxpayers. And, third, see that the output of the Ruhr Valley benefits Europe as a whole, and not merely the Germans. . . .

It is difficult to avoid the conclusion that the best chance of ending the sterile Anglo-American controversy and of allaying French suspicion is to establish a public corporation for the redevelopment of the Ruhr Valley. Shareholders should not be private individuals, but all Allied Governments represented at the Paris conference, together with the United States and certain Germans as representatives of the German state which must ultimately be established.

The corporation would not, of course, be a government but an agency of the Allied governments subject to the day-to-day authority of the Control Commission, and it would receive its policy from the governments participating in its direction. If a similar public corporation could be constructed for the development of Alpine hydroelectric power, it would meet the natural German objection that it was only the resources of enemy people which were being treated with such violation of national sovereignty.

Here, then is one example of a European problem which requires an American idea as much as American dollars for its solution. American statesmanship could bring about a unique experience by applying to the German problem the principles of the TVA and of the new federal agency for developing atomic energy.

Our second example is the Jordan Valley Authority. It is easier to describe with precision the character of JVA because the engineering phase of the project has already been worked out in detail. Technically it is known to be feasible to increase the cultivable area of Palestine by hundreds of thousands of acres if the waters of the Jordan are taken for irrigation and the level of the Dead Sea is maintained by pumping water out of the Mediterranean. But in the Middle East the technical problem is always the easiest. The real issue is: Who should control such a scheme? . . .

Here again a public corporation is the only practical solution. The governments of Lebanon, in whose mountains the Jordan rises, of Trans-Jordan and of Palestine must be stockholders with American and British financial backing and technical assistance. The JVA would become a water authority serving the interests of all people concerned. . . .

It is obvious enough that in the cases both of Germany and Palestine the establishment of such public corporations bristles with difficulties. To begin with, none of those directly concerned . . . can supply the financial resources necessary for such a project. American participation is essential, but will either Europe or America be willing to see a United States administration become the largest shareholder in such an institution?

Politics is never the choice between good and evil, but always the choice of evil. As we have seen, the issue is not whether American capital goods shall dominate the world's markets, but in what way inevitable domination can be made most beneficial to America and the rest of the world. In the Middle East, for instance, American oil companies are already the most powerful single economic force. Whatever Colonel McCormick may say, America is now committed to defend these oilfields in the event of Russian aggression; and from the Arab point of view dollar imperialism is already a reality. A JVA would commit America no further than she is already committed by her oil policy. But it would pour a little needed water onto troubled oils. It would provide a far better bulwark against communism than either the airfields now being completed in Saudi Arabia or the oil royalties which enrich a few Arab princes and leave the peasants as poor as before. So too a Ruhr Valley Authority would combine good business and good politics.

BIBLIOGRAPHY

An asterisk (*) preceding a reference indicates that the article or part of it has been reprinted in this book.

BOOKS AND PAMPHLETS

Association of American Railroads. Great delusion: facts you should know about the proposal to build a so-called St. Lawrence "seaway." 31p. The Association. Transportation Building. Washington 6, D.C. '47.

*Berthe, L. T. Should there be a Missouri Valley Authority? 28p. Mississippi Valley Association. 511 Locust Street, St. Louis, Mo. '45.

Chase, Stuart. Government in business. 296p. Macmillan Co. New York. '35.

Chase, Stuart and Tyler, Marian. What the TVA means: planning at the grass-roots. *In their* Men at work p 134-46. Harcourt, Brace & Co. New York. '45.

*Coffey, Max. Analyzing the MVA bill. 9p. Mississippi Valley Association. 511 Locust St. St. Louis, Mo. '49.
Reprinted from Omaha World-Herald.

Congress of Industrial Organizations. Magnificent Columbia. 23p. CIO Department of Education and Research. 718 Jackson Pl. N.W. Washington 6, D.C.

Davidson, Donald. The Tennessee. (Rivers of America) 2v. Rinehart & Co. New York. '46-'48.

*Duffus, R. L. Valley and its people. 167p. Alfred A. Knopf. New York. '47.

Flynn, J. T. Road ahead; America's creeping revolution. 160p. Devin Adair Co. New York. '49.
Excerpts. Reader's Digest. 56:2-19. F. '50.

Green, C. J. Analysis of the real cost of TVA power. 91p. Chamber of Commerce of the United States. Natural Resources Department. Washington 6, D.C. '48.

Gunther, John. Inside U.S.A. 979p. Harper & Bros. New York. '47.
Columbia Valley Authority. p 132-3; MVA versus behemoth river. p 183-9; St. Lawrence waterway in 606 words. p539-40; Model TVA. p731-48.

Guy, D. J. Real cost of TVA power. 16p. Chamber of Commerce of the United States. Washington 6, D.C. '48.

Hansen, A. H. and Perloff, H. S. Regional resource development. 40p. National Planning Association. Washington, D.C. '42.

Hill, Lister. Rivers and prosperity. *In* Bliven, Bruce and Mezerik, A. G. eds. What the informed citizen needs to know. p 140-51. Duell, Sloan and Pearce. New York. '45.

Howard, W. V. Authority in TVA land. 180p. Frank Glenn Publishing Co. Kansas City, Mo. '48.

*Humphrey, Tom. TVA—miracle or monster? 18p. Pacific Northwest Development Association. 205 Multnomah Hotel. Portland, Ore. '49.
 Reprinted from Oregon Journal. Mr.-Ap. '49.

King, Judson. Welfare state and the TVA. (Bulletin no237) 6p. National Popular Government League. 23 Columbia Ave. Washington 12, D.C. '50.

*Lilienthal, D. E. Democracy on the march. 191p. Harper & Bros. New York. '44.

*Macleay, Lachlan. Regional authority issue. 18p. Mississippi Valley Association. 511 Locust Street, St. Louis, Mo. '46.

Mississippi Valley Association. Analysis of Senate Bill 1160 (the MVA bill). 11p. The Association. St. Louis, Mo. '49.

Morgan, M. C. Columbia powerhouse. 295p. Superior Publishing Co. Seattle. '49.

Nash, B. D. and Lynde, Cornelius. A hook in leviathan. 234p. Macmillan Co. New York. '50.

New York (state). Power Authority. St. Lawrence project: public need for its completion. 216p. The Authority. 270 Broadway. New York 7. '48.

Nixon, H. C. Tennessee Valley, a recreation domain. 22p. Vanderbilt University Press. Nashville 4, Tenn. '45.

Osborne, Fairfield. Our plundered planet. 217p. Little, Brown & Co. Boston. '48.

Pacific Northwest Development Association. Is CVA-MVA-TVA legislation socialistic? 8p. mimeo. The Association. 205 Multnomah Hotel. Portland, Ore. '49.

Pacific Northwest Development Association. Untold story of Pacific Northwest progress. 47p. The Association. 205 Multnomah Hotel. Portland, Ore. '49.

Pacific Northwest Development Association. What CVA means (full text of S. 1645 with marginal notes). The Association. 205 Multnomah Hotel. Portland, Ore. '49.

Public Affairs Institute. Big Missouri: hope of our West. (Report, no2) 57p. The Institute. 312 Pennsylvania Ave. S.E. Washington 3, D.C. '48.

Ransmeier, J. S. Tennessee Valley Authority: a case study in the economics of multiple purpose stream planning. 486p. Vanderbilt University Press. Nashville, Tenn. '42.

*Russell, Dean. TVA idea. 108p. Foundation for Economic Education. Irvington-on-Hudson, N.Y. '49.

Shelton, Barrett. Decatur story: address before United Nations Scientific Conference on Conservation and Utilization of Resources, 1949. 11p. Distributed by Tennessee Valley Authority. Knoxville, Tenn. '49.

Tennessee Valley Authority. Annual report of the Tennessee Valley Authority, fiscal year 1948. 98,211p. Supt. of Docs. Washington 25, D.C. '48.
Reprint of text with title Valley is paying off: TVA 1949. 98p. '49.

Tennessee Valley Authority. Annual report of the Tennessee Valley Authority, fiscal year 1949. 56,206p. Supt. of Docs. Washington 25, D.C. '49.

Tennessee Valley Authority. Fifty inches of rain: a story of land and water conservation. 111p. Supt. of Docs. Washington 25, D.C. '39.

Tennessee Valley Authority. Food at the grass roots; the nation's stake in soil minerals. 100p. The Authority. Knoxville, Tenn. '47.

Tennessee Valley Authority. Progress in the valley: TVA—1947. 82p. The Authority. Knoxville, Tenn. '47.

*Tennessee Valley Authority. Rebuttal of "The TVA idea." 38p. mimeo. The Authority. Knoxville, Tenn. '49.

Tennessee Valley Authority. TVA power. 16p. The Authority. Knoxville, Tenn. '49.

Tennessee Valley Authority. Tennessee Valley resources: their development and use. 145p. The Authority. Knoxville, Tenn. '47.

Tennessee Valley Authority. Technical Library. Congressional hearings, reports, and documents relating to TVA, 1933-1946. 53p. mimeo. The Library. Knoxville, Tenn.
Continued by cumulative annual supplements.

Tennessee Valley Authority. Technical Library. Indexed bibliography of the Tennessee Valley Authority, 1935-date. The Library. Knoxville, Tenn.

Terral, Rufus. Missouri Valley; land of drought, flood and promise. 274p. Yale University Press. New Haven, Conn. '47.

*United States. Commission on Organization of the Executive Branch of the Government. Organization and policy in the field of natural resources: a report with recommendations. L. A. Miller and others. 244p. Supt. of Docs. Washington 25, D.C. '49.
Cover title: Task force report on natural resources (Appendix L) January, 1949.

*United States. Commission on Organization of the Executive Branch of the Government. Reorganization of the Department of the Interior: a report to the Congress, March 1949. 94p. Supt. of Docs. Washington 25, D.C. '49.

United States. Congress. Flood control act of 1944. 78th Congress, 1st session. [Approved December 22, 1944] 58 Statutes at Large. p899.

United States. Congress. Government corporations control act. 79th Congress, 1st session. [Approved December 6, 1946] Chapter 557, 59 Statutes at Large. p597-9.

United States. Congress. Tennessee Valley Authority Act. 73d Congress, 1st session. [Approved May 18, 1933] Chapter 32, 48 Statutes at Large. p58-72.
    Amendments: [Approved August 31, 1935] Chapter 836, 49 Statutes at Large. p 1075-80; [Approved July 26, 1939] Chapter 366, 53 Statutes at Large. p 1083; [Approved July 18, 1941] Chapter 309, 55 Statutes at Large. p599; [Approved November 21, 1941] Chapter 480, 55 Statutes at Large. p773.

United States. Congress. Joint Committee on Labor-Management Relations. Labor-management relations in the Tennessee Valley Authority. 63p. S.Rept. 372. 81st Congress, 1st session. Supt. of Docs. Washington 25, D.C. '49.

United States. Department of the Interior. Bureau of Reclamation. Annual report of the commissioner, Bureau of Reclamation, to the Secretary of the Interior, fiscal year 1948. 134p. Supt. of Docs. Washington 25, D.C. '49.

United States. Department of the Interior. Bureau of Reclamation. Columbia River. 399p. Supt. of Docs. Washington 25, D.C. '47.

United States. Department of the Interior. Bureau of Reclamation. Fact sheet on the Missouri River plan (Pick-Sloan plan). 9p. mimeo. The Bureau. Washington 25, D.C. '47.

United States. Department of the Interior. Bureau of Reclamation. Putting the Missouri to work. 29p. The Bureau. Washington 25, D.C. '45.

United States. Department of the Interior. Bureau of Reclamation. Reclamation program, 1948-54. 24p. Supt. of Docs. Washington 25, D.C. '48.

United States. Federal Power Commission. Report on review of allocations of costs of the multiple-purpose water control system in the Tennessee River basin. 90p. Federal Power Commission. Washington, D.C. '49.
    Also distributed by Tennessee Valley Authority. Knoxville, Tenn.

United States. House. Audit of Tennessee Valley Authority for fiscal year ended June 30, 1945. 65p. H.Doc. 172. 80th Congress, 1st session. Supt. of Docs. Washington 25, D.C. '45.

*United States. House. Message from the President of the United States requesting establishment of a Columbia Valley Administration. 6p. H.Doc. 158. 81st Congress, 1st session. Supt. of Docs. Washington 25, D.C. '49.
    Same. Congressional Digest. 29:16-18. Ja. '50; Congressional Record. 95: 4552-4. Ap. 13, '49.

United States. House. Missouri River basin agricultural program. 183p. H.Doc. 373. 81st Congress, 1st session. Supt. of Docs. Washington 25, D.C. '49.

United States. House. Reconciliation report on problems of the Missouri Valley project [Pick-Sloan plan]. 10p. H.Doc. 784. 78th Congress, 2d session. Supt. of Docs. Washington 25, D.C. '44.

United States. House. Recreation development of the Tennessee River system. 99p. H.Doc. 565. 76th Congress, 3d session. Supt. of Docs. Washington 25, D.C. '40.

United States. House. Regionalized freight rates: barrier to national productiveness—a report to the Tennessee Valley Authority. 203p. H.Doc. 137. 78th Congress, 1st session. Supt. of Docs. Washington 25, D.C. '43.

United States. House. Report on audit of Tennessee Valley Authority, fiscal year 1945, letter from comptroller general transmitting report. 6p. H.Doc. 673. 79th Congress, 2d session. Supt. of Docs. Washington 25, D.C. '46.

United States. House. Report on audit of Tennessee Valley Authority, fiscal years 1946 and 1947, letter from comptroller general transmitting report. 48p. H.Doc. 748. 80th Congress, 2d session. Supt. of Docs. Washington 25, D.C. '48.

United States. House. Report on audit of Tennessee Valley Authority, fiscal year 1948, letter from comptroller general transmitting report. 73p. H.Doc. 203. 81st Congress, 1st session. Supt. of Docs. Washington 25, D.C. '49.

United States. House. Report on Columbia basin project on the Columbia River. 28p. H.Doc. 172. 79th Congress, 1st session. Supt. of Docs. Washington 25, D.C. '45.

United States. House. Review by Corps of Engineers, U.S. Army, of reports on the Missouri River for flood control [Pick plan]. 213p. H.Doc. 475. 78th Congress, 2d session. Supt. of Docs. Washington 25, D.C. '44.

United States. Senate. Bill to establish a Columbia Valley Administration. 45p. S. 1645. 81st Congress, 1st session. Supt. of Docs. Washington 25, D.C. '49.

United States. Senate. Bill to establish a Missouri Valley Authority. 63p. S. 1160. 81st Congress, 1st session. Supt. of Docs. Washington 25, D.C. '49.

United States. Senate. History of appropriations made by the Congress of the United States for the Tennessee Valley Authority. 27p. S.Doc. 35. 79th Congress, 1st session. Supt. of Docs. Washington 25, D.C. '45.

United States. Senate. Missouri River basin; conservation, control and use of water resources; report by Secretary of the Interior on Bureau of Reclamation's plan for basin development. 146p. S.Doc. 191. 78th Congress, 2d session. Supt. of Docs. Washington 25, D.C. '44.

United States. Senate. Missouri Valley Authority Act. (2 pts.) 41p. S.Rept. 639. 79th Congress, 1st session. Supt. of Docs. Washington 25, D.C. '45.

United States. Senate. Missouri Valley Authority: background and analysis of proposal. C. F. Keyser. 116p. S.Doc. 555. 79th Congress, 1st session. Supt. of Docs. Washington 25, D.C. '45.

United States. Senate. Opinion of the Supreme Court of the United States in Ashwander et al., petitioners, vs. Tennessee Valley Authority. 35p. S.Doc. 186. 74th Congress, 2d session. Supt. of Docs. Washington 25, D.C. '36.

Also separate. United States Supreme Court Reports. 80 Law Edition U.S. 296-8. p688-728.

United States. Senate. Report of committee representing Corps of Engineers and Bureau of Reclamation reviewing features of plans presented by Corps of Engineers (H.Doc. 475). 6p. S.Doc. 247. 78th Congress, 2d session. Supt. of Docs. Washington 25, D.C. '44.

United States. Senate. Report of the Bureau of Reclamation on development of the Missouri River basin [Sloan plan]. 211p. S.Doc. 191. 78th Congress, 2d session. Supt. of Docs. Washington 25, D.C. '44.

Vestal, Stanley. The Missouri. (Rivers of America) 368p. Farrar & Rinehart. New York. '45.

Vogt, William. Road to survival. 334p. William Sloane Associates. New York. '48.

Whitman, Willson. David Lilienthal: public servant in a power age. 245p. Henry Holt & Co. New York. '48.

Willkie, W. L. American program. 58p. Simon & Schuster. New York. '44.

Yale University. Directive Committee for Regional Planning (M. S. McDougal and M. E. H. Rotival, chairmen). Regional planning with special reference to New England. 94p. Yale University Press. New Haven, Conn. '47.

PERIODICALS

Advertising and Selling. 40:39-40+. Ap. '47. What is the color of the T.V.A.? Maurice Henle and A. C. Spurr.

America United. 1, no51:1-7. '45. Radio forum conducted by the Chamber of Commerce of the United States on regional authorities.

American City. 60:112-13. O. '45. Missouri Valley compromise: regional council or advisory board to coordinate plans and programs of both federal and state agencies. P. H. Elwood.

American City. 60:139. O. '45. Republican banker visits the TVA. W. E. Pearson.

American Economic Review. 33:sup 184-9. Mr. '43. Problem of union relations in public agencies. G. R. Clapp.

American Mercury. 64:618-23. My. '47. St. Lawrence River project. Eugene Rachlis.

*American Political Science Review. 40:62-70. F. '46. Proposed "valley authority" legislation. W. C. Clark.

American Political Science Review. 40:935-49. O. '46. TVA-state-local relationships. M. H. Satterfield.

American Political Science Review. 43:922-32. O. '49. Influence of the Tennessee Valley Authority on government in the South. J. M. Ray.

American Scholar. 14, no4:479-84. [O.] '45. Some social aspects of TVA. J. A. Dombrowski.

Atlantic Monthly. 175:72-6. My. '45. Why an MVA? Robert Lasch.

Atlantic Monthly. 177:101-5. Ja. '46. Your electricity and your money. C. W. Kellogg.
    Reply with rejoinder. TVA: an American invention. 177:105-10. Ja. '46. D. E. Lilienthal.

Business Week. p 17. Ap. 5, '47. End of TVA yardstick?

Business Week. p24. D. 18, '48. St. Lawrence back.

Business Week. p22-3. D. 25, '48. Missouri Valley: vast development coming.

*Business Week. p91-3. Ap. 23, '49. TVA for Columbia Valley.

Canadian Geographical Journal. 36:52-69. F. '48. St. Lawrence seaway: navigation aspects. D. W. Hoan.

Canadian Geographical Journal. 36:70-1. F. '48. Power potentialities of the St. Lawrence River.

Christian Century. 62:649-51. My. 30, '45. From TVA to MVA. Ernest Kirschten.

Christian Century. 64:923-5. Jl. 20, '47. Stop floods with MVA! T. A. Tripp.
    Reply with rejoinder. 64:1209-10. O. 8, '47. Lachlan Macleay.

Christian Century. 66:1429. N. 30, '49. Celebrate decade of TVA benefits. A. W. Taylor.

Christian Science Monitor Magazine Section. p5. F. 28, '48. Water power sparks a town; Decatur, Ala. Sidney Ross.

Christian Science Monitor Magazine Section. p. 11. O. 8, '49. Record for TVA.

Collier's. 116:22-3+. Ag. 11, '45. Taming the Tennessee. W. L. Chenery.

Commercial and Financial Chronicle. 169:1953+. My. 5, '49. St. Lawrence "duplicity" project. C. B. Huntress.

Commonweal. 42:446-9. Ag. 24, '45. Missouri Valley Authority; America's greatest single peace project. Edward S. Skillin.

Commonweal. 45:364. Ja. 24, '47. TVA: profit or loss?

Commonweal. 47:97-8. N. 7, '47. M.V.A. James Rorty.

Commonweal. 47:412. F. 6, '48. Midwest to the sea.

Commonweal. 49:412. F. 4, '49. CVA.
    Reply. 49:492. F. 25, '49. H. A. Reinhold.

Commonweal. 49:579. Mr. 25, '49. Valley staffs and operations.

Commonweal. 50:60-1. Ap. 29, '49. Columbia Valley Authority.

*Commonweal. 50:145+. My. 20, '49. Missouri Valley task force.
E. S. Skillin.

Commonweal. 51:172. N. 18, '49. Existing vested rights.

Congressional Digest. 25:225-56. O. '46. Congress again studies
question of Great Lakes-St. Lawrence seaway; fact material and pro
and con discussion.

Congressional Digest. 29:5-32. Ja. '50. New "valley authorities" for
the U.S.? Congress studies a policy for the future; with pro and con
discussion.

Congressional Record. 90:8056. S. 21, '44. Message of the President
to Congress recommending establishment of a Missouri Valley
Authority.

*Congressional Record. 94:531-43. Ja. 26, '48. On St. Lawrence sea-
way project. H. C. Lodge, Jr.

*Congressional Record. 94:531-43. Ja. 26, '48. On St. Lawrence sea-
way project. A. R. Wiley.

*Congressional Record. 95:1740-4. Mr. 2, '49. Provisions of the MVA
bill. J. E. Murray.
    Also separate. Supt. of Docs. Washington, D.C. '49.

*Congressional Record. 95:1744-8. Mr. 2, '49. On a Missouri Valley
Authority. G. E. Gillette.
    Also separate. Supt. of Docs. Washington, D.C. '49.

*Congressional Record. 95:1748-52. Mr. 2, '49. On a Missouri Valley
Authority. H. H. Humphrey.
    Also separate. 13p. Supt. of Docs. Washington, D.C. '49.

*Congressional Record. 95:14869-905. O. 14, '49. On a Columbia
Valley Administration. Wayne Morse.
    Also separate. 37p. From Senator Morse. Senate Office Building. Wash-
ington 25, D.C.

*Country Gentleman. 120:21+. F. '50. "The farmer must make money
—first." Howard Bloomfield.
    Same abridged with title Government didn't have to do it. Reader's Digest.
56:73-5. Ap. '50.

Department of State Bulletin. 16:1126-8. Je. 8, '47. Relation of St.
Lawrence seaway and power project to national security.

Editorial Research Reports. 1, no 1:1-19. '45. Regional development.
F. P. Huddle.

Fortune. 40:59-67. Ag. '49. Missouri Valley; story of the Pick-Sloan
plan.

*Forum. 109:176-92. Mr. '48. St. Lawrence seaway project; Senate
debate from Congressional Record.

Harper's Magazine. 190:511-24. My. '45. Golden river. J. K. Howard.

*Harper's Magazine. 190:569-76. My. '45. These government cor-
porations. M. E. Dimock.

*Harper's Magazine. 191:206-15. S. '45. Hard look at TVA. C. H.
Grattan.

Iowa Law Review. 32:193-406. Ja. '47. Regional planning; a symposium.

Partial contents: Interstate cooperation in river basin development. L. K. Caldwell; TVA in court—a study of TVA's constitutional litigation. J. C. Swidler and R. H. Marquis; Transplantability of the TVA. C. H. Pritchett; What kind of "valley authority"? R. W. Greenleaf; Plain talk about a Missouri Valley Authority. M. L. Cooke; Critical review of the proposed Missouri Valley Authority. J. M. Drabelle.

Journal of Farm Economics. pt2, 31:1010-34. N. '49. Missouri River development program. H. A. Steele and others.

Journal of Politics. 3:318-34. Ag. '41. Payments in lieu of taxes by the Tennessee Valley Authority. L. L. Durisch and H. L. Macon.

Journal of Politics. 9:31-58. F. '47. Intergovernmental cooperation in the Tennessee Valley. M. H. Satterfield.

Journal of Politics. 12:3-12. F. '50. States and decentralized administration of federal functions. L. L. Durisch.

Land. 5:411-19. Winter '46-'47. Science and stewardship. D. E. Lilienthal; Plot against democracy: TVA. Lachlan Macleay.

Life. 19:71-9. Ag. 13, '45. MVA: Missouri Valley argues question of what to do with its willful river.

*Monthly Labor Review. 69:41-2. Jl. '49. Labor-management relations in TVA.

Nation. 160:544-5. My. 12, '45. Lilienthal and the valley. B. C. Shelton.

Nation. 160:622-3, 645-7, 693-4. Je. 2-9, 23, '45. Northwest needs a CVA. Carey McWilliams.

*Nation. 164:655-8. My. 31, '47. Dixie in black and white; big push against the valley. A. G. Mezerik.

Nation. 165:139+. Ag. 9, '47. Hell, high water, and the MVA. Ernest Kirschten.

*Nation. 166:656-9. Je. 12, '48. TVA, the first fifteen years. Ernest Kirschten.

Reply with rejoinder. 167:214-17. Ag. 21, '48. D. L. Harley.

Nation. 167:38. Jl. 10, '48. A. P. lends a hand to TVA wreckers. Miles McMillin.

Nation. 167:655. D. 11, '48. St. Lawrence seaway project.

National Geographic Magazine. 88:569-98. N. '45. Taming the outlaw Missouri River. Frederick Simpich.

*Nation's Business. 37:34-6. O. '49. Why a Columbia Valley Authority? R. O. Case.

Also separate. 8p. Pacific Northwest Development Association. 205 Multnomah Hotel. Portland, Ore. '49.

Nature Magazine. 43:33. Ja. '50. What about CVA?

New Republic. 111:266-8. S. 4, '44. For a Missouri Valley Authority. Ralph Coghlan and J. L. Coghlan.

New Republic. 112:498-9. Ap. 16, '45. Who shall boss the MVA? M. L. Cooke.

New Republic. 113:281-2. S. 3, '45. TVA from war to peace. Bruce Bliven.

New Republic. 113:312-14. S. 10, '45. TVA rescues the farmer. Bruce Bliven.

New Republic. 113:340-2. S. 17, '45. Human welfare in the TVA. Bruce Bliven.

New Republic. 115:406-9. S. 30, '46. TVA pioneers. D. E. Lilienthal.

New Republic. 116:9. My. 5, '47. In danger.

New Republic. 117:9-10. Jl. 28, '47. Truman's big no.

New Republic. 117:36-8. Ag. 4, '47. Floods and the MVA. Angus McDonald.

New Republic. 120:sup 18. Ja. 10, '49. Developing our resources.

New Republic. 120:14-16. Ap. 11, '49. Growing need for CVA. Joe Miller.

New Republic. 120:7-8. My. 2, '49. CVA sabotage.

*New Republic. 121:8. O. 24, '49. Piecemeal planning.

New Republic. 121:10. N. 7, '49. Propaganda against TVA.

*New York Times. 98:26. F. 23, '49. St. Lawrence power.

*New York Times. 99:22. Ja. 13, '50. Battle of the rivers.

New York Times Magazine. p 10+. Ja. 7, '45. Shall we have more TVA's? essential principles. D. E. Lilienthal.

New York Times Magazine. p 17+. Jl. 21, '46. From monkey trial to atomic age. Russell Owen.

*New York Times Magazine. p 12+. Ag. 24, '47. TVA's for world peace. R. H. S. Crossman.

New York Times Magazine. p 18-19. Ja. 18, '48. Double harness for the St. Lawrence.

New York Times Magazine. p 14-15+. Ap. 2, '50. Again a land battle in the West. R. L. Neuberger.

New York Times Magazine. p 14-15+. My. 7, '50. More T.V.A.'s? the issues weighed. W. R. Espy.

Newsweek. 24:49. N. 27, '44. Who will harness the rivers? valley authorities comparable to the TVA. E. K. Lindley.

Newsweek. 29:71. Ja. 20, '47. Red ink valley?

Newsweek. 31:26. F. 16, '48. Seaway thriller.

Newsweek. 31:29. My. 17, '48. No steam for TVA.

Newsweek. 32:52. D. 27, '48. Nearer the seaway.

Newsweek. 33:66. Mr. 28, '49. Steam plant issue.

Newsweek. 33:23. Ap. 25, '49. Plan for Bunyan's river.

*Newsweek. 34:84. Ag. 15, '49. Death sentence for state government. Raymond Moley.

Same abridged. Reader's Digest. 55:71-2. D. '49; *Also separate.* 1 p. Pacific Northwest Development Association. 205 Multnomah Hotel. Portland, Ore. '49.

Nieman Reports. 4:3. Ja. '50. The press and the CVA. R. L. Neuberger.

Oregon Voter. 35:1175-6+. O. 29, '49. Papers object: preponderant majority in Oregon want no CVA.

Public Administration Review. 1, no4:326-34. '41. Local government and the T.V.A. program. L. L. Durisch.

Public Administration Review. 8, no 1:1-11. '48. Valley development and valley administration in the Missouri basin. H. C. Hart.

Public Utilities Fortnightly. 40:547-55. O. 23, '47. Grass-root sentiment does not favor an MVA. Chan Gurney.

Public Utilities Fortnightly. 43:544-53. Ap. 28, '49. Why not states' rights for the Columbia Valley? D. B. Noble.

Public Utilities Fortnightly. 44:427-8. S. 29, '49. Three-way feud on river development.

Public Utilities Fortnightly. 45:105-6+. Ja. 19, '50. TVA, agency of the welfare state; discussion of sixteenth annual report.

Queen's Quarterly. 55, no 1:1-19. [F.] '48. Great public utility: Tennessee Valley Authority. S. M. Woodward and V. M. Hare.

*Reader's Digest. 50:75-8. My. '47. Alternative to big government. D. E. Lilienthal.

*Reader's Digest. 51:129-34. D. '47. Hidden red ink in TVA's books. J. T. Flynn.

Rotarian. 70:12-13+. Ja. '47. Build the Great Lakes-St. Lawrence seaway? J. L. Dansereau; C. C. Thompson.
    Discussion. 70:1-2. Mr.; 3+. Ap. '47.

*Saturday Evening Post. 218:22-4+. Ja. 19, '46. What you can believe about MVA. Wesley Price.
    Same abridged with title Battle over the Missouri Valley. Reader's Digest. 48:69-73. O. '46.

Saturday Evening Post. 218:17+. Je. 22, '46. No glamour boy. Rufus Jarman.

Saturday Evening Post. 222:12. O. 15, '49. Who's behind CVA propaganda drive? Interior's bright boys, of course. R. O. Case.
    Also separate. 12p. Pacific Northwest Development Association. 205 Multnomah Hotel. Portland, Ore. '49.

Saturday Review of Literature. 32:60+. Ag. 6, '49. Machines with and without freedom. D. E. Lilienthal.

Science News Letter. 47:297. My. 12, '45. Regional development of great river basins; escape from over-centralization.

Science News Letter. 53:41. Ja. 17, '48. Warns quakes may damage St. Lawrence waterway.

Science News Letter. 56:60. Jl. 23, '49. River basin planning.

Senior Scholastic. 46:13. My. 14, '45. Great Lakes-St. Lawrence seaway: pro and con.

Senior Scholastic. 48:10-11. Mr. 25, '46. Battle of the St. Lawrence seaway.

Senior Scholastic. 52:7-8. Mr. 1, '48. Saga of the seaway.

Senior Scholastic. 54:12. F. 9, '49. CVA: fast-growing Northwest needs more power and water.

*Senior Scholastic. 54:6-7. My. 4, '49. More authorities for river valleys? C. L. Thompson.

Senior Scholastic. 56:5-7. F. 15, '50. Missouri basin.

Senior Scholastic. 56:10T. Ap. 5, '50. How to see TVA. Maurice Henle.

State Government. 21:214-18. O. '48. Federal-state-local cooperation: the Tennessee Valley. H. B. Johnson.

*Survey. 85:259-62. My. '49. MVA: order out of chaos. Rufus Terral.

Survey. 85:320-4. Je. '49. TVA idea. James Rorty.

*Survey. 85:362-6. Jl. '49. CVA, order on the frontier. R. L. Neuberger.

Survey Graphic. 33:376-81. S. '44. Big magic for the Big Muddy. Rufus Terral.

Time. 47:88. Ja. 14, '46. New giant.

Time. 51:14. Ja. 12, '48. Still going strong.

Town Meeting (Bulletin of America's Town Meeting of the Air). 13, no44:1-24. '48. Should the St. Lawrence seaway plan now before Congress be adopted? G. D. Aiken and others.

*United States News & World Report. 27:17-20. D. 2, '49. Thirty-seven billions to remake the West.

Vital Speeches of the Day. 12:55-7. N. 1, '45. Great age; valleys of America await full development; address, October 10, 1945. H. S. Truman.

Vital Speeches of the Day. 14:253-6. F. 1, '48. Labor and the St. Lawrence waterway. Matthew Woll.

SPEECH AND DEBATING

Competitive Debate: Rules and Strategy. By G. M. Musgrave. 151p. rev. ed. 1946. $1.25.

Extempore Speaking: A Handbook for the Student, the Coach, and the Judge. By D. L. Holley. 115p. 1947. $1.50.

High School Forensics: An Integrated Program. By A. E. Melzer. 153p. 1940. 90c.

How to Debate. By H. B. Summers, F. L. Whan, and T. A. Rousse. rev. ed. 349p. 1950. $2.75.

Oral Interpretation of Literature in American Colleges and Universities. By M. M. Robb. 242p. 1941. $2.75.

Representative American Speeches. By A. C. Baird, comp. Published annually in The Reference Shelf. Prices vary.

Each volume contains representative speeches by eminent men and women on public occasions during the year. Each speech is prefaced by a short sketch of the speaker and the occasion.

Selected Readings in Rhetoric and Public Speaking. By Lester Thonssen, comp. 324p. 1942. $3.